for Peter Fleud

W.N. Honey

29ᵃ Nov. 1940

D1491538

THE
SACRED FIRE

THE SACRED FIRE

AN ANTHOLOGY OF ENGLISH POEMS FROM THE FOUR-TEENTH CENTURY TO THE PRESENT DAY CHOSEN AND ARRANGED WITH AN INTRODUCTION BY WILLIAM BOWYER HONEY

GEORGE ROUTLEDGE & SONS, LTD.
BROADWAY HOUSE, CARTER LANE, LONDON E.C.

First published 1939

Printed in Great Britain by Butler & Tanner Ltd., Frome and London

TO
A. W. W.

CONTENTS

Contents

Contents

Contents

ACKNOWLEDGEMENTS

THE grateful thanks of the editor are due to those living authors, and to the literary executors of some others, who have given their consent to the inclusion of poems in this book. The editor is further indebted to many publishers for permission to include copyright poems. Acknowledgements are due—

for a poem by Lascelles Abercrombie, to the author and Messrs. John Lane, The Bodley Head (*Emblems of Love*);

for a poem by W. H. Auden, to the author and Messrs. Faber & Faber (*Letters from Iceland*, 1937, and *Selected Poems*);

for poems by Rupert Brooke, to Messrs. Sidgwick & Jackson (*Collected Poems of Rupert Brooke*, 1918, *Complete Poems*, 1932, *Selected Poems*, 1917, and *Twenty Poems*, 1935);

for poems by Robert Bridges, from *The Shorter Poems of Robert Bridges* (1931), The Clarendon Press, Oxford, and *The Poetical Works of Robert Bridges*, 6 vols., Oxford University Press (1929), to the publishers who have in each case given permission to reprint;

for poems by Walter de la Mare, to the author (through Messrs. J. B. Pinker & Son) and Messrs. Constable & Co. (*Poems: 1901 to 1918*);

for a poem by John Davidson, to Messrs. John Lane, The Bodley Head (*The Testament of a Man Forbid* and *Selected Poems*);

for poems by Ernest Dowson, to Messrs. John Lane, The Bodley Head (*The Poems of Ernest Dowson*);

for poems by T. S. Eliot, to the author and Messrs. Faber & Faber (*Collected Poems: 1909–35*);

for poems by Robert Frost, to the author and Messrs. Henry Holt & Co. (*North of Boston*, 1914, and *Mountain Interval*, 1916);

for poems by Thomas Hardy, to the author's executors and Messrs. Macmillan & Co. (*The Collected Poems of Thomas Hardy*);

for poems by Gerard Manley Hopkins, to the author's family and The Oxford University Press (*The Poems of Gerard Manley Hopkins*, 1937);

for poems by A. E. Housman, to the Trustees of the author's Estate (through Messrs. J. B. Pinker & Son) and The Richards Press (*A Shropshire Lad*);

Acknowledgements

for poems by D. H. Lawrence, to Mrs. Frieda Lawrence (through Messrs. Pearn, Pollinger & Higham) and Messrs. William Heinemann (*Collected Poems* and *Last Poems*);

for a poem by C. Day Lewis, to the author and The Hogarth Press (*Collected Poems 1929–33*, 1935);

for a poem by Louis MacNeice, to the author and Messrs. Faber & Faber (*Poems*, 1935);

for a poem by George Meredith, to the Trustees of the author's Estate and Messrs. Constable & Co. (*The Complete Poetical Works of George Meredith*);

for poems by Charlotte Mew, to Mrs. Alida Monro and The Poetry Bookshop (*The Rambling Sailor*);

for a poem by Wilfred Owen, to Mrs. Susan Owen and Messrs. Chatto & Windus (*Poems by Wilfred Owen*, edited by Edmund Blunden);

for a poem by Stephen Phillips, to Messrs. John Lane, The Bodley Head (*Poems by Stephen Phillips*);

for poems by Herbert Read, to the author and Messrs. Faber & Faber (*Poems 1914–34*);

for a poem by Stephen Spender, to the author and Messrs. Faber & Faber (*Poems*, 1934);

for poems by Edward Thomas, to Mrs. Helen Thomas and Messrs. Faber & Faber (*Collected Poems*);

for a poem by Francis Thompson, to Mr. Wilfred Meynell and Messrs. Burns, Oates and Washbourne (*The Works of Francis Thompson*, Vol. II, and *The Collected Poems of Francis Thompson*);

for poems by W. B. Yeats, to the author (through Messrs. A. P. Watt & Son) and Messrs. Macmillan & Co. (*The Collected Poems of W. B. Yeats*, and *A Full Moon in March*).

THE
SACRED FIRE

THE SACRED FIRE

INTRODUCTION

I AM aware that the publication of another anthology is an act
calling for serious justification, for something more than the mere
avowal of a wish to see one's favourite poems assembled in a fittingly
austere and beautiful typographical dress. In the present case,
perhaps, a sufficient excuse may be found in the somewhat unusual
point of view of the anthologist. Familiarity with the arts of
form and colour usually called decorative, with the history of their
styles and modes of creation, may (if small things may be compared
with great) suggest parallels, and throw light on the theory of this
art of poetry. An acquaintance with those styles must, I think,
lend an unusual tolerance of changing fashions. A choice of master-
pieces of English silversmith's work, for example, or of furniture
or pottery, covering several centuries, must obviously take account
of widely different criteria of beauty and excellence prevailing at
different times, and a taste that proposed to measure every style
by a single standard derived from what at the moment was regarded
as the best period, or from some theoretical consideration of fitness
or ideal beauty, would accuse itself at once of a want of sensibility
and imagination. An informed and adaptable taste would accept
rather the dictum of Lessing when he wrote: *"Man hat keinen
Geschmack wenn man nur einen einseitigen Geschmack hat; aber
oft is man desto parteiischer. Der wahre Geschmack is der allge-
meine, der sich über Schönheiten von jeder Art verbreitet, aber von
keiner mehr Vergnügen und Entzückung erwartet, als sie nach ihrer
Art gewähren kann."*[1] In poetry, on the contrary, it is usual to
find the anthologist and critic relying upon an implied theory of
pure poetry, or, worse still, of some particular sort of subject-
matter supposed to be "poetical" or "realistic", as the case may be
(such as the more agreeable aspects of nature, or the more dis-

The Sacred Fire

agreeable aspects of civilization, both alike called Truth), by which whole movements in the history of English poetry are judged to be without merit. It is as though painting should be tied exclusively to landscape in the manner of Constable and his followers or to some other restricted school. The unfortunate poet of the "bad period" is represented in anthologies if at all by his least characteristic work. Whatever holds most strongly the peculiar interests or aspirations or flavour of its time tends to be suppressed, and by the fashionable practice of mingling the most diverse manners in what Palgrave called "the most poetical order" nothing receives the support of its proper setting; all styles tend to be dissolved into a mere common measure of like and unlike. It is therefore one of the purposes of this anthology, and of this introductory essay, to show how by disregarding the fashions of the moment and by accepting the fact of difference, even to the point of applauding extravagance and excess, a sharper, more vivid impression and deeper understanding may be had of English verse in the whole range of its excellences.

Such a recognition of diversity brings an additional advantage in fitting the mind for the reception of modern work, of whatever is genuinely new and creative in one's own time, and this is surely the final test of a sensibility to poetry. The academic single standard presumes likeness, and every innovation, every extension of subject-matter, imagery, rhythm and vocabulary, calls for the familiar reluctant remaking of the canon. But if every movement in the past is thought of as having its own aesthetics the mind is at least left free to perceive if it can the merit of original work, however unlike that may be to what has been done before.

That we are satisfied to call so many various compositions alike by the name of poetry would at first sight seem to imply the existence of a common standard, or at least some common essence, and the extent to which the attempted isolation or definition of this has in fact occupied men's minds is shown by a vast body of criticism, ancient as well as modern, attempting to answer the question, "What is poetry?" Of most of this it may be said that it was concerned with the justification of the poetry of its own age. But every well-founded and comprehensive theory has shown the essential quality to belong to form (an adequate word to be further defined in a moment) rather than to subject-matter,

– 2 –

Introduction

and much play has been made in consequence with the conception of pure poetry, something akin to absolute music, something which has risen clear of meaning and rests only on the power of syllables and words when placed in a certain order to evoke what we call poetic emotion, to bear what we recognize as a purely poetic significance. This conception of pure poetry has given colour to the theory of a single essence, but every attempt to isolate some aspect of rhythm or imagery as constituting this essence has always failed in face of the inseparable union of sound and meaning. And though it is not difficult to find poetry which has attained to this "condition of music", to which in Pater's excellent phrase all art should aspire, it seems certain that no great poetry has ever been composed with the deliberate intention of achieving it, of directly reaching this state of abstract perfection and purity. A living painter has well said of his own art that "the deliberate pursuit of purely formal qualities as ends in themselves can lead only to an empty and lifeless formalism; real formal significance seems only to arise when the artist is at least partially preoccupied with one or other of the secondary . . . or impure emotions". In poetry, equally, a purely formal intention can, it seems, produce nothing better than a "Jabberwocky".

For though an abstract, purely formal, beauty may be achieved, it must be regarded as a final state, reached through a preoccupation, an excitement about some in the strict sense irrelevant concern. What is called the subject-matter of poetry has included in the past an endless variety of such exciting causes. Sometimes personal affairs of love or lust, hate or indignation, or revelation of truth or beauty, passionately experienced, they are as often matters of communal aspiration, concerned with religious or political movements which have fired the imagination of their time. No subject can in fact be excluded as beyond the bounds of poetry. Occasionally, but seldom in England, we find a group of men united in a devotion to certain kinds of imagery or symbolism, or even to some technical principle or innovation, such as free verse or the use or avoidance of certain words or forms. These movements are more familiar in other arts, where we commonly find the artists claiming such innovations as the essence of their art, and by this preoccupation leaving themselves free for the more or less unconscious creation of formal beauty. This is or was the

The Sacred Fire

case with many handicrafts, where the craftsman (who may not have called himself an artist at all) was wholly occupied in doing a job with some practical purpose. The abstract qualities which we call beauty then came like a benediction upon work in itself utilitarian. The material, in both the wide and restricted sense of the word, was used up in this occupation, and the result was a work of art unconsciously created. Thus too for Wilfred Owen the poetry was "in the pity"; it could not come directly from any dilettante trifling with words.

But excitement or passion or devotion to a cause are not enough to make a poet. It has often happened that a man sincerely moved has chosen to write in verse but has achieved nothing more than an ephemeral *pastiche* of the worn and obsolete counters of an earlier or lately current poetical language. The impulse to rhythmical speech must be united to a conscience and sensibility that reject all language and imagery that are not fire-new, as it were, and beyond this there must be that positive creative gift by which words and images can·be chosen and arranged in precisely that order whose poetical significance and music we can recognize if not so easily define. Without this gift not the most sensitive taste and intelligence, nor metrical ingenuity and skill, nor extensive vocabulary and facility, nor vision alone, can ever make a poet. Swinburne had many of these gifts, and the empty clang of his writing is the result as much of a want of genuine poetic fire as of a lack of deep and sincere feeling; the words in true poetry seem to be supercharged with meaning, not to be in excess of it. In Shelley too (as for example in much of the famous *Ode to the West Wind*) and in Emily Brontë, we often find a flood of words carried rapidly along by the mere force of the poet's vehemence, but lacking altogether that intensity which marks the finest poetry. The words and phrases are severally flat and insignificant, even suggesting makeshifts or "fill-ups"; they are not the "right" words, but just ordinary words.[2] Given however the double excitement of creative fire and human passion the most intractable material may be consumed, the most far-fetched imagery may be fused to white heat and the most everyday language be transfigured; every word may be given a life of its own and out of the amorphous matrix of common speech the jewel of poetry may be crystallized.

Poetry is thus a state to which language may attain, and no one part or aspect of a poem—neither a special kind of subject-matter in its content, nor imagery alone, nor any particular sort of words —can be claimed as its essence Attempts at definition in these terms must always fail. It is like light which must needs be coloured by some transmitting medium or reflected from some object not itself on which it strikes before we can ever become aware of it. "Pure poetry" can no more exist for us apart, than life can be made known to us without a material embodiment.[3] And its recognition is a direct act of the intuition or "imaginative reason", never a matter of taking thought. It is "felt in the blood, and felt along the heart", or as Housman more bluntly put it, you recognize it by a sensation in the pit of the stomach which can never be mistaken by one who has experienced it.

Of the ultimate source and nature of this poetic fire and sensibility I know of no satisfying account. Nor do I know of any adequate description of its outward manifestation in words. Often described as music, with a disastrous implication of smoothness, dignity or jingling prettiness, the rhythms and patterns of poetic language are obviously of an order very different from those of instrumental or vocal music, with their precise notation of pitch. The science of prosody may suggest a kinship, with its concern for the measurement of syllables and pauses and the counting of accents; but it must ignore not only the colours which words may acquire in the texture of a poem but the pattern of meanings in conjunction also. As with every other science concerned with quantities the essential living values will always elude the instruments. Even the metrical schemes on which prosody insists are not to be mistaken for the rhythms themselves with their strange vitality, any more than the trellis which supports a vine is to be mistaken for the living plant, though we should perhaps be less aware of the true rhythm if the metrical beat or background were not there to reveal it by inflections and infractions, the living opposed to and revealed by the mechanical. The point need not have been stressed had not the confusion encouraged the setting (sometimes with the consent of poets) of the words of poetry into irrelevant vocalizations called songs. Little but the mere content, with something perhaps of the imagery, can survive this process, and even these must be robbed of their urgency. In spite of the original meaning of the word lyric and a full consciousness of heresy I have no hesitation in asserting that poetry in its fully developed form (I shall speak of ballads later) is destroyed by this attempted union. Form and content are in a poem fused and one. Impose the melody of the musician upon the entirely different music of the poet, and the delicate structure of the latter is distorted and destroyed; the mere value of the words as meaning alone can survive, with hardly more evocative power than they had before the poet had transmuted them. That Campion was willing to write for his own composing is hardly to the point, though it shows perhaps that he was more aware of his gifts as a musician than of the character of his powers as a poet, while Milton's acclamation of the union of voice and verse reveals an equally surprising failure. Only such cold perfections as the songs of Ben Jonson (which to my sense scarcely ever stir into poetic life for all their fine taste and intelligence and craftsman's polishing) can bear without loss the distortions that music must inflict on verse. But this is because they have nothing of true poetry to lose. It is indeed rare to hear one's favourite poems satisfyingly read aloud, but who has ever enjoyed them in a musical setting? [4] This distinction is important since it helps to define by elimination the distinguishing characters of poetry, but it also raises a rather difficult question of the relation of written to spoken verse which must be briefly answered here.

In its secular origin English poetry had a tradition of spoken (not written) popular use; narrative poetry and the drama usually, and ballads always, existed by oral tradition, even after literary uses had become general, and much play has recently been made by traditionalists and others, particularly in America, with the conception of a new popular art of spoken verse concerned with objective things, vivid and direct, such as the ballads and mystery plays are supposed to have been. Such compositions had a strong metrical framework, with bold rhymes in a robust text upon which improvised variations could be made without injury; they could be altered in a dozen ways at the whim of the speaker or singer. Now having in mind the whole body of our written poetry, from which this anthology has been chosen, I cannot but regard these popular creations as the crude precursors rather than the austere primitives of the art of poetry. They are not even the sole precursors, any more than the music of such ballads (whose descendants

Introduction

in more than name are modern drawing-room songs) is the source of the art of concerted music, which has the chants of the mediaeval church and ultimately the music of the Greek ritual drama to look to for its ancestors. And I am not prepared for the sake of this theory of popular tradition to regard English poetry from the 16th Century almost to the present day as a decadent growth arising from the morbid preoccupation of romantic individualist poets with their private destiny and troubles. (Even the least individualist modern poet seeks the precise word with as great a regard for his personal inspiration as any romantic.) To me the written poetry is a mature art, while the other is childish; and so entirely personal is it in its private communication that the presence of a professional or any other speaker comes as a blatant and intolerable intrusion. I have called the ballad sort of poetry childish, and it is this in more than a figurative sense; it is such an art as appeals to children, with its vivid external play-acting or fairy-tale character and its obvious metrical beat. The mature art of poetry, on the other hand, requires not only a mature sensibility and a cultivated feeling for the overtones of language, but a body of adult experience which children fortunately cannot have. The true music of poetry is thus something they can hardly be expected to hear.[5]

Now if we accept the distinction just made, and in the absence of a better terminology continue to speak of the music of poetry, we may proceed to describe a poem as a composition of evocative words passing beyond meaning into music. It may well be a composition of such a compelling power that we find ourselves accepting any words having the "right" sounds, however remote their meaning, if once the thing has come to poetic life, if in the familiar words it has fired our imagination. This is not merely the operation of Coleridge's dictum that a poet must be judged by his best lines and that a poem cannot be all poetry, but a proof of the willing suspension of the rational faculty before what I would call the parallel or unwritten poem. Much seems to depend on the right onset, the initial flight. Many instances could be cited. In such a poem as John Donne's *Dream*, the enchanting tenderness of the first lines, with their caressing sounds, might have carried us past harshnesses of diction far more disturbing than those actually used. This opening movement, with its sense of darkness and trembling quiet, sustained throughout, begins the "actual" poem to which the words with their meaning seem in the end the mere accompaniment. The calm faith, again, of the first lines of Wordsworth's *Ode* inspires a serene perfection and simplicity of utterance which sustains us through long passages which as meaning are as empty as anything Wordsworth ever wrote. The glow persists until a new burst of poetic passion flames out, and so to the end. How far the poet is himself conscious of this parallel poem, beyond meaning, which accompanies the articulate expression with which he must in the first place be concerned is a matter on which I cannot offer an opinion of any value; and for reasons at which I have already hinted I do not think the poets themselves are always the best judges of their own work, or fully conscious of the nature of their inspiration. But this is to me and to those whose sensibility I most respect quite certainly the essence of the matter; it is the absolute poem or incantation. There is an insoluble paradox in this. While we may read a contemporary poet for his matter, which heartens us by its zeal for a cause we have at heart, it may be, or by its praise of scenes we love or its description of ideas and experiences we may have shared with him, and while these passions are needed to make him a poet, it is on that other obscurer gift that his power to move us to the depths must ultimately depend; and that other quality alone can give a poem an enduring appeal long after the cause is lost or won or forgotten. What a poet means is important, especially to his contemporaries and to himself; his message or observations may be original and thrilling or they may be commonplace. But his ultimate rank as a seer must depend on what he says, on the enchantment he can make with words, giving them a significance beyond intelligible meaning. It is this music, this pattern, which like beauty of every kind has "something in it of Divinity more than the ear discovers: it is an Hieroglyphical and shadowed lesson of the whole World and creatures of GOD".

*   *   *   *   *

This choice of poems, then, has been made in the belief that poetry is a state to which impassioned writing of many kinds can attain, that there have been poets in every age to tend its sacred fire, and that each movement is to be judged by its own standard

Introduction

in regard not only to its choice of poetical subject-matter but also to its special order of technical accomplishment. Each has its own language. It would be logical to carry the argument a stage farther and contend that each poet is a law unto himself, and this we should not hesitate to do.[6] But it is in fact hardly necessary to apply the principle, since the poets themselves have always (though no doubt to some extent unconsciously) belonged to more or less distinct movements sharing the same ideals. Often enough they have had the same human aspirations; but even when outwardly at variance they have had in common with their contemporaries a certain poetic character which we recognize as peculiar to their time. That essential character is more easily recognized in the work of times long past, but I believe it to be always there. The broad divisions by style are generally admitted and are in fact commonplaces of literary history. There are, however, to my ear and sense briefer "periods" of this kind, with less obvious characters in common and frequently overlapping. These form the separate sections of this book, representing the successive impulses which have inspired our English poetry, and I shall presently survey them very briefly in the light of the foregoing observations. Particular instances may make the special characters clear. But before proceeding to this I must pause for a moment and try to account for the changes of taste and outlook which mark this procession. Mere action and reaction provide a partial explanation. The sons revolt against the fathers, and every generation of young poets rejects the manner of its immediate predecessors, grown lifeless and academic, even to the point of denying all merit to the creative work which founded the departing fashion. Disgusted by the host of *pasticheurs* who have picked up the tone and vocabulary of a once vital mode, they are blind to all the genuine achievement that went to make it. Such blindness is excusable in a creative artist who can be interested only in the kind of art he is himself intent on achieving and naturally denies the worth of all else; and he will of course be a leader of fashion in criticism. But others less preoccupied need not share this narrowness, hard though it is not to be prejudiced against the exploiters of borrowed sentiments and phrases. These, lacking authentic fire, set up a paper flame to be lit by reflected light. The "poetic sentiments" they indulge in are the empty shells of a once-living mode of poetry.

The Sacred Fire

Even to-day, in spite of a so-called classical reaction, vibrations from the Romantic Movement still persist—moonlit scenes, noble suffering, the songs of birds, and the like, are still called "poetical" by people to whom these things are the necessary apparatus of poetry, the only "poetical" subjects, by people who would be shocked and alarmed by the strangeness of a genuine poetical experience. Reactions against an exhausted mode, however, account only for the fact of change; they do not determine its direction. If we were convinced that the stuff of poetry lay in what it dealt with we could say that the poets of a period are united in the communal hopes, aspirations or despairs (as the case might be) of their own time. But since we find that the special character is bound up with a quality we have called formal, something shared occasionally with a contemporary who stands outside the common enthusiasms, we are driven to conjecture some deeper source. I have discussed this problem elsewhere [7] in considering the origin of the 18th-Century styles of decorative art. I do not think that the art of any period is to be regarded as the mere product "of the political, economic, social and scientific influences of the age" (as is usually supposed), though obviously it is subject to such influences and derives its occasions from them. Its essential nature is due to some deeper creative cause. Movements in thought or social evolution cannot account for what is characteristic in form in any of the arts. However readily the critic may find this or that aspect of a style appropriate or "expressive" of an age, it is found so, I believe, by a rationalizing process, and the essentials—a preference for a particular sort of curve or rhythm, for symmetry or the lack of it—remain a mystery as obscure as the source of inspiration in music, where there can be no articulate reference to the life of a time. I cannot equate an idea with a curve or complex of lines; though if I believed in a connection I might fancy some kind of fitness or symbolical relation between them. The materialism that would find a complete and easy explanation of everything in its surroundings and antecedents is naturally popular at the present time; it gives the critic matter to write about and the public lacking a sense of form is satisfied to find the arts explained as little more than illustration. In poetry the same conditions hold and the difficulty is increased by the fact that words are also normally used to convey information,

Introduction

which the literal-minded insist on regarding as the whole of the matter.[8] It is tempting to postulate as the source a subconscious communal mind of the age or race to which all poets have at times access; and though it begs the question to some extent, the hypothesis is suggestive enough to explain the undoubted fact that the deeper despairs and liberations of the whole race of Englishmen, which are scarcely perceptible to contemporaries but are plain enough in a long view, do in fact find expression in poetry. The following notes must of necessity touch upon little else and only in briefest, crudest outline, with many glimpses of the obvious as well as some strongly held preferences and dislikes. I have avoided however the customary "period" labels.

*   *   *   *   *

A word is first needed on the scope of the book. I have begun it with a small group of poems written not in English, but in the language from which our modern tongue has grown. To this belongs (I am heretic enough to say) the language of Chaucer. I am aware that it is usual "to begin with" him. It is not unusual too to rewrite him, and the conclusion is the obvious one I have just stated. But I am conscious that in including these poems I am breaking a rule I have otherwise observed in confining my choice to English work and not including pieces in Scots dialect, since in these the words cannot to the English mind have the same evocative power as they have to a Scotsman. (Nor have I with one exception included any poems written in America, since these belong to another national consciousness with its own movements.) These pre-Tudor poems, however, may usefully convey an impression of the origins of the art to which this volume is devoted, and they will themselves be found beautiful by anyone caring to take a little trouble with them. The doctrine of verbal inspiration implied in this essay of course forbids absolutely any attempt to "modernize" these poems,[9] and on the same ground I have throughout the book preserved the poets' own spelling, setting-out, and use of capitals and italics; the texts wherever possible have been taken from volumes seen through the press by the authors themselves. There can be no justification for altering a poet's text save a belief that poetry is a single thing in its origin as well as its final state, and this I have attempted to show is false.

The Sacred Fire

The fact of difference, revealed principally in outlook and mode of expression, covers also such smaller matters as typographical dress.

Contrary to the usual custom I have not hesitated to include a few long poems (as well as paragraphs from others still longer), exceeding the length conventionally assigned to what is called the lyric. In my view the academic classification of poetry under the names used in the ancient world is on several grounds indefensible and impracticable where English poetry is concerned. Precisely the same poetic qualities are to be found in *Paradise Lost* and parts of the plays of Shakespeare as in shorter works, and even the subsidiary qualities of form, of design in the architecture of a poem, are as conspicuous in the easily detachable paragraphs of Milton's epic as in "lyrics" more obviously complete in themselves. The arbitrary division moreover excludes much of the most beautiful blank verse, which in its many varieties is among the chief glories of our language.

I have naturally made no distinction between "classical" and modern; modern should mean nothing more or less than original. I have further endeavoured as far as possible to disregard the reactions of the present day, and I am well aware that some of the poets whose characteristic work I have included are at the moment decidedly unfashionable; each being represented by his most individual (even his most extravagant) work there is naturally much that may be found mannered and artificial, or gushing and sentimental, by the single standard of the present day. On the other hand I have ventured to omit deliberately some "accepted classics" which in my opinion are derivative or owe their fame to qualities not strictly poetical. The arrangement though in the main chronological is not rigidly or pedantically so, and it is hoped that the grouping into periods and the deliberate ordering within the groups will give a sense of vital order and rhythmical progression which are naturally lacking in a wholly arbitrary arrangement (however ingenious) due merely to the whim of an editor.

*　　*　　*　　*　　*

English poetry proper may be said to begin with the emergence of the new spirit in Europe which we call the Renaissance, and here as in every other art Italy was the leader. The Italian and

Introduction

Italian-Classical forms and manners were everywhere copied at first. Like the contemporary Tudor architecture this early Renaissance poetry is awkward in movement but with unmistakable fire and life beneath the often absurd apparel. Sir Thomas Wyat was our first considerable master in the new manner; his immediate successors—even the estimable Henry Howard, Earl of Surrey—were clumsy practitioners by comparison, with their laborious versification, conceits and ill-considered extravagance. A more sensitive instrument was created by Edmund Spenser, though not (it is worth remarking) until Queen Elizabeth had reigned for nearly twenty years. Of the supposed Elizabethan morning freshness there is little enough in his early poems, even in the *Shepheardes Calender*. This was a grey sunrise, deeply charged with a despondency due no doubt to the troubles of the Reformation and the threat of a Spanish war.[10] Not until the latter part of the reign, with the emergence of a new national consciousness and hope, do we find the zest, animation, fresh colour and limpid calm of the characteristic Elizabethan poetry. Spenser had been a forerunner, but shared in the movement in its final form. The precocious Marlowe, too, was a herald, maturing a few years earlier than his contemporaries and expressing more plainly than they the hard masculinity (not to say brutality) which is as much a part of the Elizabethan temper as the too-easily-prettified sensuous feeling for physical beauty. It was an age of widespread fashion and accomplishment in the writing of verses, especially of songs, though only a small part of the enormous literary production can be considered as creative or more than gracefully turned. That the Elizabethan poets were a school or movement, however, united by common literary ideals (as well as by the deeper sub-consciousness of which I have spoken), is in spite of minor squabbles among them fully testified by literary history, and not least by the remarkable outburst of sonnet-writing between the years 1590 and 1595.

Before the end of the Century the Elizabethan zest, product of a quick-witted and sensitive but not as a rule deeply reflective age, already showed signs of breaking down before a newly awakened sense of futility and despair. The prescient spirit of John Donne in his poems, the rugged melancholy Chapman, and occasional passages in the work of Shakespeare, all may be said to foreshadow the beginning of a new phase. In place of a happy outward-looking enjoyment we see the mind of the age turned in upon itself, and for nearly forty years the most moving English poetry was inspired by the thought of death and speculation about the meaning and purpose of life. Much of this was the poetry absurdly called metaphysical, abused by Johnson and others as frigid and contorted, but capable of a flaming intensity which was all the fiercer for the refractory nature of its material. Shakespeare's tragedies, and even his last plays for all their note of reconciliation, belong to this movement of the English poetic spirit, as do the sombre plays of Webster, and Donne's twilit poems also. The Authorized Version of the Bible is most moving in precisely those terrible moods which stirred the poets most deeply.[11] George Herbert and Henry King were almost the first to give expression in modern English to the emotions called religious, and the movement they started still produced vital poetry as late as the middle of the 17th Century, in the work of Vaughan and Crashaw and Thomas Traherne, and by this time a new movement had come and almost gone. The impulse that stirred so profound a searching as this cannot be accounted for by a mere dissatisfaction with James I or a sense of the vanity of conquest (though these may have given it additional force); it would be better explained by an awakening conscience—a vision sharpened and intensified by national misfortune but essentially an access of deeper understanding and embitterment.

After such an experience, it was impossible ever to recapture completely the earlier mood of unselfconscious acceptance and delight. A quality of chastened happiness, of dewy morning sunshine deeply and not unthinkingly enjoyed, is characteristic of a new movement, which appeared early in the reign of Charles I. This I like to think of as led by the young Milton, though perhaps the smiling irony and deep sensibility of Marvell, the graceful mockery of Suckling and grave simplicity of Sidney Godolphin are in their several ways just as typical. Only Herrick may appear to be still the true blithe-hearted rather stupid Elizabethan, but even Herrick had his moments of misgiving. This beautiful running of streams after a night of terror slackened and ceased within a couple of decades. Marvell lapsed into a writer of dull satires and Milton ceased to write poetry altogether. The failure is usually accounted for by the arid puritan atmosphere of the

Introduction

Commonwealth, but the explanation is much too simple; both alike were the consequence of some less obvious cause.

When at length the obstruction was broken down, two new streams of poetry were liberated, with entirely different characters and direction: on the one hand the movement led by John Dryden looked forward to new forms and manners, while *Paradise Lost* and *Samson Agonistes* at once ended an epoch and stand as the final culmination of its achievement. Milton in middle life had dreamed of "a still time, when there shall be no more chiding" and it should be possible for him to write the long poem he had meditated since his boyhood. His dream was never fulfilled, but it was finally granted to him, in solitude and disgrace, to pour out in the greatest single poem in the English language all those treasures of learning and imagination he had accumulated during a lifetime devoted to the public service. It is, I suppose, a commonplace now to say that Milton was the inheritor of all that the Renaissance had to give in humanist learning and imagery. Much too came to him from the Hebrew literature so inspiringly translated just before he began to write. But these were no more than the material he used. Far more important in his writings is the sheer and unaccountable poetic gift that could charge with living splendour of colour and varied harmony all that mass of often absurd material. The great poem is lit up again and again in long passages with a poetic fire unsurpassed in our language. No anthology of English poetry can be complete without some of these, and though in time it falls in another age with quite different poetic ideals the later work of Milton must take rank in my series as a whole movement in itself. To me it has been like a great mountain range with a thousand beautiful places waiting to be discovered and rediscovered amongst its undeniable stretches of waste and bog. No more flagrant instance could be found of the confusion of the poetic spirit with its mere apparel than the contemporary disparagement of Milton on account of his opinions and the puritanism he is supposed to have served.

The other poets of the century which followed the Restoration have of course been the chief victims of the prejudice I have mentioned, by which a regard for certain aspects of nature and the acceptance of certain conventions about the passion of love became the touchstones of poetic "truth". Naturalness and artifice were set in opposition as a pair of mutually exclusive alternatives, the latter wholly evil. That prejudice was an inheritance from the nineteenth century, when an excessive admiration prevailed for the poets of what is called the Romantic Movement. Now I have tried to show that poetry may be engendered by many various passions, and those which possessed the minds and hearts of this period were as valid as any others. Outwardly it began as a period of reaction against the sort of life imposed by the puritan rule; the pleasures of the town and the more profane Classical literature had been forbidden and were now to be enjoyed. That is sufficient to explain the new direction taken in the choice of matter. We find that satire, cynical wit, and truth to reason, have taken the place of romantic love, country pleasures and mystical or emotional religious themes as the exciting causes of poetry. Over all, as a unifying convention, was the new care for smooth versifying, born apparently of a new admiration for the Latin classics. This regard for conventional correctness and a revived fashion for the writing of verses united in what is outwardly a common form the elegant versifier with the poet of true vocation. This new Classicism has in our own time been applauded by critics of two fashionable schools so diverse as the adherents of tradition on the one hand and on the other those who deplore any romantic individualist departure from the general line. If what is called technical mastery, in the Classical manner, were the whole poetic achievement this would be the greatest period in English poetry; but in my own view poetic technique is simply the poet's power to embody his vision or express his feelings in rhythmical speech, not necessarily of one kind only and not always measured, orderly and rigidly restrained, and a convention that treats the English language as if it were a precise instrument like Latin or French is as arbitrary and limiting as the demand for "poetic feeling" and "truth to Nature" made by the opposing school. Much of the greatness of English poetry springs from the very fact that the language is not precise but suggestive, evocative, and full of echoes. It is reasonable to say, however, of this period that it was one of those rare times when a passion for the art of versification, rather than any larger issue,[12] was a main preoccupation of some (but not all) of the poets themselves, and the Latin fashion merely stressed the more coldly formal and artificial aspects of poetry. But where so much is manner, it is harder to distinguish what is truly creative. Romantic criticism frankly abandoned the task, accepting several impostors and preferring (for example) the costive tenderness of Pope's *Elegy* to his harder and more artificial but more brilliantly inspired and characteristic work, of which *The Rape of the Lock* is typical.

Within the Century, at least three distinct movements may be detected. The hard, strong and clear but still animated and baroque art of Dryden had its outrider in the precocious Cowley, while the easy manners of the time had a reflection in the songs of Etherege and the Restoration dramatists and the poems of Cotton, who might have seemed to belong to the age of Marvell but for a certain slipshod cynicism. The songs of the period have the same wit and grace and ironic sentiment and are the townsman's version of Marvell's country poems. Pope and Swift, with Matthew Prior, John Gay and other lesser men of the early part of the 18th Century, belong to a more strictly classical generation, with whom high finish and smoothness of diction were ruling passions. (But the most rigid verbal discipline could not mask the passion of indignation that flamed in Swift, nor could the utmost facility in Thomson hide an entire lack of poetic power.) The graceful art then created was widely practised or imitated throughout the next hundred years or so, and to the great mass of pleasant but uninspired and "insincere" verses so produced is no doubt due the long-standing prejudice against the 18th Century. The poets of the next generation, with this expressive instrument at their command, added a rich and complex harmony to the rather bare writing of the previous period. Gray and Collins, and in a more casual way Oliver Goldsmith in his one serious work, were poets as true as any in the centuries before and after, and only the occasional flatness of a conventional epithet could obscure the fact. Collins indeed is one of the greatest of all English poets, a magician capable of every enchantment. His case is especially valuable since he showed that the highest level may be reached by a poet working in and through the idiom of his time, however "artificial" and unpromising that may appear to later generations.

The poets of the last thirty years of the 18th Century belong in some senses to a transition. Conscious in the period just mentioned of the graceful fancy of the contemporary Rococo, one is tempted to see in the sometimes cloying sweetness of Cowper a parallel with the Neo-Classical sentiment of the age of Josiah Wedgwood and the early *Louis-Seize*. When this was kept in check by the restraint of his beautiful and very personal sort of blank verse Cowper showed himself a poet of the highest rank. In his best work there is a new naturalness of diction which anticipates the Romantics, though the gap is usually held to be bridged rather by the wayward and rebellious art of William Blake. But while Blake's irregular rhythms and individual fancy may justify this, his diction and much of his sentiment show him I think to be in the direct line of the 18th-Century poets.[13] No man can avoid sharing the poetic atmosphere or inspiration of his time, however much he may outwardly rebel or try to escape from it.[14] Even the unfortunate Christopher Smart, whose madness is supposed to have freed him from the evil conventions which tied his fellow poets, was obviously of their number, as a study of the language of the *Song to David* will quickly show.

The revolution in poetry that came just before the turn of the century was undoubtedly due to the same ferment or wave of ideas and aspirations which had produced the political revolution in France. Claimed as a return to Nature and a rediscovery of Truth, it secured also an exciting return to simple diction, purged of the conventional pomposities into which the 18th Century had often lapsed. The movement was also sustained by another influence. It is difficult now to assess the extent to which the movement was indebted to the traditional ballads, whose rediscovery and publication by Bishop Percy in 1765 stands as a landmark in English poetry.[15] In the preface to their *Lyrical Ballads*, published in 1798, Wordsworth and Coleridge announced their intention of ascertaining "how far the language of conversation . . . is adapted for the purpose of poetic pleasure". They protested against the "gaudiness" of "modern writers" and feared that their language would seem "too familiar". To this doctrine Coleridge, with his metaphysical bent, imaginative gifts and ear for the subtlest undertones, was less faithful than Wordsworth, whose art lay more in the transfiguration of common events than the narration of extraordinary ones, as in the old ballads with which by their title they claimed a kinship of aim. To Shelley the liberation meant the indulgence at the prompting of the passions of the time in a riot of abstractions, whose very facility and lack of discipline too often allow their poetic force to spend itself ineffectively in a torrent of empty words. But Shelley's onsets are sometimes magnificent and sustain to the end compositions that would otherwise lapse into wordiness and insignificance. The parallels between the Romantic poets and the English landscape painters are not always noticed. The former stand in much the same relation to Collins and Gray and William Cowper as J. R. Cozens and Thomas Girtin stand to Richard Wilson and Francis Towne. The romantic naturalism of the followers of Cozens, with their increasing disregard of formal qualities and reliance on "expression" reveals the same hint of ultimate failure as the contemporary poetic creed of Wordsworth and Shelley. A parallel still less often observed is that linking the late Classical or *Empire* style in building and decoration [16] with the more grandiloquent manner at times adopted by Shelley and with the forthright rhythms of Walter Scott. In Byron too this aspect is conspicuous, though in my own opinion his facile and witty verses are not poetry at all. Keats, as the youngest and most gifted of the group, inherited all their discoveries and fulfilled all their promises. The hint of an excessive sweetness in his early poems, the hyperboles and romantic languishments so little tolerable to us to-day, have largely disappeared in his later work, which culminates in the *Odes* and the matchless *Hyperion*.

Of the aftermath of the Romantic movement, still not ended, it is difficult to offer a calm opinion, so disastrous has it been for poetry. Sincerity and an individual accent may no doubt be claimed for some of the numerous poets of the second quarter of the 19th Century, for the outpourings of Elizabeth Barrett Browning and the picturesque defiance and shrill heroics of Emily (or Branwell) Brontë, but as poetry it is largely derivative, while the bellowings of the unspeakable Macaulay are simply not poetry at all.[17] The romantic vocabulary had become as empty and the poetic attitude or posture as false as the productions of that Gothic Revival which also enjoyed its heyday in this very period.

The impulse to a new or renascent mode came when a younger generation of poets found something deeply felt to write about, when they were stirred by a new passion of indignation and protest. The colour and imagery of the later Romantics were then taken

The Sacred Fire

up and put to a new use by a new sensibility and seriousness. The decades following the Napoleonic Wars were a period of the grossest materialism, when the Industrial Revolution made its greatest advances, and out of the revolt against this and the reaffirmation of religious belief in early Victorian times was born the movement to which belonged such diverse poets as Browning, Tennyson and Arnold. Each felt himself a defender of truth, and each created for himself a new poetic instrument. Browning was at his most personal and most truly a poet when ruggedly arguing in blank verse, with flashes of imagery and bursts of fierce compelling rhythm, than when tied to rhymed metres, unconvincingly mellifluous.[18] Tennyson too wrote some of his most moving poetry on themes that challenged his faith in the ultimate goodness of existence. His astonishing command of language at once descriptively exact and charged with vibrant poetic feeling was intensified by a didactic or reforming purpose; left to narrative his art often declined into little more than decoration. Arnold's was a smaller gift, springing at first less directly from the problems of the time though finally caught up and destroyed rather than made by them, while Rossetti and his sister, by race more than half Italian, shared only in that part of the early Victorian inspiration which was sensuous and emotional rather than intellectual.

The early Victorian upheaval, with its optimism and its doubt, its challenge to a complacent materialism, in my view lapsed soon after the middle of the Century into a dull and heavy indifference, stifling to the poetic spirit. It is difficult, no doubt, when so recent a period is discussed, to avoid a charge of picking one's examples to suit one's arguments, and an accusation of poetic sterility brought against the mid-Victorian age must appear at first sight entirely unjustified. Tennyson and Arnold were still writing and Swinburne pouring out volume after volume. A charge of hardness too will bring a storm of protest; but I find it inescapable. Meredith, born in the same year as Rossetti, could (when not showing off) find a difficult vein of poetry in a didactic admonitory utterance that was stirring and beautiful as well as hard. The hard nature and fluent pen of Coventry Patmore combined to produce a mere simulacrum of poetry. Swinburne, with all his metrical skill and violence was never stirred deeply enough to become a poet; his nature was too shallow. The art of William Morris was decorative only, in verse as in the other arts he practised, charming but with no great depth or resonance. Stevenson again was a *poseur* and a graceful decorator; while no harder or shallower man of genius ever wrote verses than W. E. Henley. Gerard Manley Hopkins, unlike his friend Robert Bridges, was scarcely a cloistered craftsman quietly experimenting with rhythms and metrical devices; but excitingly beautiful as his best poems are I feel that they show overmuch self-conscious ingenuity and belong essentially if only invertedly to a stony period of complacency and repression, when artists were not allowed to be more than decorators, when "applied art" became the recognized term used to describe the decorated products of mechanized industry. Thomas Hardy alone of the poets who began to write in that time had the sensibility, the simple transmuting gift, that the others lacked. His was a prophetic inspiration, contradicting in some degree the generalizations made on previous pages. Living on through the '90's (whose melancholy he may have inspired) he had with his jigging ballad metres as little in common with the stylists and rhetoricians of that time as with his own contemporaries, and found his poetic kindred at last in the Georgians, only when an old man. Altogether and in spite of this one exception I am forced to believe that the two or three decades after about 1860 were poetically sterile from some spiritual cause, hard to diagnose or describe, but probably similar to that which had afflicted the Commonwealth and was later on to blight the decade after the Boer War.

In the distinct period known in literary history as the Eighteen-Nineties a new movement was born, of a kind rare in England but common in France, on the one hand inspiring a new conscience in craftsmanship, conveniently summed up in the phrase "art for art's sake", and on the other rejecting the long-current scientific and middle-class optimism in a profound melancholy, cynical hedonism, or *fin-de-siècle* despair. That may be thought to be an inadequate description of Francis Thompson, but a behaviourist criticism will always clearly separate performance from a profession of belief, and distinguish the burden of what I have called the actual poem from the dogmas the poet was consciously stating. Ernest Dowson, A. E. Housman and Mr. W. B. Yeats were plainly if not avowedly of this school, as was Stephen Phillips, whose total loss of critical favour to-day is due I think as much to reaction after his spell of extreme popularity, as to an excess of sweetness in a spring of unquestionable poetry. The hard but strongly coloured art of John Davidson is similarly disregarded with the same injustice, largely for reasons of fashion.

The highly wrought and always deliberate and self-conscious poetry of the '90's was apt to stiffen into a pompous grandiloquence (as in William Watson) and its non-moral hardness of content to become mere insensitive crudeness and brutality (as in Kipling), and it was chiefly in this manner that verse continued to be written in the years after the Boer War. No more stifling atmosphere has ever weighed upon English poetry than that of the Edwardian era. Mr. de la Mare had begun to write, but had not found his true voice; others unquestionably sincere seemed fated to use the worn poetic *clichés* of the previous decade. Davidson was still to compose some of his most beautiful blank verse, but its tormented spirit is as much a mirror of the age as of his own personal sufferings, while Thomas Hardy alone continued to write in the effortless and beautiful manner already created by him thirty years before.

Reaching the second decade of the present century I am conscious that an impartial critical attitude is at this point impossible for me. The poets who became collectively aware of their reforming and creative mission when "E. M." published his first anthology of *Georgian Poetry* in 1911 were the poets of my first adult understanding of their art. Their sensitive and flexible rhythms and living natural language, no less than their delight in the English country scene, their irony and wit, and hatred of cant and overstatement, were qualities that seemed then to me, and must still seem, the most valuable side of the English poetic temperament.[19] All those by whom that period is represented here (and they could well be more) shared in their several ways in that renascence, which the work of Thomas Hardy had heralded. Above all, D. H. Lawrence, Robert Frost, Edward Thomas and Mr. Walter de la Mare remain for me poets in the greatest English tradition. The genius of Lawrence was often obscured in peevish complainings, but in his inspired moments, with his apparently effortless choice of the significant word, with his haunting music and transfiguring power, he is to be ranked with Shakespeare himself. Such a movement was bound to be short-lived, lasting hardly as long as the early Caroline renascence with which it had so much in common. It was ultimately destroyed by the War, sometimes lapsing at the end into a grievous sentimentality. What was in some ways a reaction was in fact started in the year before the War in the self-styled Imagist movement, whose members announced that it stood for hard precision and concentration in language and imagery. In actual performance, however, the most significant Imagist poetry depended for its value on associations and symbolism often of a vague and elusive kind, wrought in a manner subsequently developed by Mr. T. S. Eliot, who was in fact for a time associated with the movement. It is this relationship rather than its positive achievement which gives the short-lived movement its historical importance. In my own opinion the most beautiful poetry of the original Imagist inspiration was written not by a member of the group but by Mr. Herbert Read in his early *Eclogues*.

These and later movements concern contemporaries, and are therefore perhaps (in Saintsbury's excellent phrase) subjects for conversation, not criticism. They are too near for a final judgement. What is genuinely creative in much that is excitingly experimental can be distinguished only after many readings, always with an open mind and listening ear, and the small choice of recent poems included in this anthology is put forward as no more than a tentative and personal one. I would claim no more than that these poems seem to me to belong to significant movements of the same order as those of the past here demonstrated. They are also a few of the modern poems I like best. But this admission of uncertainty cannot I think affect the claims of the two rather older men already mentioned, whose poetry reveals more than any other the deep spiritual wounds left by the War. I find the beauty of Mr. Eliot's poems and their profound despair—a despair apparently too great for direct utterance—entirely at variance with his professed belief, as critic, in impersonal forms and the traditions of Church and State. Mr. Read's beautiful and terrible poems though so different in colour and movement must surely have a like spiritual origin. The younger men, united in a justifiable pessimism about the state of the world, find a natural fitness in an art in revolt against facile music and poetic *clichés*, against anything that could be accused of prettiness, glossing, or acceptance. The right to use any theme, however prosaic or unpleasant, is once more affirmed.[20]   The poetry they write has a hard bony texture and vivid dissonant colour not unlike that of contemporary painting and music. The use of harsh contrasts, oblique reference and ironical laughter, has much in common with Surrealism and seems to have been derived from Mr. Eliot; but Mr. Yeats also has employed this new technique for some of his finest recent poems, and this is as remarkable a case as Hardy's anticipation of the poetic outlook of the Georgians. Much has been written lately about these younger poets, but hitherto their apologists have been content to explain them, more or less obscurely, in terms of their meaning, language or imagery and their relation to the world of to-day and its "problems". From a more detached point of view their poetic merit would appear to lie rather in a singular beauty of rhythm, of words brought into a new and striking pattern of sound and sense depending on none of the more obvious resources of the poetry of the past; it is a melody that is comparable with that of much contemporary music, hard to recognize at a first hearing, when every note seems wrong. A detached point of view moreover allows it to be seen that this original character, achieved in common by at least three of these younger men, may readily be linked through Wilfred Owen to the English tradition of Herbert, Wordsworth and Thomas Hardy. It is in fact original work growing out of the tradition, extending and enriching it. That the tradition exists is undeniable, and though I have in this note stressed the fact of differences it is obvious that some common characters may be found, especially by strangers, in all English poetry. It is unlikely, however, that these characters have ever been consciously felt or sought after by original poets (they are like the air we breathe), and what has been called respect for tradition is in this matter best shown, not by adherence to any rules, or the attempted suppression of personality, but by a respectful attitude towards the achievements of the past, which have created our language, with its wealth of evocative words, and on which all contemporary effort rests. Like the final state of perfection which is poetry itself, this living traditional character is attained not by renouncing personality but through it. For it seems certain that the greatest work in poetry as in other arts has never been done with a full consciousness of its ultimate aesthetic value. That value comes, as I have said, like a benediction on sincere, passionate and individual effort towards another end.

*   *   *   *   *

The anthology thus gathered from all these movements has been deliberately made short enough to be read and re-read through as a book, suitably proportioned in its parts; it is not intended to be "representative" or to be a repository for the whole treasure of English verse. I have chosen only what I consider the best, however well-known or unfamiliar it may be. But I make no claim to have read everything. I write here as a layman, not as a "professed" or professional "student of literature", and I should be sorry to think that there are not many beautiful poems, well known to others, still waiting to be discovered by me. Ignorance is fortunately not here a matter of professional disgrace. My intrusion into this field has been justified only if I have by suggesting a fresh and rewarding point of view enabled some others to share the various delights and profound satisfactions that English poetry may give.

As I have explained, the book is intended primarily as the clear record of a succession of distinct creative movements, and if lengthened at all would include more of the same poets rather than something of many others. For by the definition of poetry here indicated most of the latter are to be regarded as followers, using the current poetical idiom in verse which shines as much by reflected light as by its own interior fires. I have been concerned here only with the creators. That writers of what is in the strict sense unoriginal verse do often achieve a measure of beauty I would not deny. But my concern here has been to demonstrate the several phases of our incomparable English poetry in their purity and integrity.

I

LATE-MEDIAEVAL POEMS

The Sacred Fire

1. Lenten is come . . .

LENTEN is come with love to toune
With blosmen and with briddès roune,
 That al this blissè bryngeth,
Dayès-eyès in this dales,
Notès suete of nyhtègales;
 Uch foul song singeth.
The threstelcoc him threteth oo;
Away is huere wynter woo,
 When wodèrovè springeth.
This foulès singeth ferly fele
Ant wlyteth on huere wynter wele,
 That al the wodè ryngeth.

The rosè rayleth hire rode;
The levès on the lyhtè wode
 Waxen al with wille.
The monè mandeth hire bleo
The lilie is lossom to seo,
 The fenyl ant the fille
Wowès thisè wildè drakes;
Milès murgeth huere makes,
 Ase strem that striketh stille.
Mody meneth, so doht mo,
Ichot ycham on of tho,
 For love that likès ille.

The monè mandeth hire lyht;
So doth the semly sonnè bryht,
 When briddès singeth breme.
Deawès donketh the dounes,
Deorès with huere dernè rounes,
 Domès fortè deme.
Wormès woweth under cloude;
Wymmen waxeth wounder proude,

So wel hit wol hem seme.
Yef me shal wontè wille of on,
This wunnè weole I wole forgon,
     Ant wyht in wode be fleme.

early 14th Century   ANONYMOUS

2. When the nyhtègalè singes . . .

WHEN the nyhtègalè singes,
     The wodès waxen grene,
Lef ant gras ant blosmè springes
     In averyl, I wene;
Ant love is to myn hertè gon
     With onè spere so kene,
Nyht ant day my blod hit drynkes,
     Myn hertè deth to tene.

Ich have lovèd al this yer
     That I may love namore;
Ich have sikèd moni syk,
     Lemmon, for thin ore.
Me nis love never the ner,
     Ant that me reweth sore.
Suetè lemmon, thench on me,
     Ich have lovèd thee yore.

Suetè lemmon, I preyè thee
     Of love onè speche.
Whil I lyve in world so wyde
     Other nulle I seche.
With thy love, my suetè leof,
     My blis thou mihtès eche;
A suetè cos of thy mouth
     Mihtè be my leche.

early 14th Century   ANONYMOUS

– 30 –

3. Lollai, lollai, litil child!

LOLLAI, lollai, litil child!
  Whi wepistou so sore?
Nedis mostou wepe,
  Hit was iyarkid the yore
Ever to lib in sorow,
  And sich and mourne evere,
As thin eldren did er this,
  Whil hi alivès were.
      Lollai, lollai, litil child,
        Child, lolai, lullow!
      Into uncuth world
        Icommen so ertow.

Bestis and thos foules,
  The fisses in the flode,
And euch schef alives
  Makid of bone and blode,
Whan hi commith to the world
  Hi doth ham silf sum gode,
Al bot the wreche brol
  That is of Adamis blode.
      Lollai, lollai, litil child.
        To kar ertow bemette;
      Thou nost noght this worldis wild
        Bifor the is isette.

Child, if it betidith
  That thou ssalt thrive and the,
Thench thou wer ifostred
  Up thi moder kne;
Ever hab mund in thi hert
  Of thos thingès thre
Whan thou commist, whan thou art,
  And what ssal com of the.
      Lollai, lollai, litil child,
        Child, lollai, lollai!
      With sorow thou come into this world,
        With sorow ssalt wend awai.

The Sacred Fire

Ne tristou to this world;
   Hit is thi ful fo.
The rich he makith pouer,
   The porè rich also.
Hit turneth wo to wel,
   And ekè wel to wo.
Ne trist no man to this world,
   Whil hit turnith so.
      Lollai, lollai, litil child!
        The fote is in the whele.
      Thou nost whoder turne
        To wo other wele.

Child, thou ert a pilgrim
   In wikidnis ibor;
Thou wandrest in this fals world;
   Thou lokè the bifor.
Deth ssal come with a blast
   Ute of a wel dim horre,
Adamis kin dun to cast,
   Him silf hath ido befor.
      Lollai, lollai, litil child!
        So wo the worth Adam
      In the lond of Paradis
        Throgh wikidnes of Satan.

Child, thou nert a pilgrim,
   Bot an uncuthe gist;
Thi dawès beth itold;
   Thi iurneis beth icast.
Whoder thou salt wend,
   North other est,
Deth the sal betide,
   With bitter bale in brest.
      Lollai, lollai, litil child!
        This wo Adam the wroght,
      Whan he of the appil ete,
        And Eve hit him betacht.

early 14th Century   ANONYMOUS

An Anthology

4. Balade

HYDE, Absolon, thy giltè tresses clere;
Ester, ley thou thy meknesse al adoun;
Hyde, Jonathas, al thy frendly manere;
Penalopee, and Marcia Catoun,
Mak of your wyfhod no comparisoun;
Hyde ye your beautès, Isoude and Eleyne.
My lady cometh, that al this may disteyne.

Thy fairè body, lat hit not appere,
Lavyne; and thou, Lucresse of Romè toun,
And Polixene, that boghten love so dere,
And Cleopatre, with al thy passioun,
Hyde ye your trouthe of love and your renoun;
And thou, Tisbe, that hast of love swich peyne.
My lady cometh, that al this may disteyne.

Herro, Dido, Laudomia, alle yfere,
And Phyllis, hanging for thy Demophoun,
And Canace, espyèd by thy chere,
Ysiphile, betraysèd with Jasoun,
Make of your trouthe in love no bost ne soun;
Nor Ypermistre or Adriane, ye tweyne.
My lady cometh, that al this may disteyne.

about 1385   GEOFFREY CHAUCER

5. I synge of a mayden . . .

I SYNGE of a mayden
That is makèles,
Kyng of all kynges
To her sone sche ches.
He cam al so stylle
There his moder was,
As dew in Aprille
That fallyt on the gras.

- 33 -   c

The Sacred Fire

He came al so stylle
To his moderès bour,
As dew in Aprille
That fallyt on the flour.
He came al so stylle
There his moder lay,
As dew in aprille
That fallyt on the spray.
Moder and mayden
Was never non but sche;
Wel may swych a lady
Godès moder be.

early 15th Century ANONYMOUS

6. Cleveland Lyke-Wake Dirge

THIS ae nighte, this ae nighte,
    Every nighte and alle,
Fire and sleete and candle lighte;
    And Christe receive thye saule.

When thou from hence away art past,
    Every nighte and alle,
To Whinny-muir thou com'st at last;
    And Christe receive thye saule.

If ever thou gavest hosen and shoon,
    Every nighte and alle,
Sit thee down and put them on;
    And Christe receive thye saule.

If hosen and shoon thou ne'er gav'st nane,
    Every nighte and alle,
The whinnes sall pricke thee to the bare bane;
    And Christe receive thye saule.

— 34 —

An Anthology

From Whinny-muir when thou may'st pass,
Every nighte and alle,
To Brigg o' Dread thou com'st at last;
And Christe receive thye saule.

If ever thou gave of thy silver and gold,
Every nighte and alle,
At Brigg o' Dread thou 'lt find foothold;
And Christe receive thye saule.

If silver and gold thou ne'er gav'st nane,
Every nighte and alle,
Thou 'lt tumble down towards Hell's flame;
And Christe receive thye saule.

From Brigg o' Dread when thou may'st pass,
Every nighte and alle,
To purgatory fire thou com'st at last;
And Christe receive thye saule.

If ever thou gavest meat or drink,
Every nighte and alle
The fire shall never make thee shrink;
And Christe receive thye saule.

If meate or drinke thou ne'er gav'st nane,
Every nighte and alle
The fire will burn thee to the bare bane;
And Christe receive thye saule.

This ae nighte, this ae nighte,
Every nighte and alle
Fire and sleete, and candle lighte;
And Christe receive thye saule.

TRADITIONAL

II

EARLY-TUDOR POEMS

7. Song

THE maydens came
When I was in my mothers bower
I have all that I wolde.
The bayly berith the bell away
The lyllè the rose the rose I lay
The sylver is whit red is the golde
The robes thay lay in fold.
The bayly berith the bell away
The lyllè the rose the rose I lay
And through the glasse window shines the sone
How shuld I love and I so young
The bayly berith the bell away
The lylle the rose the rose I lay.

first half of 16th Century.   ANONYMOUS

8. Song

WESTRON wynde when wyll thou blow,
The smalle rayne downe can rayne,
Cryst yf my love wer in my armys
And I yn my bed agayne.

early 16th Century   ANONYMOUS

9. The lover sheweth how he is forsaken of such as he sometime enjoyed

THEY flee from me, that sometyme did me seke
With naked fote stalking within my chamber.
I have sene them gentill, tame, and meke,
That now are wyld, and do not remember
That sometyme they have put theimself in daunger
To take bred at my hand: and now they raunge
Besily seking with a continuell change.

Thancked be fortune it hath ben othrewise
Twenty tymes better; but ons, in speciall,
In thinne arraye, after a pleasant gyse,
When her lose gowne did from her shoulders fall,
And she me caught in her armes long and small,
Therewith all swetely did me kysse
And softely saide: "Dere hert how like you this."

It was no dreme: I lay brode waking
But all is turnde, thorough my gentilnes,
Into a straunge fashion of forsaking:
And I have leve to goo of her goodenes:
And she also to use new fangilnes:
But syns that I unkyndely so am served,
I wold fain knowe what hath she now deserved.

about 1535   THOMAS WYAT

10. The lover complayneth of the unkindnes of his love

MY lute awake! perfourme the last
Labor that thou and I shall wast,
And end that I have now begon:
For when this song is song and past,
My lute be still, for I have done.

As to be herd where eare is none,
As lede to grave in marbill stone,
My song may perse her hert as sone:
Should we then sigh or sing or mone.
No! no! my lute, for I have done.

The rokkes do not so cruelly
Repulse the waves continuelly
As she my sute and affection:
So that I am past remedy,
Whereby my lute and I have done.

Proud of the spoyll that thou hast gott
Of simple herts, thorough loves shot:
By whome, unkynd, thou hast theim wone,
Thinck not he hath his bow forgot,
All tho my lute and I have done.

Vengeaunce shall fall on thy disdain
That makest but game on ernest pain:
Think not alone under the sonne
Unquyt to cause thy lovers plain,
All tho my lute and I have done.

Perchaunce thee lie witherd and old
The wynter nights that are so cold,
Playning in vain unto the mone:
Thy wisshes then dare not be told:
Care then who list, for I have done.

And then may chaunce thee to repent
The tyme that thou hast lost and spent
To cause thy lovers sigh and swone:
Then shalt thou knowe beautie but lent,
And wisshe and want as I have done.

Now cesse, my lute: this is the last
Labor that thou and I shall wast,
And ended is that we begon:
Now is this song both song and past
My lute be still, for I have done.

about 1535 THOMAS WYAT

11. He ruleth not though he raigne over realmes that is subject to his owne lustes

IF thou wilt mighty be, flee from the rage
Of cruell wyll, and see thou kepe thee free
From the foule yoke of sensuall bondage,
For though thy empyre stretche to Indian sea,
And for thy feare trembleth the fardest Thylee,
If thy desire have over thee the power,
Subject then art thou and no governour.

If to be noble and high thy minde be meved,
Consider well thy grounde and thy beginnying:
For he that hathe eche starre in heaven fixed,
And geves the Moon her hornes and her eclipsying:
Alike hath made the noble in his workyng,
So that wretched no way thou may bee,
Except foule lust and vice do conquere thee.

All were it so thou had a flood of golde,
Unto thy thirst yet should it not suffice.
And though with Indian stones a thousande folde,
More precious then can thy selfe devise,
Ycharged were thy backe: thy covitise
And busye bytyng yet should never let,
Thy wretched life ne do thy death profet.

about 1540 THOMAS WYAT

– 42 –

12. Description of Spring, wherein eche thing
    renewes, save onlie the lover

THE soote season, that bud and blome furth brings,
With grene hath clad the hill and eke the vale:
The nightingale with fethers new she singes:
The turtle to her make hath told her tale:
Somer is come, for every spray now springes,
The hart hath hong his olde hed on the pale:
The buck in brake his winter cote he flinges:
The fishes flote with new repaired scale:
The adder all her sloughe awaye she slinges:
The swift swalow pursueth the flyes smale:
The busy bee her honye now she minges:
Winter is worne that was the flowers bale:
And thus I see among these pleasant thinges
Eche care decayes, and yet my sorow springes.

about 1545　　　HENRY HOWARD, EARL OF SURREY

III

from The Shepheardes Calender

The Sacred Fire

13. *from* The Shepheardes Calender: December

THE gentle shepheard satte beside a springe
All in the shadowe of a bushye brere,
That *Colin* hight, which wel could pipe and singe
For he of *Tityrus* his songs did lere.
    There as he satte in secreate shade alone,
    Thus gan he make of love his piteous moan.

O soveraigne *Pan* thou God of shepheards all,
Which of our tender Lambkins takest keep:
And when our flocks into mischance might fall,
Dost save from mischiefe the unwary sheep:
    Als of their maisters hast no less regard
    Than of their flocks, which thou dost watch and ward.

I thee beseche (so be thou deigne to heare,
Rude ditties tund to shepheards oaten reede,
Of if I ever sonet song so cleare,
As it with pleasaunce might thy fancie feede)
    Hearken awhile from thy greene cabinet,
    The rurall song of carefull Colinet.

Whilome in youth, when flowrd my joyfull Spring,
Like swallow swift I wandred here and there:
For heate of heedless lust me so did sting,
That I of doubted danger had no feare.
    I went the wastefull woodes and forest wyde,
    Withouten dreade of Wolves to bene espyed.

I wont to raunge amydde the mazie thickette,
And gather nuttes to make me Christmas game:
And joyed oft to chase the trembling Pricket,
Or hunt the hartlesse hare, till she were tame.
    What wreaked I of wintrye ages waste,
    Tho deemed I my spring would ever laste.

The Sacred Fire

How often have I scaled the craggie Oak,
All to dislodge the Raven of her neste:
How have I wearied with many a stroke
The stately Walnut tree, the while the rest
    Under the tree fell all for nuts at strife:
    For ylike to me was libertee and lyfe.

And for I was in thilke same looser yeares,
(Whether the Muse so wrought me from my birth,
Or I too much beleeved my shepheard peers)
Somedele ybent to song and musicks mirth.
    A good olde shepheard, *Wrenock* was his name,
    Made me by arte more cunning in the same.

Fro thence I durst in derring doe compare
With shepheards swayne, whatever fedde in field:
And if that *Hobbinol* right judgement bare,
To *Pan* his owne selfe pype I need not yield.
    For if the flocking Nymphes did follow *Pan*,
    The wiser Muses after *Colin* ran.

But ah such pryde at length was ill repayde,
The shepheards God (perdie God he was none)
My hurtless pleasaunce did me ill upbraide,
My freedom lorne, my life he left to mone
    Love they him called, that gave me checkmate
    But better might they have behote him Hate.

Tho gan my lovely Spring bid me farewel,
And Sommer season sped him to display
(For love then in the Lyons house did dwel)
The raging fyre, that kindled at his ray.
    A comett stird up that unkindly heate,
    That reigned (as men sayd) in *Venus* seate.

Forth was I ledde, not as I wont afore,
When choise I had to choose my wandering waye:
But whether luck or loves unbridled lore
Would leade me forth on Fancies bitte to playe,
    The bush my bedde, the bramble was my bowre,
    The Woodes can witness many a wofull stowre.

Where I was wonte to seeke the honey Bee,
Working her formall rowmes in Wexen frame:
The grieslie Todestoole growne there mought I see
And loathed Paddocks lording on the same.
    And where the chaunting birds luld me asleepe,
    The ghastlie Owle her grievous ynne doth keepe.

Then as the springe gives place to elder time,
And bringeth forth the fruit of sommers pryde:
All so my age now passed youngthly pryme,
To things of riper reason selfe applied.
    And learnd of lighter timber cotes to frame,
    Such as might save my sheep and me fro shame.

To make fine cages for the Nightingale,
And Baskets of bulrushes was my wont:
Who to entrappe the fish in winding sale
Was better seene, or hurtful beastes to hont?
    I learned als the signes of heaven to ken,
    How *Phoebe* fayles, where *Venus* sittes and when.

And tryed time yet taught me greater things,
The sodain rysing of the raging seas;
The soothe of birds by beating of their winges,
The power of herbs, both which can hurt and ease;
    And which be wont t'enrage the restlesse sheepe,
    And which be wont to work eternall sleepe.

But ah unwise and witlesse *Colin cloute*
That kydst the hidden kinds of many a wede:
Yet kydst not ene to cure thy sore hart roote,
Whose ranckling wound as yet does rifelye bleede.
    Why livest thou still, and yet hast thy deaths wound?
    Why dyest thou still, and yet alive art founde?

Thus is my sommer worne away and wasted,
Thus is my harvest hastened all to rathe:
The care that budded faire, is burnt and blasted,
And all my hoped gaine is turned to scathe.
    Of all the seede, that in my youth was sowne,
    Was nought but brakes and brambles to be mowne.

My boughes with bloosmes that crowned were at firste,
And promised of such timely fruite such store,
Are left both bare and barren now at erst
The flattring fruite is fallen to grownd before,
    And rotted, ere they were halfe mellow ripe:
    My harvest wast, my hope away dyd wipe.

The fragrant flowres, that in my garden grewe,
Bene withered, as they had bene gathered long.
Theyr rootes bene dryed up for lacke of dewe,
Yet dewed with teares they han be ever among.
    Ah who has wrought my *Rosalind* this spight
    To spill the flowers, that should her girlond dight?

And I, that whilome wont to frame my pipe,
Unto the shifting of the shepheards foote:
Sike follies nowe have gathered as too ripe,
And cast hem out, as rotten and unsoote.
    The loser Lasse I cast to please nomore,
    One if I please, enough is me therefore.

And thus of all my harvest hope I have
Nought reaped but a weedy crop of care:
Which when I thought have thresht in swelling sheave,
Cockel for corne, and chaffe for barley bare.
   Soon as the chaffe should in the fan be fyned,
   All was blowne away of the wavering wynd.

So now my yeare drawes to his latter terme
My spring is spent, my sommer burnt up quite:
My harveste hasts to stirre up winter sterne,
And bids him clayme with rigorous rage hys right.
   So nowe he stormes with many a sturdy stoure,
   So nowe his blustring blast eche coste doth scoure.

The carefull cold hath nypt my rugged rynde,
And in my face deepe furrowes eld hath pight:
My head besprent with hoary frost I fynd,
And by myne eie the Crow his claw dooth wright.
   Delight is layd abedde, and pleasure past,
   No sonne now shines, cloudes han all overcast.

Now leave ye shepheard boyes your merry glee,
My Muse is hoarse and weary of thys stounde:
Here will I hang my pype upon this tree,
Was never pype of reede did better sounde.
   Winter is come, that blowes the bitter blaste,
   And after Winter drearie death does hast.

Gather ye together my little flocke
My little flocke, that was to me so liefe:
Let me, ah lette me in your folds ye lock,
Ere the breme Winter breede you greater griefe.
   Winter is come, that blowes the balefull breath
   And after Winter commeth timely death.

The Sacred Fire

Adieu delightes, that lulled me asleepe,
Adieu my deare, whose love I bought so deare:
Adieu my little Lambes and loved sheepe,
Adieu ye Woodes that oft my witnesse were:
    Adieu good *Hobbinol*, that was so true,
    Tell *Rosalind*, her *Colin* bids her a dieu.

about 1578–9   EDMUND SPENSER

IV

Christopher Marlowe
from Venus and Adonis
Thomas Lodge
Edmund Spenser

14. *from* The Second Part of The Bloody Conquests of Mighty Tamburlaine

I WILL with Engines never exercisde,
Conquer, sacke, and utterly consume
Your cities and your golden pallaces,
And with the flames that beat against the clowdes
Incense the heavens and make the starres to melt
As if they were the teares of *Mahomet*,
For hot consumption of his countries pride.
And til by vision or by speach I heare
Immortal *Jove* say, Cease my *Tamburlaine*
I will persist a terrour to the world,
Making the meteors, that like arm'd men
Are seene to march upon the towers of heaven,
Run tilting round about the firmament
And breake their burning Lances in the aire,
For honor of my woondrous victories.

about 1588   CHRISTOPHER MARLOWE

15. *from* Hero and Leander

THE men of wealthie *Sestos*, everie yeare
(For his sake whom their goddesse held so deare,
Rose-cheekt *Adonis*) kept a solemne fest.
Thither resorted many a wandring guest
To meet their loves; such as had none at all,
Came lovers home from this great festivall.
For everie street like to a Firmament
Glistered with breathing stars, who where they went
Frighted the melancholie earth, which deem'd
Eternall heaven to burne, for so it seem'd
As if another Phaeton had got
The guidance of the sunnes rich chariot.
But far above the loveliest *Hero* shin'd,
And stole away th' inchaunted gazers mind.

The Sacred Fire

For like Sea-nimphs inveigling harmony
So was her beautie to the standers by
Nor that night-wandring pale and watrie starre
(When yawning dragons draw her thirling carre
From *Latmus* mount up to the glomie sky
Where crown'd with blazing light and majestie,
She proudly sits) more overrules the flood,
Than she the hearts of those that neere her stood.

*   *   *

On this feast day, O cursed day and hour,
Went *Hero* thorow *Sestos*, from her tower
To Venus temple, where unhappilye,
As after chaunc'd, they did each other spye.
So faire a church as this had *Venus* none;
The walls were of discoloured *Jasper* stone,
Wherein was *Proteus* carved, and o'rehead,
A livelie vine of green sea-agate spread;
Where by one hand, light headed *Bacchus* hung
And with the other wine from grapes outwroong.
Of Christall shining faire the pavement was,
The town of *Sestos* call'd it *Venus'* glasse.
There might you see the gods in sundrie shapes,
Committing headdie ryots, incests, rapes:
For know, that underneath this radiant floure
Was *Danaes* statue in a brazen tower,
Jove slylie stealing from his sisters bed,
To dallie with *Idalian Ganimed*,
And for his love *Europa* bellowing loud
And tumbling with the Rainbow in a cloud:
Blood-quaffing *Mars* heaving the yron net,
Which limping *Vulcan* and his *Cyclops* set:
Love kindling fire to burne such townes as *Troy*:
Sylvanus weeping, for the lovely boy
That now is turn'd into a *Cypres* tree,
Under whose shade the Wood-gods love to bee.
And in the midst a silver altar stood;
There *Hero* sacrificing turtles blood
Vaild to the ground, vailing her eie-lids close,

And modestly they opened as she rose:
Thence flew Loves arrow with the golden head,
And thus *Leander* was enamoured.
Stone still he stood, and evermore he gazed,
Till with the fire that from his count'nance blazed,
Relenting *Heroe*, gentle heart was strooke,
Such force and vertue has an amorous looke.
  It lies not in our power to love or hate
For will in us is over-rul'd by fate.
When two are stripp'd, long ere the course begin,
We wish that one should loose, the other win.
And one especiallie doe we affect
Of two gold Ingots, like in each respect.
The reason no man knowes; let it suffise,
What we behold is censur'd by our eies.
Where both deliberat, the love is slight,
Who ever lov'd, that lov'd not at first sight?
  He kneel'd, but unto her devoutly praid;
Chaste *Hero* to her selfe thus softly said:
Were I the saint he worships, I would heare him.
And as shee spake these words, came somewhat nere him.
He started up, she blusht as one asham'd,
Wherewith *Leander* much more was inflam'd.
He toucht her hand, in touching it she trembled,
Love deepely grounded, hardly is dissembled.
These lovers parled by the touch of hands,
True love is mute, and oft amazed stands.
Thus while dum signs their yeelding harts entangled,
The aire with sparkes of living fire was spangled,
And night deepe drencht in mystie *Acheron*
Heav'd up her head, and halfe the world upon
Breath'd darkenesse forth (darke night is *Cupids* day)
And now begins *Leander* to display
Loves holy fire, with words, with sighs and teares,
Which like sweet musicke entred *Heroe's* eares,
And yet at everie word she turn'd aside,
And alwaies cut him off as he replide.

about 1593   CHRISTOPHER MARLOWE

The Sacred Fire

16. *from* Venus and Adonis

Looke how a bird lyes tangled in a net,
So fastned in her armes Adonis lyes;
Pure shame and aw'd resistance made him fret,
Which bred more beautie in his angrie eyes:
  Raine added to a river that is ranke
  Perforce will force it overflow the banke.

Still she intreats, and prettily intreats,
For to a prettie eare she tunes her tale;
Still is he sullein, still he lowres and frets,
Twixt crimson shame and anger ashie pale;
  Being red she loves him best, and being white,
  Her best is betterd with a more delight.

Looke how he can, she cannot chuse but love;
And by her faire immortall hand she sweares,
From his soft bosome never to remove,
Till he take truce with her contending teares,
  Which long have raind, making her cheeks all wet,
  And one sweet kisse shall pay this comptlesse debt.

Upon this promise did he raise his chin,
Like a dive-dapper peering through a wave,
Who, being lookt on, ducks as quickly in;
So offers he to give what she did crave;
  But when her lips were ready for his pay,
  He winks, and turnes his lips another way.

Never did passenger in summer heat
More thirst for drinke, then she for this good turne,
Her helpe she sees, but helpe she cannot get;
She bathes in water, yet her fire must burne:
  O pitie, gan she crie, flint-hearted boy,
  Tis but a kisse I begge, why art thou coy?

I have bene wooed, as I intreat thee now,
Even by the sterne and direfull god of warre,
Whose sinowy necke in battell nere did bow,
Who conquers where he comes in everie jarre,
    Yet hath he bene my captive, and my slave,
    And begd for that which thou unaskt shalt have.

Over my altars hath he hung his launce,
His battred shield, his uncontrolled crest,
And for my sake hath learnd to sport and daunce,
To toy, to wanton, dallie, smile and jest;
    Scorning his childish drumme and ensigne red,
    Making my armes his field, his tent my bed.

Thus he that over-ruld I over-swayed,
Leading him prisoner in a red rose chaine:
Strong-temperd steele his stronger strength obayed,
Yet was he servile to my coy disdaine.
    Oh be not proud, nor brag not of thy might,
    For maistring her that foyld the god of fight.

Touch but my lips with those faire lips of thine,
Though mine be not so faire, yet are they red,
The kisse shall be thine owne as well as mine,
What seest thou in the ground? hold up thy head,
    Looke in mine eyeballs, there thy beauty lyes,
    Then why not lips on lips, since eyes in eyes?

Art thou asham'd to kisse? then winke againe,
And I will winke; so shall the day seeme night.
Love keepes his revels where there are but twaine;
Be bold to play, our sport is not in sight:
    These blew-veind violets whereon we leane,
    Never can blab, nor know not what we meane.

The Sacred Fire

The tender spring upon thy tempting lip,
Shews thee unripe; yet maist thou well be tasted,
Make use of time, let not advantage slip,
Beautie within itself should not be wasted,
    Fair flowers that are not gathred in their prime,
    Rot, and consume themselves in little time.

Were I hard-favour'd, foule, or wrinckled old,
Ill-nurtur'd, crooked, churlish, harsh in voice,
Ore-worne, despised, reumatique, and cold,
Thick-sighted, barren, lean, and lacking juyce,
    Then mightst thou pause, for then I were not for thee,
    But having no defects, why dost abhor me?

Thou canst not see one wrinckle in my brow,
Mine eyes are grey, and bright, and quicke in turning;
My beautie as the spring doth yearelie grow,
My flesh is soft, and plumpe, my marrow burning;
    My smooth moist hand, were it with thy hand felt,
    Would in thy palm dissolve, or seeme to melt.

Bid me discourse I will enchant thine eare,
Or like a Fairie, trip upon the greene,
Or, like a Nimph, with long disheveled haire,
Daunce on the sands, and yet no footing seene.
    Love is a spirit all compact of fire,
    Not grosse to sinke, but light, and will aspire.

Witnesse this Primrose banke whereon I lie;
These forcelesse flowers like sturdy trees support me:
Two strengthless doves will draw me through the skie,
From morne till night, even where I list to sport me.
    Is love so light sweet boy, and may it be
    That thou shouldst think it heavy unto thee?

Is thine owne heart to thine own face affected?
Can thy right hand ceaze love upon thy left?
Then woo thy selfe, be of thy selfe rejected:
Steale thine own freedom, and complain on theft.
    Narcissus so him selfe him self forsooke,
    And died to kisse his shadow in the brooke.

Torches are made to light, jewels to weare,
Dainties to tast, fresh beautie for the use,
Herbes for their smell, and sappy plants to beare.
Things growing to them selves are growths abuse,
    Seeds spring from seeds and beauty breedeth beauty,
    Thou wast begot, to get it is thy duty.

Upon the earths increase why shouldst thou feed,
Unlesse the earth with thy increase be fed?
By law of nature those art bound to breed,
That thine may live, when thou thy selfe art dead:
    And so in spite of death thou dost survive,
    In that thy likenesse still is left alive.

about 1593   **WILLIAM SHAKESPEARE**

17. Rosalynde's Madrigall

LOVE in my bosome, like a bee
    Doth sucke his sweete;
Now with his wings he playes with me,
    Now with his feete.
Within mine eyes he makes his nest,
His bed amidst my tender brest
My kisses are his dayly fest
And yet he robs me of my rest
    Ah wanton will ye?

And if I sleepe, then pearcheth he,
  With pretty flight,
And makes a pillow of my knee
  The livelong night.
Strike I my lute, he tunes the string,
He musicke playes if so I sing
He lends me every lovely thing:
Yet cruell he my heart doth sting.
    Whist wanton still ye.

Else I with roses, every day
  Will whip you hence,
And binde you when you long to play
  For your offence.
Ile shut my eyes to keepe you in,
Ile make you fast it for your sinne,
Ile count your power not worth a pinne
Alas, what hereby shall I winne,
    If he gainsay me?

What if I beate the wanton boy
  With many a rod?
He will repay me with annoy,
  Because a god.
Then sit you safely on my knee
And let thy bower my bosome be:
Lurke in mine eies, I like of thee:
O Cupid, so thou pittie me,
    Spare not but play thee.

about 1590   THOMAS LODGE

18. Rosaders Sonnet: sent to Rosalynde

Two sunnes at once from one fair heaven there shinde,
Ten branches from two boughes tipt all with roses,
Pure lockes more golden than is golde refinde,
Two pearled rowes that Natures pride incloses.

Two mounts faire marble white, down-soft and dainty,
A snow died orbe: where love increast by pleasure
Full wofull makes my heart, and body faintie:
Hir faire (my woe) exceeds all thought and measure.

In lines confusde my lucklesse harme appeareth,
Whom sorrow cloudes, whom pleasant smiling cleareth.

about 1590   THOMAS LODGE

19. Song
Imitated from the Italian of Martelli

O SHADIE vales, O faire inriched meades,
O sacred woodes, sweete fields, and rising mountaines,
O painted flowers, greene herbes, where Flora treads,
Refresht by wanton windes and watrie fountaines!

O all you winged queristers of woode,
That pierched aloft your former paines report,
And strait againe recount with pleasant moode,
Your present joyes in sweete and seemely sort.

O all you creatures, whosoever thrive,
On mother earth, in seas, by aire or fire,
More blest are you then I here under sunne:
Love dies in me, whenas he doth revive
In you; I perish under beauties ire,
Where after stormes, windes, frosts, your life is wonne.

about 1595   THOMAS LODGE

20. Epithalamion

YE learned sisters which have oftentimes
Beene to me ayding, others to adorne,
Whom ye thought worthy of your gracefull rymes,
That even the greatest did not greatly scorne
To hear theyr names sung in your simple layes,
But joyed in theyr prayse.
And when ye list your owne mishaps to mourne,
When death, or love, or fortunes wreck did rayse,
Your string could soone to sadder tenor turne,
And teach the woods and waters to lament
Your dolefull dreriment.
Now lay those sorrowfull complaints aside,
And having all your heads with girland crownd,
Help me mine owne loves prayses to resound,
Ne let the same of any be envide:
So Orpheus did for his owne bride,
So I unto my selfe alone will sing,
The woods shall to me answer and my eccho ring.

Early before the worlds light-giving lampe
His golden beame upon the hils doth spred,
Having disperst the nights unchearefull dampe,
Doe ye awake, and with fresh lusty hed,
Go to the bowre of my beloved love,
My truest turtle dove,
Bid her awake; for Hymen is awake,
And long since ready forth his maske to move,
With his bright Tead that flames with many a flake,
And many a bachelor to waite on him,
In theyr fresh garments trim.
Bid her awake therefore and soone her dight,
For lo the wished day is come at last,
That shall for al the paynes and sorrowes past,
Pay to her usury of long delight:
And whylest she doth her dight,
Doe ye to her of joy and solace sing,
That all the woods may answer and your eccho ring.

Bring with you all the Nymphes that you can heare
Both of the rivers and the forrests greene:
And of the sea that neighbours to her neare,
Al with gay girlands goodly wel besene.
And let them also with them bring in hand,
Another gay girland
For my fayre love of lillyes and of roses,
Bound truelove wize with a blew silke riband.
And let them make great store of bridale poses,
And let them eeke bring store of other flowers
To deck the bridale bowers.
And let the ground whereas her foot shall tread,
For feare the stones her tender foot should wrong
Be strewed with fragrant flowers all along,
And diapred lyke the discolored mead.
Which done, do at her chamber dore awayt,
For she will waken strayt,
The whiles doe ye this song unto her sing,
The woods shall to you answer and your eccho ring.

Ye Nymphes of Mulla which with carefull heed,
The silver scaly trouts doe tend full well,
And greedy pikes which use therein to feed,
(Those trouts and pikes all others do excell)
And ye likewise which keepe the rushy lake,
Where none doo fishes take,
Bynd up the locks the which hang scatterd light,
And in the waters which your mirror make,
Behold your faces as the christall bright,
That when you come whereas my love doth lie,
No blemish she may spie.
And eke ye lightfoot mayds which keepe the deere,
That on the hoary mountayne use to towre,
And the wylde wolves which seeke them to devoure,
With your steele darts do chase from comming neer,
Be also present heere,
To helpe to decke her and to help to sing,
That all the woods may answer and your eccho ring.

The Sacred Fire

Wake, now my love, awake: for it is time,
The Rosy Morne long since left Tithones bed
All ready to her silver coche to clyme,
And Phoebus gins to show his glorious hed.
Hark how the cheerefull birds do chaunt theyr laies
And carroll of loves praise.
The merry Larke hir mattins sings aloft,
The Thrush replies, the Mavis descant playes,
The Ouzell shrills, the Ruddock warbles soft,
So goodly all agree with sweet consent,
To this dayes merriment.
Ah my deere love why doe ye sleepe thus long,
When meeter were that ye should now awake,
T' awayt the comming of your joyous make,
And hearken to the birds lovelearned song,
The deawy leaves among.
For they of joy and pleasance to you sing.
That all the woods them answer and theyr eccho ring.

My love is now awake out of her dreame,
And her fayre eyes like stars that dimmed were
With darksome cloud, now show their goodly beams
More bright then Hesperus his head doth rere,
Come now ye damzels, daughters of delight,
Helpe quickly to her dight,
But first come ye fayre hours which were begot
In loves sweet paradice of Day and Night,
Which doe the seasons of the yeare allot,
And all that ever in this world is fayre
Doe make and still repayre.
And ye three handmayds of the Cyprian Queene,
The which doe still adorne her beauties pride,
Help to addorne my beautifullest bride:
And as ye her array, still throw betweene
Some graces to be seene,
And as ye use to Venus, to her sing
The whiles the woods shal answer and your eccho ring.

Now is my love all ready forth to come,
Let all the virgins therefore well awayt,
And ye fresh boyes that tend upon her groome
Prepare your selves; for he is comming strayt.
Set all your things in seemely good array
Fit for so joyfull day,
The joyfulst day that ever sunne did see.
Fair Sun, shew forth thy favourable ray,
And let thy lifull heat not fervent be
For fear of burning her sunshyny face,
Her beauty to disgrace.
O fayrest Phoebus, father of the Muse,
If ever I did honour thee aright,
Or sing the thing, that mote thy mind delight,
Doe not thy servants simple boone refuse,
But let this day let this one day be myne,
Let all the rest be thine.
Then I thy soverayne prayses loud wil sing,
That all the woods shal answer and theyr eccho ring.

Harke how the minstrels gin to shrill aloud
Their merry musick that resounds from far,
The pipe, the tabor, and the trembling Croud,
That well agree withouten breach or jar.
But most of all the damzels doe delite,
When they their tymbrels smyte,
And thereunto doe daunce and carrol sweet,
That all the sences they doe ravish quite,
The whyles the boyes run up and downe the street,
Crying aloud with strong confused noyce
As if it were one voyce:
Hymen io Hymen, Hymen, they do shout,
That even to the heavens their shouting shrill
Doth reach, and all the firmament doth fill,
To which the people standing all about,
As in approvance do thereto applaud
And loud advaunce her laud,

And evermore they Hymen, Hymen, sing
That all the woods them answer and theyr eccho ring.

Loe where she comes along with portly pace
Lyke Phoebe from her chamber of the East,
Arysing forth to run her mighty race,
Clad all in white, that seemes a virgin best.
So well it her beseemes that ye would weene
Some angell she had beene.
Her long loose yellow locks lyke golden wyre,
Sprinckled with perle, and perling flowres a tweene,
Doe lyke a golden mantle her attyre,
And being crowned with a girland greene,
Seeme lyke some mayden Queene.
Her modest eyes abashed to behold
So many gazers, as on her do stare,
Upon the lowly ground affixed are.
Ne dare lift up her countenance too bold,
But blush to heare her prayses sung so loud,
So farre from being proud.
Nathelesse doe ye still loud her prayses sing
That all the woods may answer and your eccho ring.

Tell me ye merchants daughters did ye see
So fayre a creature in your towne before,
So sweet, so lovely, and so milde as she,
Adornd with beautyes grace and vertues store,
Her goodly eyes lyke Saphyres shining bright,
Her forehead yvory white,
Her cheekes lyke apples which the sun hath rudded,
Her lips lyke cherryes charming men to byte,
Her brest lyke to a bowl of cream uncrudded,
Her paps lyke lyllies budded,
Her snowy neck lyke to a marble towre
And all her body like a pallace fayre
Ascending uppe with many a stately stayre,
To honors seat and chastities sweet bowre.
Why stand ye still ye virgins in amaze,
Upon her so to gaze,

Whiles ye forget your former lay to sing,
To which the woods did answer and your eccho ring.

But if ye saw that which no eyes can see,
The inward beauty of her lively spright,
Garnisht with heavenly guifts of high degree,
Much more then would ye wonder at that sight,
And stand astonisht lyke to those which red
Medusaes mazeful hed.
There dwels sweet love and constant chastity,
Unspotted fayth and comely womanhood,
Regard of honour and mild modesty,
There vertue raynes as Queene in royal throne,
And giveth lawes alone.
The which the base affections doe obay,
And yeeld theyr services unto her will,
Ne thought of thing uncomely ever may
Thereto approch to tempt her mind to ill.
Had ye once seene these her celestial threasures,
And unrevealed pleasures,
Then would ye wonder and her praises sing,
That al the woods should answer and your echo ring.

Open the temple gates unto my love,
Open them wide that she may enter in,
And all the postes adorne as doth behove,
And all the pillours deck with girlands trim,
For to recyve this Saynt with honour dew,
That commeth in to you.
With trembling steps and humble reverence,
She commeth in, before th' almighties vew,
Of her ye virgins learne obedience,
When so ye come into these holy places,
To humble your proud faces:
Bring her up to th' high altar, that she may
The sacred ceremonies there partake,
The which do endlesse matrimony make,
And let the roring Organs loudly play
The praises of the Lord in lively notes

The Sacred Fire

The whiles with hollow throates
The Choristers the joyous Antheme sing,
That al the woods may answere and their eccho ring.

Behold whiles she before the altar stands
Hearing the holy priest that to her speakes
And blesseth her with his two happy hands,
How the red roses flush up in her cheekes,
And the pure snow with goodly vermill stayne,
Like crimsin dyde in grayne,
That even th' Angels which continually,
Above the sacred Altare do remaine,
Forget their service and about her fly,
Ofte peeping in her face that seemes more fayre,
The more they on it stare.
But her sad eyes still fastened on the ground,
Are governed with goodly modesty,
That suffers not one looke to glaunce awry,
Which may let in a little thought unsownd.
Why blush ye love to give to me your hand,
The pledge of all our band?
Sing ye sweet Angels, Alleluya sing,
That all the woods may answere and your eccho ring.

Now al is done; bring home the bride againe,
Bring home the triumph of our victory,
Bring home with you the glory of her gaine,
With joyance bring her and with jollity.
Never had man more joyfull day than this,
Whom heaven would heap with blis.
Make feast therefore now all this live long day,
This day for ever to me holy is,
Poure out the wine without restraint or stay,
Poure not by cups, but by the belly full,
Poure out to all that wull,
And sprinkle all the postes and wals with wine,
That they may sweat and drunken be withall.
Crowne ye God Bacchus with a coronall,
And Hymen also crowne with wreathes of vine,

And let the graces daunce unto the rest;
For they can doo it best:
The whiles the maydens doe theyr carroll sing,
To which the woods shal answer and theyr eccho ring.

Ring ye the bels, ye yong men of the towne,
And leave your wonted labors for this day:
This day is holy; doe ye write it downe,
That ye for ever it remember may.
This day the sunne is in his chiefest hight,
With Barnaby the bright,
From whence declining daily by degrees,
He somewhat loseth of his heat and light,
When once the Crab behind his back he sees.
But for this time it ill ordained was
To choose the longest day in all the yeare,
And shortest night, when longest fitter weare:
Yet never day so long, but late would passe.
Ring ye the bels, to make it weare away,
And bonefiers make all day,
And daunce about them, and about them sing:
That all the woods may answer, and your eccho ring.

Ah when will this long weary day have end,
And lende me leave to come unto my love?
How slowly do the houres theyr numbers spend?
How slowly does sad Time his feathers move?
Hast thee O fayrest Planet to thy home
Within the Western fome:
Thy tyred steedes long since have need of rest.
Long though it be, at last I see it gloome,
And the bright evening star with golden creast
Appeare out of the East.
Fayre childe of beauty, glorious lampe of love
That all the host of heaven in rankes doost lead,
And guydest lovers through the nightes dread,
How chearefully thou lookest from above,
And seemst to laugh atweene thy twinkling light
As joying in the sight

Of these glad many which for joy doe sing,
That all the woods them answer and their eccho ring.

Now ceasse ye damsels your delights forepast:
Enough is it, that all the day was youres:
Now day is doen, and night is nighing fast:
Now bring the Bryde into the brydall boures.
Now night is come, now soone her disaray,
And in her bed her lay;
Lay her in lillies and in violets,
And silken courteins over her display,
And odourd sheets, and Arras coverlets.
Behold how goodly my faire love does ly
In proud humility;
Like unto Maia, when as Jove her tooke,
In Tempe, lying on the flowry gras,
Twixt sleepe and wake, after she weary was,
With bathing in the Acidalian brooke.
Now it is night, ye damsels may be gon,
And leave my love alone,
And leave likewise your former lay to sing:
The woods no more shal answere, nor your eccho ring.

Now welcome night, thou night so long expected,
That long daies labour doest at last defray,
And all my cares, which cruell love collected,
Hast sumd in one, and cancelled for aye:
Spread thy broad wing over my love and me,
That no man may us see,
And in thy sable mantle us enwrap,
From feare of perrill and foule horror free.
Let no false treason seeke us to entrap,
Nor any dread disquiet once annoy
The safety of our joy:
But let the night be calme and quietsome,
Without tempestuous stormes or sad afray:
Lyke as when Jove with fayre Alcmena lay,
When he begot the great Tirynthian groome:
Or lyke as when he with thy selfe did lie,

And begot Majesty.
And let the mayds and yongmen cease to sing:
Ne let the woods them answer, nor theyr eccho ring.

Let no lamenting cryes, nor dolefull teares,
Be heard all night within nor yet without:
Ne let false whispers, breeding hidden feares,
Breake gentle sleepe with misconceived dout.
Let no deluding dreames, nor dreadful sights
Make sudden sad affrights;
Ne let housefyres, nor lightnings helplesse harmes,
Ne let the Pouke, nor other evill sprights,
Ne let mischivous witches with theyr charmes,
Ne let hob Goblins, names whose sence we see not,
Fray us with things that be not.
Let not the shriech Oule, nor the Storke be heard:
Nor the night Raven that still deadly yels,
Nor damned ghosts cald up with mighty spels,
Nor griesly vultures make us once affeard:
Ne let th' unpleasant Quyre of Frogs still croking
Make us to wish theyr choking.
Let none of these theyr drery accents sing;
Ne let the woods them answer, nor theyr eccho ring.

But let stil Silence trew night watches keepe,
That sacred peace may in assurance rayne,
And tymely sleep, when it is tyme to sleepe,
May poure his limbs forth on your pleasant playne,
The whiles an hundred little winged loves,
Like divers fethered doves,
Shall fly and flutter round about your bed,
And in the secret darke, that none reproves,
Their prety stealthes shal worke, and snares shal spread
To filch away sweet snatches of delight,
Conceald through covert night.
Ye sonnes of Venus, play your sports at will,
For greedy pleasure careless of your toyes,
Thinks more upon her paradise of joyes,
Then what ye do, albeit good or ill.

The Sacred Fire

All night therefore attend your merry play,
For it will soone be day:
Now none doth hinder you, that say or sing,
Ne will the woods now answer, nor your eccho ring.

Who is the same, that at my window peepes?
Or whose is that faire face, that shines so bright?
Is it not Cinthia, she that never sleepes,
But walkes about high heaven al the night?
O fayrest goddesse, do thou not envy
My love with me to spy:
For thou likewise didst love, though now unthought,
And for a fleece of woll, which privily,
The Latmian shephard once unto thee brought,
His pleasures with thee wrought.
Therefore to us be favourable now;
And sith of wemens labours thou hast charge,
And generation goodly dost enlarge,
Encline thy will t'effect our wishfull vow,
And the chast wombe informe with timely seed,
That may our comfort breed:
Till which we cease our hopefull hap to sing
Ne let the woods us answer, nor our Eccho ring.

And thou great Juno, which with awful might
The lawes of wedlock still dost patronize
And the religion of the faith first plight
With sacred rites hast taught to solemnize:
And eeke for comfort often called art
Of women in their smart,
Eternally bind thou this lovely band,
And all thy blessings unto us impart.
And thou glad Genius in whose gentle hand,
The bridall bowre and geniall bed remaine,
Without blemish or staine,
And the sweet pleasures of theyr loves delight
With secret ayde doest succour and supply,
Till they bring forth the fruitful progeny,
Send us the timely fruit of this same night.

- 74 -

And thou fayre Hebe, and thou Hymen free,
Grant that it may so be.
Til which we cease your further praise to sing,
Ne any woods shal answer, nor your Eccho ring.

And ye high heavens, the temple of the gods,
In which a thousand torches flaming bright
Doe burne, that to us wretched earthly clods,
In dreadful darknesse lend desired light;
And all ye powers which in the same remayne,
More then we men can fayne,
Poure out your blessing on us plentiously,
And happy influence upon us raine,
That we may raise a large posterity,
Which from the earth, which they may long possesse,
With lasting happinesse,
Up to your haughty pallaces may mount,
And for the guerdon of theyr glorious merit
May heavenly tabernacles there inherit,
Of blessed Saints for to increase the count.
So let us rest, sweet love, in hope of this,
And cease till then our tymely joyes to sing,
The woods no more us answer, nor our eccho ring.

Song made in lieu of many ornaments,
With which my love should duly have been dect,
Which cutting off through hasty accidents,
Ye would not stay your dew time to expect,
But promist both to recompens,
Be unto her a goodly ornament,
And for short time an endlesse moniment.

about 1595   EDMUND SPENSER

V

ELIZABETHAN SONGS

21. Song

TELL me where is fancie bred,
Or in the heart or in the head?
How begot, how nourished?
    (Replie, replie.)
It is engendred in the eyes,
With gazing fed, and Fancy dies,
In the cradle where it lies:
Let us all ring Fancies knell:
Ile begin it—Ding, dong, bell
    (Ding, dong, bell).

about 1595   WILLIAM SHAKESPEARE

22. Song

COME away! come, sweet love!
The golden morning breaks:
All the earth, all the air,
Of love and pleasure speaks;
Teach thine arms then to embrace,
And sweet rosy lips to kiss
And mix our souls in mutual bliss:
Eyes were made for beauty's grace
Viewing, ruing, love's long pains
Procured by beauty's rude disdain.

Come away! come, sweet love!
Do not in vain adorn
Beauty's grace, that should arise
Like to the naked morn:
Lilies on the river's side
And fair Cyprian flowers newly blown
Desire no beauties but their own:
Ornament is Nurse of Pride
Pleasure measure, love's delight
Haste then, sweet love, our wished flight.

about 1595   ANONYMOUS

23.

My golden locks, Time hath to silver turnd.
(O Time too swift!   O swiftnes never ceasing.)
My youth 'gainst Age and Age at youth hath spurnd,
But spurnd in vaine, Youth waneth by encreasing,
Beauty, Strength, Youth are flowers but fading seen.
Duty, Faith, Love are rootes, and ever greene.

My Helmet now shall make a hive for Bees,
And lover's Sonnets turn to holy Psalms;
A man at Armes, must now serve on his knees,
And feed on prayrs, which are old Ages almes.
But though from Court to cottage I depart
My Saint is sure of mine unspotted heart.

And when I sadly sit, in homely cell,
I'll teach my Swaines this Carrol for a song:
Blest be the hearts that wish my Sovereigne well,
Curs't be the soules that thinke to do her wrong.
Goddesse, vouchsafe this aged man his right,
To be your Beadsman now, that was your knight.

about 1590   GEORGE PEELE

24. Song

Rose-cheekt *Laura*, come;
Sing thou smoothly with thy beauty's
Silent musick, either other
       Sweetely gracing.

Lovely forms do flowe
From concent divinely framed;
Heav'n is musick and thy beauties
       Birth is heavenly.

These dull notes we sing
Discords need for helps to grace them,
Only beautie purely loving
    Knowes no discord.

But still mooves delight,
Like cleare springs renu'd by flowing,
Ever perfect, ever in them-
    selves eternall.

about 1600   THOMAS CAMPION

25. Song

FOLLOW thy faire sunne, unhappy shadowe!
Though thou be blacke as night,
And she made all of light,
Yet follow thy faire sun, unhappie shadowe!

Follow her whose light thy light depriveth;
Though here thou liv'st disgrac't,
And she in heav'n is plac't,
Yet follow her whose light the world reviveth!

Follow those pure beames, whose beautie burneth,
That so have scorched thee
As thou still blacke must be
Til her kind beames thy blacke to brightnes turneth.

Follow her while yet her glorie shineth:
There comes a luckles night,
That will dim all her light;
And this the blacke unhappie shade devineth.

Follow still since so thy fates ordained;
The Sunne must have his shade
Till both at once doe fade:
The Sunne still provd, the shadow still disdained.

about 1600   THOMAS CAMPION

26. Song

Now winter nights enlarge
The number of their houres;
And clouds their stormes discharge
Upon the ayrie towres.
Let now the chimneys blaze
And cups o'erflow with wine,
Let well-tund words amaze
With harmonie divine.
Now yellow waxen lights
Shall wait on honey love
While youthful Revels, Masks, and Courtly sights,
Sleepes leaden spells remove.

This time doth well dispence
With lovers' long discourse;
Much speech hath some defence,
Though beauty no remorse.
All doe not all things well;
Some measures comely tread,
Some knotted Ridles tell,
Some Poems smoothly read.
The Summer hath his joys,
And Winter his delights;
Though Love and all his pleasures are but toyes,
They shorten tedious nights.

about 1615   THOMAS CAMPION

27.

TAKE, oh take those lips away,
That so sweetly were forsworne,
And those eyes, the breake of day,
Lights that do mislead the morn.
But my kisses bring againe, bring againe,
Seales of love, but seal'd in vaine, seal'd in vaine.

about 1603   WILLIAM SHAKESPEARE

28. Song

FULL fathom five thy father lies;
Of his bones are Corrall made.
Those are pearles that were his eies;
Nothing of him that doth fade
But doth suffer a Sea-change
Into something rich and strange.
Sea-Nimphs hourly ring his knell.
          (Ding-dong)
     Harke now I heare them—
          (Ding-dong, bell).

about 1611   WILLIAM SHAKESPEARE

29. Song

FAIN would I change that note
To which fond Love hath charmd me
Long long to sing by rote
Fancying that that harmd me.
Yet when this thought doth come:
Love is the perfect sum
          Of all delight,
I have no other choice
Either for pen or voice
          To sing or write.

O love! they wrong thee much
That say thy sweet is bitter,
When thy ripe fruit is such
As nothing can be sweeter.
Fair house of joy and bliss,
Where truest pleasure is,
          I do adore thee.
I know thee what thou art.
I serve thee with my heart,
          And fall before thee.

about 1605   ANONYMOUS

30.

CARE charming Sleep, thou easer of all woes,
Brother to Death, sweetly thy self dispose
On this afflicted Prince. Fall like a cloud
In gentle showrs, give nothing that is loud
Or painfull to his slumbers; easie, sweet,
And as a purling stream, thou son of night,
Pass by his troubled senses; sing his pain
Like a hollow murmuring Wind or silver Rain.
Into this Prince gently, Oh gently slide
And kiss him into slumbers like a Bride!

about 1618   JOHN FLETCHER

31.

ROSES, their sharp spines being gone
Not royal in their smells alone,
But in their hew.
Maiden-Pinks, of odour faint,
Daizies smell-less, yet most quaint
And sweet Tyme true.

Primrose first born child of Ver,
Merry Spring time's Harbinger,
With her bels dimm.
Oxlips in their Cradles growing,
Marigolds on death-beds blowing,
Larks-heels trim.

All dear natures children sweet,
Lie fore Bride and Bridegrooms feet,
Blessing their sence.
Not an Angel of the Air,
Bird melodious, or Bird fair
Is absent hence.

The Crow, the slanderous Cuckooe, nor
The boading raven, nor Chough hoar,
Nor chatt'ring Pie,
May on our Bridehouse pearch or sing,
Or with them any discord bring,
But from it fly.

about 1610   WILLIAM SHAKESPEARE or JOHN FLETCHER

VI

ELIZABETHAN SONNETS

Sir Philip Sidney
Edmund Spenser
William Shakespeare
Michael Drayton

The Sacred Fire

32. Sonnet

Leave me, O love, which reachest but to dust;
And thou, my mind, aspire to higher things;
Grow rich in that which never taketh rust;
Whatever fades, but fading pleasure brings.
Draw in thy beames, and humble all thy might
To that sweet yoke where lasting freedomes be;
Which breakes the cloudes, and opens forth the light,
That doth both shine, and give us light to see.
O take fast hold: let that light be thy guide
In this small course which birth drawes out to death,
And thinke how ill becommeth him to slide,
Who seeketh heav'n and comes of heav'nly breath.
    Then farewell, world: thy uttermost I see:
    Eternall Love, maintaine thy life in me.

about 1584   PHILIP SIDNEY

33. Sonnet

Lyke as a ship, that through the Ocean wyde
  by conduct of some star doth make her way,
  whenas a storme hath dimd her trusty guyde,
  out of her course doth wander far astray.
So I whose star, that wont with her bright ray
  me to direct, with cloudes is overcast,
  doe wander now in darknesse and dismay
  through hidden perils round about me placed.
Yet hope I well, that when this storm is past
  my *Helice*, the lodestar of my lyfe
  will shine again, and looke on me at last,
  with lovely light to cleare my cloudy grief.
Till then I wander, carefull, comfortlesse,
  in secret sorrow and sad pensivenesse.

about 1595   EDMUND SPENSER

The Sacred Fire

34. Sonnet

BEING myeself captyved here in care,
    my hart whom none with servile bands can tye
    but the fayre tresses of your golden hayr,
    breaking his prison, forth to you doth fly.
Lyke as a byrd that in ones hand doth spy
    desired food, to it doth make his flight,
    even so my hart, that wont on your fayre eye
    to feed his fill, flyes backe unto your sight.
Do you him take, and in your bosome bright
    gently encage, that he may be your thrall,
    perhaps he there may learne with rare delight
    to sing your name and prayses over all.
That it hereafter may you not repent
    him lodging in your bosome to have lent.

about 1595   EDMUND SPENSER

35. Sonnet

MOST glorious Lord of lyfe, that on this day
    didst make thy triumph over death and sin:
    and having harrowd hell, didst bring away
    captivity thence captive, us to win:
This glorious day, deare Lord, with joy begin,
    and grant that we for whom thou diddest dye
    being with thy deare blood clene washt from sin
    may live forever in felicity.
And that thy love we weighing worthily
    may likewise love thee for the same again:
    and for thy sake that all lyke deare didst buy
    with love may one another entertayne.
So let us love, deare love, lyke as we ought:
    love is the lesson which the Lord us taught.

about 1595   EDMUND SPENSER

36. Sonnet

Lyke as a huntsman after weary chace,
  seeing the game from him escapt away,
  sits downe to rest him in some shady place,
  with panting hounds beguiled of their pray.
So after long pursuit and vaine assay,
  when I all weary had the chace forsooke,
  the gentle deare returnd the selfe-same way,
  thinking to quench her thirst at the next brooke.
There she beholding me with mylder looke,
  sought not to fly, but fearlesse still did bide:
  till I in hand her yet halfe trembling tooke,
  and with her owne goodwill hir fyrmely tyede.
Strange thing, meseemd, to see a beast so wyld,
  so goodly wonne with her owne will beguyld.

about 1595   EDMUND SPENSER

37. Sonnet

That time of yeeare thou maist in me behold,
When yellow leaves, or none, or few, doe hange
Upon those boughes which shake against the cold,
Bare ruin'd quiers where late the sweet birds sang.
In me thou seest the twilight of such day,
As after Sunset fadeth in the West,
Which by and by blacke night doth take away,
Death's second selfe that seels up all in rest.
In me thou seest the glowing of such fire,
That on the ashes of his youth doth lye,
As the death-bed, whereon it must expire,
Consum'd with that which it was nurrish't by.
  This thou perceiv'st, which makes thy love more strong,
  To love that well, which thou must leave ere long.

about 1591–94   WILLIAM SHAKESPEARE

The Sacred Fire

38. Sonnet

THE expence of Spirit in a waste of shame
Is lust in action, and till action, lust
Is perjurd, murdrous, blouddy, full of blame,
Savage, extreame, rude, cruell, not to trust,
Injoy'd no sooner but dispised straight,
Past reason hunted, and no sooner had
Past reason hated, as a swollowed bayt,
On purpose layd to make the taker mad.
Mad in pursuit, and in possession so;
Had, having, and in quest to have, extreame,
A bliss in proofe, and proved, a very wo,
Before, a joy proposd, behind a dreame,
    All this the world well knowes; yet none knowes well,
    To shun the heaven that leads men to this hell.

about 1591–94   **WILLIAM SHAKESPEARE**

39. Sonnet

SINCE brasse, nor stone, nor earth, nor boundlesse sea,
But sad mortality ore-swaies their power,
How with this rage shall beautie hold a plea,
Whose action is no stronger than a flower?
O how shall summers honey breath hold out
Against the wrackfull siege of battring dayes,
When rocks impregnable are not so stoute,
Nor gates of steele so strong, but time decayes?
O fearfull meditation, where, alack,
Shall times best Jewell from times chest lie hid?
Or what strong hand can hold his swift foote back?
Or who his spoile of beautie can forbid?
    O none, unlesse this miracle have might,
    That in black inck my love may still shine bright.

about 1591–94   **WILLIAM SHAKESPEARE**

40. Sonnet

WHEN, in disgrace with Fortune and mens eyes,
I all alone beweepe my outcast state,
And trouble deafe heaven with my bootlesse cries,
And looke upon my selfe, and curse my fate,
Wishing me like to one more rich in hope
Featur'd like him, like him with friends possest,
Desiring this man's art and that mans skope,
With what I most injoy contented least;
Yet in these thoughts my selfe almost despising,
Haplye I thinke on thee, and then my state,
(Like to the Larke at breake of daye arising)
From sullen earth sings himns at Heavens gate.
  For thy sweet love remembred such welth brings
  That then I skorne to change my state with Kings.

about 1591–94   WILLIAM SHAKESPEARE

41. Sonnet

SINCE ther's no helpe, Come let us kisse and part,
Nay, I have done: You get no more of Me,
And I am glad, yea glad with all my heart,
That thus so cleanly I my selfe can free.
Shake hands for ever, Cancell all our vowes,
And when We meet at any time againe,
Be it not seene in either of our Browes
That We one jot of former Love reteyne;
Now at the last gaspe of Loves latest Breath,
When, his pulse fayling, Passion speechlesse lies,
When Faith is kneeling by his bed of Death,
And Innocence is closing up his Eyes,
  Now if thou would'st, when all have given him over,
  From Death to Life thou might'st him yet recover.

about 1595   MICHAEL DRAYTON

The Sacred Fire

42. Sonnet

CLEERE *Ankor*, on whose Silver-sanded shore,
My Soule-shrin'd Saint, my faire *Idea* lies,
O blessed *Brooke*, whose milk-white Swans adore,
Thy Cristall streame refined by her Eyes,
Where sweet Myrrh-breathing *Zephire* in the Spring,
Gently distills his Nectar-dropping showres,
Where Nightingales in *Arden* sit and sing,
Amongst the daintie Dew-impearled flowres;
Say thus faire Brooke, when thou shalt see thy Queene,
Loe, heere thy Shepheard spent his wandering yeeres;
And in these Shades, deare Nymph, he oft hath beene,
And heere to Thee he sacrific'd his Teares:
    Fair *Arden*, thou my *Tempe* art alone,
    And thou, sweet *Ankor*, art my *Helicon*.

about 1595   MICHAEL DRAYTON

VII

Michael Drayton

43. To the Virginian Voyage

You brave Heroique Minds,
Worthy your Countries Name,
    That Honour still pursue,
    Goe, and subdue,
Whilst loyt'ring Hinds
Lurke here at home, with shame.

Britans, you stay too long,
Quickly aboord bestow you,
    And with a merry Gale
    Swell your stretch'd Sayle,
With Vowes as strong,
As the Winds that blow you.

Your Course securely steere,
West and by South forth keepe,
    Rocks, Lee-shores, nor Sholes,
    When Eolus scowles
You need not feare,
So absolute the Deepe.

And cheerfully at Sea,
Successe you still intice,
    To get the Pearle and Gold:
    And ours to hold,
Virginia,
Earth's onely Paradise.

Where Nature hath in store
Fowle, Venison, and Fish:
    And the fruitfull'st Soyle,
    Without your Toyle,
Three Harvests more,
All greater then your Wish.

E

The Sacred Fire

And the ambitious Vine
Crownes with his purple Masse,
    The Cedar reaching hie
    To kisse the Sky,
The Cypresse, Pine,
And use-full Sassafras.

To whose, the Golden Age
Still Natures lawes doth give,
    No other Cares that tend,
    But Them to defend
From Winters age,
That long there doth not live.

When as the Lushious smell
Of that delicious Land,
    Above the Sea that flowes
    The cleere Wind throwes,
Your Hearts to swell
Approching the deare Strand.

In kenning of the Shore
(Thanks to God first given,)
    O you the happy'st men,
    Be Frolike then,
Let Cannons roare,
Frighting the wide Heaven.

And in Regions farre
Such *Heroes* bring yee foorth,
    As those from whom We came,
    And plant Our name
Under that Starre
Not knowne unto our North.

And as there Plenty growes
Of Lawrell everywhere,
    APOLLO's Sacred tree:
    You it may see,
A Poets Browes
To crowne, that may sing there.

Thy *Voyages* attend
Industrious HACKLUIT
    Whose Reading shall inflame
    Men to seeke Fame;
And much commend
To after-Times thy wit.

about 1605   MICHAEL DRAYTON

VIII

John Donne

George Chapman

Fulke Greville

William Shakespeare

John Webster

John Ford

44. The Funerall

WHO ever comes to shroud me, do not harme,
    Nor question much
That subtile wreath of haire, which crownes my arme;
The mystery, the signe, you must not touch,
    For 'tis my outward soul,
Viceroy to that, which, then to heav'n being gone,
    Will leave this to controule,
And keepe these limbes, her provinces, from dissolution.

For if the sinewie thread my braine lets fall
    Through every part,
Can tye those parts, and make mee one of all;
These haires which upward grow, and strength and art
    Have from a better braine,
Can better do't; Except she meant that I
    By this should know my pain,
As prisoners then are manacled, when they're condemned to die.

What ere she meant by it, bury it with me,
    For since I am
Loves martyr, it might breed idolatrie
If into other hands these Reliques came;
    As 'twas humility
To afford to it all that a soule can doe
    So, 'tis some bravery,
That since you would have none of mee, I bury some of you.

about 1595–1600   JOHN DONNE

45. The Anniversary

ALL Kings, and all their favorites,
    All glory of honors, beauties, wits,
The Sun it selfe, which makes times, as they passe,
Is elder by a yeare, now, then it was

When thou and I first one another saw:
All other things, to their destruction draw,
    Only our love hath no decay;
This, no to morrow hath, nor yesterday,
Running it never runs from us away,
But truly keepes his first, last, everlasting day.

about 1595–1600   JOHN DONNE

46. Farewell to Love

    WHILST yet to prove
I thought there was some Deitie in love
    So did I reverence, and gave
Worship; as Atheists in their dying houre
Call, what they cannot name, an unknowne power,
As ignorantly did I crave:
        Thus when
Things not yet knowne are coveted by men,
    Our desires give them fashion, and so
As they waxe lesser, fall, as they size, grow.

    But, from late faire
His highnesse sitting in a golden Chaire,
    Is not lesse cared for after three dayes
By children, then the thing which lovers so
Blindly admire, and with such worship wooe;
    Being had, enjoying it decayes;
        And thence,
What before pleas'd them all, takes but one sense,
    And that so lamely, as it leaves behind
A kinde of sorrowing dullnesse to the minde.

about 1595–1600   JOHN DONNE

47. The Dreame

DEARE love, for nothing lesse then thee
Would I have broke this happy dreame;
      It was a theme
For reason, much too strong for phantasie,
Therefore thou wakd'st me wisely; yet
My Dreame thou brok'st not, but continued'st it,
Thou art so true that thoughts of thee suffice
To make dreames truths; and fables histories;
Enter these armes, for since thou thought'st it best,
Not to dreame all my dreame, let's act the rest.

As lightning, or a Taper's light,
Thine eyes, and not thy noise, wak'd mee;
      Yet I thought thee
(For thou lov'st truth) an Angell, at first sight,
But when I saw thou saw'st my heart,
And knew'st my thoughts beyond an Angel's art,
When thou knew'st what I dreamt, when thou knew'st when
Excess of joy would wake me, and cam'st then,
I must confesse, it could not chuse but bee
Prophane, to thinke thee any thing but thee.

Comming and staying show'd thee, thee,
But rising makes me doubt, that now
      Thou art not thou.
That Love is weake, where feare's as strong as hee;
'Tis not all spirit, pure, and brave,
If mixture it of *Feare, Shame, Honor,* have.
Perchance as torches, which must ready bee,
Men light and put out, so thou deal'st with mee;
Thou cam'st to kindle, goest to come; then I
Will dreame that hope againe, but else would die.

about 1595–1600　　　　　　　　　　　　JOHN DONNE

48. *from* A Coronet for his Mistresse Philosophie

Muses that sing loves sensuall emperie,
    And Lovers kindling your enraged fires
At *Cupids* bonfires burning in the eye,
    Blowne with the emptie breath of vaine desires,
You that prefer the painted Cabinet
    Before the welthy Jewels it doth store yee,
    That all your joyes in dying figures set,
    And staine the living substance of your glory,
Abjure those joyes, abhor their memory,
    And let my love the honord subject be
    Of love, and honors compleate historie;
    Your eyes were never yet, let in to see
The majestie and riches of the minde,
But dwell in darknes; for your God is blinde.

But dwell in darknes, for your God is blinde,
    Humour poures downe such torrents on his eyes;
    Which (as from Mountaines) fall on his base kind,
    And eate your entrails out with ecstasies.
Colour (whose hands for faintnes are not felt)
    Can bind your waxen thoughts in Adamant;
    And with her painted fires your harts doth melt,
    Which beate your souls in peeces with a pant.
But my love is the cordiall of soules,
    Teaching by passion what perfection is,
    In whose fixt beauties shine the sacred scroule,
    And long-lost records of your human blisse,
Spirit to flesh, and soule to spirit giving,
Love flowes not from my lyver, but her living.

Love flows not from my lyver but her living,
    From whence all stings to perfect love are darted,
    All powre, and thought of pridefull lust depriving.
    Her life so pure and she so spotles harted,

In whome sits beautie with so firme a brow
    That age, nor care, nor torment can contract it;
    Heaven's glories shining there, do stuffe alow,
    And vertues constant graces do compact it.
Her mind (the beam of God) drawes in the fires
    Of her chast eyes, from all earths tempting fewell;
    Which upward lifts the lookes of her desires,
    And makes each precious thought in her a Jewell,
And as huge fires comprest more proudly flame,
So her close beauties further blaze her fame.

about 1595   GEORGE CHAPMAN

49. *from* Euthymiæ Raptus; or the Teares of Peace

But this is Learning; to have skill to throwe
Reins on your bodies powres that nothing knowe,
And fill the soules powres, so with act, and art,
That she can curbe the bodies angrie part;
All perturbations; all affects that stray
From their one object, which is to obay
Her Soveraigne empire; as her selfe should force
Their functions onely to serve his discourse;
And that, to beat the streight path of one ende,
Which is, to make her substance still contend
To be Gods image; in informing it
With knowledge; holy thoughts, and all formes fit
For that eternitie, ye seeke in way
Of his sole imitation; and to sway
Your lifes love so that he may still be Center
To all your pleasures; and you, here, may enter
The next lifes peace; in governing so well
Your sensuall parts, that you, as free may dwell,
Of vulgare Raptures, here, as when calme death
Dissolves that learned Empire with your Breath.
To teach, and live thus, is the only use
And end of Learning. Skill that doth produce

The Sacred Fire

But tearmes, and tongues, and Parrotting of Arte,
Without that powre to rule the errant part,
Is that which some call learned ignorance;
A serious trifle, error in a trance.
And let a Scholler, all earths volumes carrie,
He will be but a walking dictionarie.
A meere articulate Clocke, that doth but speake
By others arts; when wheels weare, or springs breake,
Or any fault is in him, hee can mend
No more than clockes; but at set hours must spend
His mouth, as clocks do; if too fast, speech goe,
He cannot stay it, nor haste if too slowe,
So that, as Travaylers seek their peace through storms,
In passing many Seas for many forms
Of forreigne government, endure the paine
Of many faces seeing; and the gain
That Strangers make, of their strange-loving humours
Learn tongues; keep note books; all to feed the tumors
Of vaine discourse at home; or serve the course
Of State employment, never having force
To employ themselves; but idle compliments
Must pay their paines, costs, slaveries, all their Rents;
And though they many men knowe, get few friends.
So covetous Readers, setting many endes
To their much skill to talke; studiers of Phrase;
Shifters in art; to flutter in the Blaze
Of ignorant count'nance; to obtaine degrees
And lye in Learning's bottome, like the lees,
To be accounted deepe by shallow men;
And carve all language, in one glorious pen;
May have much fame for learning, but th' effect
Proper to perfect Learning—to direct
Reason in such an Art, as that it can
Turn blood to soule, and make both, one calm man;
So making peace with God, doth differ farre
From Clearkes that goe with God and man to war.

about 1609   GEORGE CHAPMAN

50. Chorus Sacerdotum

Oh wearisome condition of Humanity!
Born under one law, to another bound:
Vainely begot and yet forbidden vanity,
Created sicke, commanded to be sound:
What meaneth Nature by these diverse lawes?
Passion and reason selfe-division cause:
Is it the marke, or majestie of Power
To make offences that it may forgive?
Nature herself doth her own self defloure,
To hate those errors she herself doth give.
For how should man thinke that he may not doe
If Nature did not faile and punish too?
Tyrant to others, to herself unjust,
Only commands things difficult and hard.
Forbids us all things which it knowes we lust,
Makes easie pains, unpossible reward.
If Nature did not take delight in blood,
She would have made more easie waies to good.
We that are bound by vowes and by promotion,
With pompe of holy sacrifice and rites
To teach beleefe in God and stirre devotion,
To preach of Heaven's wonders and delights:
Yet when each of us in his owne heart looks,
He finds the God there, farre unlike his bookes.

about 1595–1600   FULKE GREVILLE, LORD BROOKE

51. *from* Measure for Measure

. . . Aye, but to die, and go we know not where;
To lie in cold obstruction and to rot:
This sensible warm motion to become
A kneaded clod; and the delighted spirit
To bathe in fierie floods, or to reside
In thrilling regions of thicke-ribbed Ice,
To be imprison'd in the viewlesse windes,
And blowne with restless violence round about

The pendent world; or to be worse than worst
Of those, that lawlesse and incertaine thoughts
Imagine howling, 'tis too horrible.
The weariest, and most loathed worldly life,
That Age, Ache, Penury and Imprisonment
Can lay on nature, is a Paradise
To what we feare of death.

about 1604   WILLIAM SHAKESPEARE

52. *from* Macbeth

To MORROW, and to morrow, and to morrow,
Creepes in this petty pace from day to day,
To the last Syllable of Recorded time;
And all our yesterdayes have lighted Fooles
The way to dusty death.   Out, out, breefe Candle!
Life's but a walking Shadow, a poore Player,
That struts and frets his houre upon the Stage
And then is heard no more: it is a Tale
Told by an Ideot, full of sound and fury
Signifying nothing.

about 1606   WILLIAM SHAKESPEARE

53.

FEARE no more the heate o' the Sun,
Nor the furious Winter's rages,
Thou thy worldly task hast don,
Home art gon and ta'en thy wages.
Golden Lads and Girles all must,
As Chimney-sweepers come to dust.

Feare no more the frowne o' th' Great,
Thou art past the Tirants stroake.
Care no more to cloath and eate.
To thee the Reede is as the Oake:
  The Scepter, Learning, Physicke must
  All follow this and come to dust.

Feare no more the Lightning flash.
   Nor th' all-dreaded Thunder stone.
Feare not Slander, Censure rash.
   Thou hast finish'd Joy and mone.
All Lovers young, all Lovers must
Consigne to thee and come to dust.

No Exorcisor harme thee.
Nor no witch-craft charme thee.
Ghost unlaid forbeare thee.
Nothing ill come neere thee.
Quiet consummation have,
And renowned be thy grave.

about 1610   WILLIAM SHAKESPEARE

54.

CALL for the Robin-Redbrest and the Wren,
Since ore shadie groves they hover,
And with leaves and flowres doe cover
The friendlesse bodies of unburried men.
Call unto his funerall Dole
The Ante, the Field-mouse, and the Mole,
To rear him hillockes, that shall keepe him warme,
And (when gay tombes are robb'd) sustaine no harme.
But keepe the Wolfe far thence, that's foe to men,
For with his nailes he'll dig them up agen.

about 1610   JOHN WEBSTER

55.

HEARKE, now every thing is still,
The Scritch-Owle, and the Whistler shrill
Call upon our Dame aloud
And bid her quickly don her shrowd:

The Sacred Fire

Much you had of land and rent,
Your length in clay's now competent:
A long war disturbed your mind;
Here your perfect peace is sign'd.
Of what is't fooles make such vaine keeping?
Sin their conception, their birth weeping,
Their life, a general mist of error,
Their death, a hideous storme of terror.
Strew your haire with powders sweete,
Don cleane linnen, bathe your feet.
And (the foule feend more to checke),
A crucifixe let blesse your necke.
'Tis now full tide, 'tweene night and day:
End your groane and come away

about 1620   JOHN WEBSTER

56.

ALL the Flowers of the Spring
Meet to perfume our burying:
These have but their growing prime,
And man does flourish but his time.
Survey our progresse from our birth,
We are set, we grow, we turne to earth.
Courts adieu, and all delights,
All bewitching appetites;
Sweetest Breath, and clearest Eye,
Like perfumes goe out and dye;
And consequently this is done,
As shadowes wait upon the Sunne.
Vaine the ambition of Kings
Who seeke by trophies and dead things
To leave a living name behind,
And weave but nets to catch the wind.

about 1620   JOHN WEBSTER

57. Song

Oн no more, no more, too late,
    Sighes are spent; the burning Tapers
Of a life as chast as Fate,
    Pure as are unwritten papers,
Are burnt out: no heat, no light.
Now remaines; 'tis ever night.
    Love is dead, let lovers' eyes,
    Lock'd in endlesse dreames,
    Th' extreme of all extremes,
    Ope no more, for now Love dyes.
Now Love dyes, implying
Love's martyrs must be ever, ever dying.

about 1628   JOHN FORD

IX

58. *from* The Book of Job

AND Job spake, and said:

Let the day perish wherein I was born,
And the night in which it was said,
There is a man-child conceived.
Let that day be darkness;
Let not God regard it from above,
Neither let the light shine upon it.
Let darkness and the shadow of death stain it;
Let a cloud dwell upon it,
Let the blackness of the day terrify it.
As for that night, let darkness seize upon it;
Let it not be joined unto the days of the year,
Let it not come into the number of the months.
Lo, let that night be solitary,
Let no joyful voice come therein.
Let them curse it that curse the day,
Who are ready to raise up their mourning.
Let the stars of the twilight thereof be dark;
Let it look for light, but have none;
Neither let it see the dawning of the day:
Because it shut not up the doors of my mother's womb,
Nor hid sorrow from mine eyes.
Why died I not from the womb?
Why did I not give up the ghost when I came out of the belly?
Why did the knees prevent me?
Or why the breasts that I should suck?
For now should I have lain still and been quiet,
I should have slept:
Then had I been at rest,
With kings and counsellors of the earth
Which built desolate places for themselves;
Or with princes that had gold,
Who filled their houses with silver:
Or as an hidden untimely birth I had not been;
As infants which never saw light.
There the wicked cease from troubling;

And there the weary be at rest.
There the prisoners rest together;
They hear not the voice of the oppressor.
The small and great are there;
And the servant is free from his master.
Wherefore is light given to him that is in misery?
And life unto the bitter in soul;
Which long for death, but it cometh not;
And dig for it more than for hid treasures;
Which rejoice exceedingly and are glad
When they can find the grave?
Why is light given to a man whose way is hid,
And whom God hath hedged in?
For my sighing cometh before I eat,
And my roarings are poured out like the waters.
For the thing which I greatly feared is come upon me,
And that which I was afraid of is come unto me.

*　　　*　　　*

Then the Lord answered Job out of the whirlwind and said, Who
is this that darkeneth counsel by words without knowledge?　Gird
up now thy loins like a man; for I will demand of thee, and answer
thou me:

Where wast thou when I laid the foundations of the earth?
Declare, if thou hast understanding.
Who hath laid the measures thereof, if thou knowest?
Or who hath stretched the line upon it?
Whereupon are the foundations thereof fastened?
Or who laid the corner-stone thereof?
When the morning stars sang together,
And all the sons of God shouted for joy?

Or who shut up the sea with doors, when it brake forth,
As if it had issued out of the womb?
When I made the cloud the garment thereof,
And thick darkness a swaddlingband for it,

And brake up for it my decreed place,
And set bars and doors,
And said, Hitherto shalt thou come, but no further:
And here shall thy proud waves be stayed?

Hast thou commanded the morning since thy days;
And caused the dayspring to know his place;
That it might take hold of the ends of the earth,
That the wicked might be shaken out of it?
It is turned as clay to the seal and they stand as a garment.
And from the wicked their light is withholden,
And the high arm shall be broken.

Hast thou entered into the springs of the sea?
Or hast thou walked in the search of the depth?
Have the gates of death been opened unto thee?
Or hast thou seen the doors of the shadow of death?

Hast thou perceived the breadth of the earth?
Declare if thou knowest it all.
Where is the way where light dwelleth?
And as for darkness, where is the place thereof,
That thou shouldest take it to the bound thereof,
And that thou shouldest know the paths to the house thereof?
Knowest thou it, because thou wast then born?
Or because the number of thy days is great?

Hast thou entered into the treasures of the snow?
Or hast thou seen the treasures of the hail,
Which I have reserved against the time of trouble,
Against the day of battle and war?
By what way is the light parted, which scattereth the east wind
        upon the earth?
Who hath divided a watercourse for the overflowing of waters?
Or a way for the lightning of thunder;
To cause it to rain on the earth, where no man is;
On the wilderness wherein there is no man.
To satisfy the desolate and waste ground;

And to cause the bud of the tender herb to spring forth?
Hath the rain a father?
Or who hath begotten the drops of dew?
Out of whose womb came the ice?
And the hoary frost of heaven, who hath gendered it?
The waters are hid as with a stone,
And the face of the deep is frozen.

Canst thou bind the sweet influences of the Pleiades,
Or loose the bands of Orion?
Canst thou bring forth Mazzaroth in his season?
Or canst thou guide Arcturus with his sons?
Knowest thou the ordinances of heaven?
Canst thou set the dominion thereof in the earth?
Canst thou lift up thy voice to the clouds,
That abundance of waters may cover thee?
Canst thou send lightnings that they may go,
And say unto thee, Here we are?
Who hath put wisdom in the inward parts?
Or who hath given understanding to the heart?
Who can number the clouds in wisdom?
Or who can stay the bottles of heaven,
When the dust groweth into hardness,
And the clods cleave fast together?

Wilt thou hunt the prey of the lion?
Or fill the appetite of the young lions,
When they couch in their dens
And abide in the covert to lie in wait?
Who provided for the raven his food?
When his young ones cry unto God, they wander for lack of meat.
Knowest thou the time when the wild goats of the rock bring forth?
Or canst thou mark when the hinds do calve?
Canst thou number the months that they fulfil?
Or knowest thou the time when they bring forth?
They bow themselves, they bring forth their young ones, they
     cast out their sorrows.
Their young ones are in good liking, they grow up with corn;
They go forth, and return not unto them.

Who hath sent out the wild ass free?
Or who hath loosed the bands of the wild ass?
Whose house I have made the wilderness,
And the barren land his dwellings.
He scorneth the multitude of the city,
Neither regardeth he the crying of the driver.
The range of the mountains is his pasture,
And he searcheth after every green thing.
Will the unicorn be willing to serve thee,
Or abide by thy crib?
Canst thou bind the unicorn with his band in the furrow?
Or will he harrow the valleys after thee?
Wilt thou trust him, because his strength is great?
Or wilt thou leave thy labour to him?
Wilt thou believe him, that he will bring home thy seed
And gather it into thy barn?

Gavest thou the goodly wings unto the peacocks?
Or wings and feathers unto the ostrich?
Which leaveth her eggs in the earth,
And warmeth them in the dust,
And forgetteth that the foot may crush them,
Or that the wild beast may break them.
She is hardened against her young ones,
As though they were not her's:
Her labour is in vain without fear;
Because God hath deprived her of wisdom,
Neither hath he imparted to her understanding.
What time she lifteth up herself on high,
She scorneth the horse and his rider.

Hast thou given the horse strength?
Hast thou clothed his neck with thunder?
Canst thou make him afraid as a grasshopper?
The glory of his nostrils is terrible.
He paweth in the valley and rejoiceth in his strength:
He goeth on to meet the armed men.
He mocketh at fear, and is not affrighted;
Neither turneth he back from the sword.

The quiver rattleth against him, the glittering spear and the shield.
He swalloweth the ground with fierceness and rage:
Neither believeth he that it is the sound of the trumpet.
He saith among the trumpets, Ha, ha;
And he smelleth the battle afar off, the thunder of the captains,
    and the shouting.

Doth the hawk fly by thy wisdom,
And stretch her wings toward the south?
Doth the eagle mount up at thy command,
And make her nest on high?
She dwelleth and abideth on the rock,
Upon the crag of the rock, and the strong place.
From thence she seeketh the prey,
And her eyes behold afar off.
The young ones also suck up blood:
And where the slain are,
There is she.

1611   From *The Authorized Version of the Holy Bible*

59. *from* The Book of Ecclesiastes

REMEMBER now thy Creator in the days of thy youth,
While the evil days come not, nor the years draw nigh,
When thou shalt say, I have no pleasure in them:
While the sun, or the light, or the moon, or the stars
Be not darkened,
Nor the clouds return after the rain;
In the day when the keepers of the house shall tremble,
And the strong men shall bow themselves,
And the grinders cease because they are few,
And those that look out of the windows be darkened,
And the doors shall be shut in the streets,
When the sound of the grinding is low,
And he shall rise up at the voice of the bird,
And all the daughters of musick shall be brought low.

Also when they shall be afraid of that which is high,
And fears shall be in the way,
And the almond tree shall flourish,
And the grasshopper shall be a burden,
And desire shall fail,
Because man goeth to his long home
And the mourners go about the streets.

Or ever the silver cord be loosed,
Or the golden bowl be broken,
Or the pitcher be broken at the fountain,
Or the wheel broken at the cistern
Then shall the dust return to the earth as it was:
And the spirit shall return unto God who gave it.

1611   From *The Authorized Version of the Holy Bible*

60. *from* The Epistles of St. Paul to the Corinthians

THOUGH I speak with the tongues of men and of angels,
And have not charity,
I am become as sounding brass, or a tinkling cymbal.

And though I have the gift of prophecy,
And understand all mysteries, and all knowledge;
And though I have all faith,
So that I could remove mountains,
And have not charity,
I am nothing.

And though I bestow all my goods to feed the poor,
And though I give my body to be burned,
And have not charity,
It profiteth me nothing.

Charity suffereth long, and is kind;
Charity envieth not;
Charity vaunteth not itself, is not puffed up
Doth not behave itself unseemly, seeketh not her own
Is not easily provoked, thinketh no evil;
Rejoiceth not in iniquity, but rejoiceth in the truth;
Beareth all things, believeth all things, hopeth all things, endureth
all things.

Charity never faileth:
But whether there be prophecies, they shall fail;
Whether there be tongues, they shall cease;
Whether there be knowledge, it shall vanish away.

For we know in part, and we prophesy in part,
But when that which is perfect is come,
Then that which is in part shall be done away.
When I was a child, I spake as a child, I thought as a child;
But when I became a man, I put away childish things.
For now we see through a glass, darkly; but then face to face.
Now I know in part; but then shall I know even as also I am
known.

And now abideth faith, hope, charity, these three;
But the greatest of these is charity.

1611   From *The Authorized Version of the Holy Bible*

61. Sic vita

Like to the falling of a Starre;
As the flights of Eagles are;
Or like the fresh spring's gawdy hew;
Or silver drops of morning dew;
Or like a wind that chafes the flood,
Or bubbles which on water stood;
Even such is man whose borrow'd light
Is streight call'd in, and paid to-night.

> *The Wind blows out; the Bubble dies;*
> *The Spring entombed in Autumn lies;*
> *The Dew dries up; the Starre is shot;*
> *The Flight is past;—and Man forgot.*

about 1625–30   HENRY KING

62. The Exequy

ACCEPT, thou Shrine of my dead Saint
Instead of Dirges this complaint.
And for sweet flowres to crown thy hearse,
Receive a strew of weeping verse
From thy griev'd friend, whom thou might'st see
Quite melted into tears for thee.
      Dear loss! since thy untimely fate,
My task has been to meditate
On thee, on thee: thou art the book,
The library whereon I look,
Though almost blind.   For thee (lov'd clay)
I languish out, not live, the day,
Using no other exercise
But what I practise with mine eyes:
By which wet glasses I find out
How lazily time creeps about
To one that mourns: this, onely this
My exercise and business is:
So I compute the weary houres
With sighs dissolved into showres.
Thou hast benighted me; thy set
This Eve of blackness did beget,
Who wast my day (though overcast
Before thou had'st thy Noon-tide past):
And I remember must in tears
Thou scarce had'st seen so many years
As Day tells houres.   By thy cleer sun
My love and fortune first did run;
But thou wilt never more appear

The Sacred Fire

Folded within my Hemisphear,
Since both thy light and motion
Like a fled Star, is fall'n and gon,
And 'twixt me and my soules dear wish
The earth now interposed is.
  I could allow thee for a time
To darken me and my sad Clime;
Were it a month, a year, or ten,
I would thy exile live till then;
And all that space my mirth adjourn,
So thou wouldst promise to return;
And putting off thy ashy shrowd
At length disperse this sorrows cloud.
  But woe is me! the longest date
Too narrow is to calculate
These empty hopes: never shall I
Be so much blest as to descry
A glimpse of thee, till that day come
Which shall the earth to cinders doome,
And a fierce Feaver must calcine
The body of this world like thine,
(My little world!). That fit of fire
Once off, our bodies shall aspire
To our soules bliss: then we shall rise
And view ourselves with cleerer eyes
In that calm Region, where no night
Can hide us from each others sight.
  Mean time thou hast her, earth: much good
May my harm do thee. Since it stood
With Heavens will I might not call
Her longer mine, I give thee all
My short-liv'd right and interest
In her, whom living I lov'd best.
Be kind to her, and prithee look
Thou write into thy Dooms-day book
Each parcell of this Rarity
Which in thy Casket shrin'd doth ly:
As thou wilt answer *Him* that lent—
Not gave—thee my dear Monument.

So close the ground, and 'bout her shade
Black curtains draw: my *Bride* is laid.

Sleep on, my *Love*, in thy cold bed
Never to be disquieted!
My last good-night! Thou wilt not wake
Till I thy fate shall overtake:
Till age, or grief, or sickness, must
Marry my body to that dust
It so much loves; and fill the room
My heart keeps empty in thy Tomb.
Stay for me there; I will not faile
To meet thee in that hallow Vale.
And think not much of my delay;
I am already on the way,
And follow thee with all the speed
Desire can make, or sorrows breed.
Each minute is a short degree,
And ev'ry houre a step towards thee.
At night when I betake to rest,
Next morn I rise nearer my West
Of life, almost by eight houres saile,
Then when sleep breath'd his drowsie gale.

Thus from the Sun my Bottom stears,
And my dayes Compass downward bears:
Nor labour I to stemme the tide
Through which to *Thee* I swiftly glide.
'Tis true—with shame and grief I yield—
Thou like the *Vann*, first took'st the field,
And gotten hast the victory
In thus adventuring to dy
Before me, whose more years might crave
A just precedence in the grave.
But hark! My pulse, like a soft Drum,
Beats my approch, tells *Thee* I come:
And slow howere my marches be,
I shall at last sit down by *Thee*.

The thought of this bids me go on,
And wait my dissolution
With hope and comfort. *Dear* (forgive

The crime) I am content to live
Divided, with but half a heart,
Till we shall meet and never part.

about 1625–30

HENRY KING

63. Love

Love bade me welcome; yet my soul drew back,
    Guiltie of dust and sinne.
But quick-ey'd Love, observing me grow slack
    From my first entrance in,
Drew nearer to me, sweetly questioning
    If I lack'd anything.

A guest, I answered, worthy to be here.
    Love said, you shall be he.
I, the unkinde, the ungratefull? ah, my deare,
    I cannot look on thee.
Love took my hand and smiling did reply,
    Who made the eyes but I?

Truth Lord, but I have marr'd them.   Let my shame
    Go where it doth deserve.
And know you not, sayes Love, who bore the blame?
    My deare, then I will serve.
You must sit down sayes Love, and taste my meat.
    So I did sit and eat.

about 1625

GEORGE HERBERT

64. Longing

Bowels of pitie heare!
Lord of my soul, love of my minde,
    Bow down thine eare!
    Let not the winde
Scatter my words, and in the same
    Thy name!

Behold, thy dust doth stirre,
It moves, it creeps, it aims at thee.
Wilt thou deferre
To succour me,
Thy pile of dust, wherein each crumme
Sayes, Come?

To thee help appertains.
Hast thou left all things to their course,
And laid the reins upon the horse?
Is all lockt?   Hath a sinner's plea
No key?

Thou tarriest, while I die
And fall to nothing.   Thou dost reigne
And rule on high,
While I remain
In bitter grief.   Yet am I stil'd
Thy childe.

about 1630–33   GEORGE HERBERT

65. The Collar

I STRUCK the board, and cry'd, No more!
I will abroad.
What?   Shall I ever sigh and pine?
My lines and life are free, free as the rode,
Loose as the winde, as large as store.
Shall I be still in suit?
Have I no harvest but a thorn
To let me bloud, and not restore
What I have lost with cordiall fruit?
Sure there was wine
Before my sighs did drie it: there was corn
Before my tears did drown it.
Is the yeare onely lost to me?
Have I no bayes to crown it?

No flowers, no garlands gay?   All blasted?
       All wasted?
Not so, my heart!   But there is fruit,
       And thou hast hands.
Recover all thy sigh-blown age
On double pleasures.   Leave thy cold dispute
Of what is fit and not.   Forsake thy cage,
       Thy rope of sands,
Which pettie thoughts have made, and made to thee
Good cable, to enforce and draw,
       And be thy law,
While thou didst wink and wouldst not see.
       Away!   Take heed!
       I will abroad.
Call in thy death's head there.   Tie up thy fears.
       He that forbears
    To suit and serve his need
    Deserves his load.
But as I rav'd and grew more fierce and wilde
       At every word,
Me thought I heard one calling, "*Child!*"
       And I reply'd, "*My Lord!*"

about 1630–33   GEORGE HERBERT

66. On a Prayer Book sent to Mrs. M. R.

Lo here a little Volume, but great Book!
A nest of new-born sweets;
Whose native fires disdaining
To ly thus folded, and complaining
Of these ignoble sheets,
Affect more comly bands,
Fair one, from thy kind hands,
And confidently look
To find the rest
Of a rich binding in your Brest.

It is, in one choise handfull, heaven; and all
Heav'n's Royall host; encamped thus small
To prove that true, schooles use to tell,
Ten thousand Angels in one point can dwell.
It is love's great artillery,
Which here contracts itself and comes to ly
Close couch't in your white bosom: & from thence,
As from a snowy fortresse of defence,
Against your ghostly foes to take your part
And fortify the hold of your chaste heart.
It is an armory of light;
Let constant use but keep it bright,
  You'll find it yields
To holy hands and humble hearts
  More swords and shields
Then sin hath snares, or Hell hath darts.
  Only be sure
  The hands be pure
That hold these weapons; and the eyes
Those of turtles, chast and true;
  Wakeful and wise;
Here's a friend shall fight for you
Hold but this book before your heart;
Let prayer alone to play his part.

But O the heart
That studyes this high Art
Must be a sure house-keeper;
And yet no sleeper.
Dear soul, be strong.
Mercy will come e're long.
And bring her bosome full of blessings
Flowers of never fading graces
To make immortall dressings
For worthy soules, whose wise embraces
Store up themselves for Him who is alone
The Spouse of virgins & the Virgin's Son.
But if the noble Bridegroom, when he come,
Shall find the wandering Heart from home;

The Sacred Fire

Leaving her chast abode
To gadde abroad
Amongst the gay mates of the god of flyes
To take her pleasure, & to play
And keep the devill's holyday;
To dance in the sunshine of some smiling
But beguiling
Spheare of sweet and sugared Lyes,
Some slippery Pair
Of false, perhaps as fair,
Flattering but forswearing eyes;
Doubtlesse some other heart
Will gett the start
Mean while, & stepping in before
Will take possession of that sacred store
Of hidden sweets and holy joys;
Words which are not heard with Eares
(Those tumultuous shops of noise)
Effectual whispers whose still voice
The soul it selfe more feeles than heares;
Amorous languishments; luminous trances;
Sights which are not seen with eyes;
Spirituall and soul-piercing glances,
Whose pure and subtil lightning flyes
Home to the heart, and setts the house on fire
And melts it down in sweet desire:
Yet does not stay
To ask the window's leave to pass that way;
Delicious Deaths, soft exhalations
Of soul; dear and divine annihilations;
A thousand unknown rites
Of joyes and rarefy'd delights;
A hundred thousand loves & graces,
And many a mystick thing,
Which the divine embraces
Of the deare Spouse of spirits with them will bring,
For which it is no shame
That dull mortality must not know a name.
Of all this store

Of blessings, and ten thousand more,
(If when he come
He find the Heart from home)
Doubtlesse He will unload
Himself some other where
And poure abroad
His pretious sweets
On the fair soul whom first He meets.

O fair, O fortunate! O rich, O dear!
O happy and thrice-happy she
Deare silver-breasted dove
Who ere she be,
Whose early love
With winged vowes
Makes haste to meet her morning Spouse
And close with his immortall kisses;
Happy indeed, who never misses
To improve that pretious hour
And every day
Seize her sweet prey,
All fresh and fragrant as He rises
Dropping with a baulmy Showr
A delicious dew of spices;
O let the blissfull heart hold fast
Her heavnly arm-full, she shall tast
At once ten thousand paradises;
She shall have power
To rifle and deflour
The rich and roseall spring of those rare sweets
Which with a swelling bosome there she meets;
Boundles and infinite, bottomles treasures
Of pure inebriating pleasures.
Happy proof she shal discover
What joy, what blisse,
How many Heav'ns at once it is,
To have her God become her Lover.

about 1640   RICHARD CRASHAW

67. The Morning Watch

O Joyes!   Infinite sweetnes! with what flowres
And shoots of glory, my soul breakes and buds!
            All the long houres
            Of night, and Rest,
            Through the still shrouds
            Of sleep, and Clouds,
      This Dew fell on my Breast;
            O how it *blouds*,
And *Spirits* all my Earth! heark! in what Rings,
And *Hymning Circulations* the quick world
            Awakes, and sings;
            The rising winds,
            And falling springs,
            Birds, beasts, all things
      Adore him in their kinds.
            Thus all is hurl'd
In sacred *Hymnes* and *Order*, The great *Chime*
And *Symphony* of nature.   Prayer is
            The world in tune,
      ,   A spirit voyce,
            And vocall joyes,
      Whose *Eccho* is heav'ns blisse.
            O let me climbe
When I lye down!   The Pious soul by night
Is like a clouded starre, whose beames, though sed
            To shed their light
            Under some Cloud,
            Yet are above,
            And shine, and move
      Beyond that misty shrowd.
            So in my bed,
That Curtain'd grave, though sleep, like ashes, hide
My lamp, and life, both shall in thee abide.

about 1650   HENRY VAUGHAN

68. The Salutation

THESE little Limmes
These Eys and Hands which here I find,
These rosie Cheeks wherwith my Life begins,
    Where have ye been? Behind
What Curtain were ye from me hid so long!
Where was, in what Abyss, my Speaking Tongue?

    When silent I
    So many thousand thousand yeers
Beneath the Dust did in a Chaos lie,
    How could I Smiles or Tears,
Or Lips, or Hands, or Eys, or Ears perceive?
Welcome ye Treasures which I now receive.

    I that so long
    Was Nothing from Eternitie,
Did little think such Joys as Ear and Tongue,
    To Celebrate or See:
Such Sounds to hear, such Hands to feel, such Feet,
Beneath the Skies, on such a Ground to meet.

    New Burnisht Joys!
    Which yellow Gold and Pearl excell!
Such Sacred Treasures are the Limmes in Boys,
    In which a Soul doth Dwell;
Their Organised Joynts and Azure Veins
More Wealth include than all the World contains.

    From Dust I rise
    And out of Nothing now awake,
These Brighter Regions which salute mine Eys
    A Gift from GOD I take.
The Earth, the Seas, the Light, the Day, the Skies,
The Sun and Stars are mine; if those I prize.

The Sacred Fire

Long time before
I in my Mother's Womb was born,
A GOD preparing did this Glorious Store,
The World for me adorn;
Into this Eden, so Divine and fair,
So Wide and Bright, I com his Son and Heir.

A Stranger here
Strange Things doth meet, Strange Glories see;
Strange Treasures lodg'd in this fair World appear,
Strange all, and New to me;
But that they mine should be, who nothing was,
That Strangest is of all, yet brought to pass.

about 1660   THOMAS TRAHERNE

X

John Milton

Robert Herrick

John Suckling

Sidney Godolphin

Thomas Carew

Andrew Marvel

69. At a Solemn Musick

BLEST pair of *Sirens*, pledges of Heav'ns joy,
Sphear-born harmonious Sisters, Voice, and Vers,
Wed your divine sounds, and mixt power employ
Dead things with inbreath'd sense able to pierce,
And to our high-rais'd phantasie present,
That undisturbed Song of pure concent,
Ay sung before the saphire-colour'd throne
To him that sits thereon
With Saintly shout and solemn Jubily,
Where the bright Seraphim in burning row
Their loud up-lifted Angel trumpets blow,
And the Cherubick host in thousand quires
Touch their immortal Harps of golden wires,
With those just Spirits that wear victorious Palms,
Hymns devout and holy Psalms
Singing everlastingly;
That we on Earth with undiscording voice
May rightly answer that melodious noise;
As once we did, till disproportion'd sin
Jarr'd against natures chime, and with harsh din
Broke the fair musick that all creatures made
To their great Lord, whose love their motion sway'd
In perfect Diapason, whilst they stood
In first obedience, and their state of good.
O may we soon again renew that Song,
And keep in tune with Heav'n, till God ere long
To his celestial Consort us unite,
To live with him, and sing in endles morn of light.

about 1630   JOHN MILTON

70. L'Allegro

HENCE loathed Melancholy
    Of *Cerberus*, and blackest midnight born,
In *Stygian* Cave forlorn
    'Mongst horrid shapes, and shreiks, and sights unholy,

The Sacred Fire

Find out some uncouth cell,
　　Where brooding darknes spreads his jealous wings,
And the night-Raven sings;
　　There under *Ebon* shades, and low-brow'd Rocks,
As ragged as thy Locks,
　　In dark *Cimmerian* desert ever dwell.
But com thou Goddes fair and free,
In Heav'n ycleap'd *Euphrosyne*,
And by men, heart-easing Mirth,
Whom lovely *Venus* at a birth
With two sister Graces more
To Ivy-crowned *Bacchus* bore;
Or whether (as som Sager sing)
The frolic Wind that breathes the Spring,
Zephir with *Aurora* playing
As he met her once a Maying,
There on Beds of Violets blew
And fresh-blown Roses washt in dew,
Fill'd her with thee a daughter fair,
So bucksom, blith and debonair.
Haste thee nymph, and bring with thee
Jest and youthful Jollity,
Quips and Cranks, and wanton Wiles,
Nods, and Becks, and Wreathed Smiles,
Such as hang on *Hebe's* cheek,
And love to live in dimple sleek;
Sport that wrincled Care derides,
And Laughter holding both his sides.
Com, and trip it as ye go
On the light fantastick toe,
And in thy right hand lead with thee,
The Mountain Nymph, sweet Liberty;
And if I give thee honour due,
Mirth, admit me of thy crue
To live with her, and live with thee,
In unreproved pleasures free;
To hear the Lark begin his flight,
And singing startle the dull night,
From his watch-towre in the skies,

'Till the dappled dawn doth rise;
Then to com in spight of sorrow,
And at my window bid good morrow,
Through the Sweet-Briar, or the Vine,
Or the twisted Eglantine.
While the Cock with lively din,
Scatters the rear of darknes thin,
And to the stack, or the Barne dore,
Stoutly struts his Dames before,
Oft list'ning how the Hounds and horn
Chearly rouse the slumbring morn,
From the side of som Hoar Hill,
Through the high wood echoing shrill.
Som time walking not unseen
By Hedge-row Elms, on Hillocks green,
Right against the Eastern gate,
Where the great Sun begins his state,
Rob'd in flames, and Amber light,
The clouds in thousand Liveries dight.
While the Plowman neer at hand,
Whistles ore the Furrow'd Land
And the Milkmaid singeth blithe,
And the Mower whets his sithe,
And every Shepherd tells his tale
Under the Hawthorn in the dale.
Streit mine eye hath caught new pleasures
Whilst the Lantskip round it measures,
Russet Lawns and Fallows Gray,
Where the nibling flocks do stray,
Mountains on whose barren brest
The labouring clouds do often rest:
Meadows trim with Daisies pide,
Shallow Brooks, and Rivers wide.
Towers, and Battlements it sees
Boosom'd high in tufted Trees,
Wher perhaps som beauty lies,
The Cynosure of neighbouring eyes.
Hard by, a Cottage chimney smokes,
From betwixt two aged Okes,

The Sacred Fire

Where *Corydon* and *Thyrsis* met,
Are at their savory dinner set
Of Hearbs, and other Country Messes,
Which the neat-handed *Phillis* dresses;
And then in haste her Bowre she leaves,
With *Thestylis* to bind the Sheaves;
Or if the earlier season lead
To the tann'd Haycock in the Mead,
Som times with secure delight
The up-land Hamlets will invite,
When the merry Bells ring round,
And the jocond rebecks sound
To many a youth, and many a maid,
Dancing in the Chequer'd shade;
And young and old com forth to play
On a Sunshine Holyday,
Till the live-long day-light fail.
Then to the Spicy Nut-brown Ale,
With stories told of many a feat
How *Faery Mab* the junkets eat,
She was pincht, and pull'd she sed
And he by Friar's Lanthorn led,
Tells how the drudging *Goblin* swet,
To ern his Cream-bowle duly set,
When in one night, ere glimps of morn,
His shadowy Flale hath thresh'd the Corn
That ten day-labourers could not end,
Then lies him down the Lubbar Fend.
And stretch'd out all the Chimney's length
Basks at the fire his hairy strength;
And crop-full out of dores he flings,
Ere the first Cock his Mattin rings.
Thus don the Tales, to bed they creep,
By whispering Windes soon lull'd asleep.
Towred Cities please us then,
And the busy humm of men,
Where throngs of Knights and Barons bold,
In weeds of Peace high triumphs hold,
With store of Ladies, whose bright eies

Rain influence, and judge the prise
Of wit, or Arms, while both contend
To win her Grace, whom all commend.
There let *Hymen* oft appear
In Saffron robe, with Taper clear,
And pomp, and feast, and revelry,
With mask, and antique Pageantry,
Such sights as youthfull Poets dream
On Summers eeves by haunted stream.
Then to the well-trod stage anon,
If *Jonsons* learned Sock be on,
Or sweetest *Shakespear* fancies childe,
Warble his native Wood-notes wilde,
And ever against eating Cares,
Lap me in soft *Lydian* Aires,
Married to immortal verse
Such as the meeting soul may pierce
In notes, with many a winding bout
Of lincked sweetnes long drawn out,
With wanton heed, and giddy cunning,
The melting voice through mazes running;
Untwisting all the chains that ty
The hidden soul of harmony.
That *Orpheus* self may heave his head
From golden slumber on a bed
Of heapt *Elysian* flowres, and hear
Such streins as would have won the ear
Of *Pluto*, to have quite set free
His half regain'd *Eurydice*.
These delights, if thou canst give,
Mirth with thee, I mean to live.

about 1632   JOHN MILTON

71. Il Penseroso

HENCE vain deluding joyes,
    The brood of folly without father bred,
How little you bested,
    Or fill the fixed mind with all your toyes;
Dwell in some idle brain,
    And fancies fond with gaudy shapes possess,
As thick and numberless
    As the gay motes that people the Sun Beams,
Or likest hovering dreams
    The fickle Pensioners of *Morpheus* train.
But hail thou Goddes, sage and holy,
Hail divinest Melancholy,
Whose Saintly visage is too bright
To hit the Sense of human sight;
And therfore to our weaker view,
Ore laid with black staid Wisdoms hue.
Black, but such as in esteem,
Prince *Memnons* sister might beseem
Or that Starr'd *Ethiope* Queen that strove
To set her beauties praise above
The Sea Nymphs, and their powers offended.
Yet thou art higher far descended,
Thee bright-hair'd *Vesta* long of yore,
To solitary *Saturn* bore;
His daughter she (in *Saturns* raign,
Such mixture was not held a stain)
Oft in glimmering Bowres, and glades
He met her, and in secret shades
Of woody *Ida's* inmost grove,
While yet there was no fear of *Jove.*
Com pensive Nun, devout and pure,
Sober, stedfast, and demure,
All in a robe of darkest grain,
Flowing with majestic train,
And sable stole of *Cipres* Lawn,
Over thy decent shoulders drawn.
Com, but keep thy wonted state,

With eev'n step, and musing gate,
And looks commercing with the skies,
Thy rapt soul sitting in thine eyes:
There held in holy passion still,
Forget thyself to Marble, till
With a sad Leaden downward cast,
Thou fix them on the earth as fast.
And joyn with thee calm Peace and Quiet,
Spare Fast, that oft with gods doth diet,
And hears the Muses in a ring,
Ay round about *Joves* Altar sing.
And adde to these retired Leasure,
That in trim Gardens takes his pleasure;
But first, and chiefest, with thee bring,
Him that yon soars on golden wing,
Guiding the fiery-wheeled throne,
The Cherub Contemplation.
And the mute Silence hist along,
'Less *Philomel* will daign a Song,
In her sweetest, saddest plight,
Smoothing the rugged brow of night,
While *Cynthia* checks her Dragon yoke,
Gently o're th'accustom'd Oke;
Sweet Bird that shunn'st the noise of folly,
Most musical, most melancholy!
Thee Chauntress oft the Woods among,
I woo to hear thy eeven-Song;
And missing thee I walk unseen
On the dry smooth-shaven Green,
To behold the wandring Moon,
Riding neer her highest noon,
Like one that had bin led astray
Through the Heav'ns wide pathles way;
And oft, as if her head she bow'd,
Stooping through a fleecy cloud.
Oft on a Plat of rising ground,
I hear the far-off *Curfeu* sound,
Over som wide-water'd shoar,
Swinging slow with sullen roar;

Or if the Ayr will not permit,
Som still removed place will fit,
Where glowing Embers through the room
Teach light to counterfeit a gloom,
Far from all resort of mirth,
Save the Cricket on the hearth,
Or the Belmans drousie charm,
To bless the dores from nightly harm:
Or let my Lamp at midnight hour,
Be seen in som high lonely Towr,
Where I may oft outwatch the *Bear*,
With thrice great *Hermes*, or unsphear
The spirit of *Plato* to unfold
What Worlds, or what vast Regions hold
The immortal mind that hath forsook
Her mansion in this fleshly nook:
And of those *Dæmons* that are found
In fire, air, flood, or under ground,
Whose power hath a true consent
With Planet, or with Element.
Som time let Gorgeous Tragedy
In Scepter'd Pall com sweeping by,
Presenting *Thebs*, or *Pelops* line,
Or the tale of *Troy* divine.
Or what (though rare) of later age,
Ennobled hath the Buskind stage.
But, O sad Virgin, that thy power
Might raise *Musæus* from his bower,
Or bid the soul of *Orpheus* sing
Such notes as warbled to the string,
Drew Iron tears down *Pluto's* cheek,
And made Hell grant what Love did seek.
Or call up him that left half told
The story of *Cambuscan* bold,
Of *Camball*, and of *Algarsife*,
And who had *Canace* to wife,
That own'd the vertuous Ring and Glass,
And of the wondrous Hors of Brass,
On which the *Tartar* King did ride;

And if ought els, great *Bards* beside,
In sage and solemn tunes have sung,
Of Turneys and of Trophies hung;
Of Forests, and inchantments drear,
Where more is meant then meets the ear.
Thus night oft see me in thy pale career,
Till civil-suited Morn appeer,
Not trickt and frounc't as she was wont,
With the Attick Boy to hunt,
But Cherchef't in a comly Cloud,
While rocking Winds are Piping loud,
Or usher'd with a shower still,
When the gust hath blown his fill,
Ending on the russling Leaves,
With minute drops from off the Eaves.
And when the Sun begins to fling
His flaring beams, me Goddes bring
To arched walks of twilight groves,
And shadows brown that *Sylvan* loves
Of Pine, or monumental Oake,
Where the rude Ax with heaved stroke,
Was never heard the Nymphs to daunt,
Or fright them from their hallow'd haunt.
There in close covert by som Brook,
Where no profaner eye may look,
Hide me from Day's garish eie,
While the Bee with Honied thie,
That at her flowry work doth sing,
And the Waters murmuring
With such consort as they keep,
Entice the dewy-feather'd Sleep;
And let som strange mysterious dream,
Wave at his Wings in Airy stream,
Of lively portrature display'd,
Softly on my eye-lids laid.
And as I wake, sweet musick breath
Above, about, or underneath,
Sent by som spirit to mortals good,
Or th'unseen Genius of the Wood.

But let my due feet never fail,
To walk the studious Cloysters pale,
And love the high embowed Roof,
With antic Pillars massy proof,
And storied Windows richly dight,
Casting a dimm religious light.
There let the pealing Organ blow,
To the full voic'd Quire below,
In Service high, and Anthems cleer,
As may with sweetnes, through mine ear
Dissolve me into extasies,
And bring all Heav'n before mine eyes.
And may at last my weary age
Find out the peacefull hermitage,
The Hairy Gown and Mossy Cell,
Where I may sit and rightly spell
Of every Star that Heav'n doth shew,
And every Herb that sips the dew;
Till old experience do attain
To somthing like Prophetic strain.
These pleasures *Melancholy* give,
And I with thee will choose to live.

about 1632   JOHN MILTON

72. Song

SWEET Echo, sweetest Nymph that liv'st unseen
        Within thy airy shell
    By slow *Meander's* margent green,
And in the violet-imbroider'd vale
        Where the love-lorn Nightingale
Nightly to thee her sad Song mourneth well.
Canst thou not tell me of a gentle Pair
        That likest thy *Narcissus* are?
            Or if thou have
        Hid them in som flowry Cave,
            Tell me but where,

Sweet Queen of Parly, Daughter of the Sphear,
   So maist thou be translated to the skies,
And give resounding grace to all Heav'ns Harmonies.

about 1634   JOHN MILTON

73. Sonnet

O NIGHTINGALE, that on yon bloomy Spray
   Warblest at eeve, when all the Woods are still,
   Thou with fresh hope the Lovers heart dost fill,
   While the jolly hours lead on propitious *May*,
Thy liquid notes that close the eye of Day,
   First heard before the shallow Cuccoo's bill,
   Portend success in love. O if *Jove's* will
   Have linkt that amorous power to thy soft lay,
Now timely sing, ere the rude Bird of Hate
   Foretell my hopeles doom in som Grove ny:
   As thou from yeer to yeer hast sung too late
For my relief; yet hadst no reason why,
   Whether the Muse, or Love call thee his mate,
   Both them I serve, and of their train am I.

about 1631   JOHN MILTON

74. Art above Nature: To Julia

WHEN I behold a Forrest spread
With silken trees upon thy head;
And when I see that other Dresse
Of flowers set in comlinesse:
When I behold another grace
In the ascent of curious Lace,
Which like a Pinacle doth shew
The top and the top-gallant too:
Then, when I see thy Tresses bound
Into an ovall, square, or round;

And knit into knots far more then I
Can tell by tongue; or true-love tie:
Next, when those Lawnie Filmes I see
Play with a wild civility:
And all those airie silks to flow,
Alluring me, and tempting so:
I must confesse, mine eye and heart
Dotes less on Nature then on Art.

about 1640   ROBERT HERRICK

75. To Dianeme

SWEET, be not proud of those two eyes,
Which Star-like sparkle in their skies:
Nor be you proud, that you can see
All hearts your captives; yours yet free:
Be you not proud of that rich haire,
Which wantons with the Love-sick aire:
When as that Rubie, which you weare,
Sunk from the tip of your soft eare,
Will last to be a precious Stone,
When all your world of Beautie's gone.

about 1630–40   ROBERT HERRICK

76.

I SING of *Brooks*, of *Blossomes*, *Birds*, and *Bowers*:
Of *April*, *May*, of *June*, and *July*-flowers.
I sing of *May-poles*, *Hock-carts*, *Wassails*, *Wakes*,
Of *Bride-grooms*, *Brides*, and of their *Bridall-cakes*.
I write of *Youth*, of *Love*, and have Accesse
By these, to sing of cleanly *Wantonnesse*;
I sing of *Dewes*, of *Raines*, and piece by piece,
Of *Balme*, of *Oyle*, of *Spice*, and *Ambergreece*.
I sing of *Times trans-shifting*; and I write
How *Roses* first came *Red*, and *Lillies White*.

I write of *Groves*, of *Twilights*, and I sing
The Court of *Mab*, and of the *Fairie-King*.
I write of *Hell;* I sing (and ever shall)
Of *Heaven*, and hope to have it after all.

about 1640   ROBERT HERRICK

77. Phillada flouts me

OH! what a pain is love,
How shall I bear it?
She will inconstant prove,
I greatly fear it.
She so torments my mind,
That my strength faileth;
And wavers with the wind,
As a ship that saileth.
Please her the best I may,
She looks another way
Alack and well-a-day!
   Phillada flouts me.

All the fair, yesterday
She did pass by me
She look'd another way,
And would not spy me.
I wooed her for to dine,
But could not get her.
Will had her to the wine;
He might entreat her.
With *Daniel* she did dance,
On me she look'd askance.
O thrice unhappy chance!
   Phillada flouts me.

Fair maid! be not so coy.
Do not disdain me!
I am my mother's joy.
Sweet! entertain me!

She'll give me when she dies
All that is fitting:
Her poultry and her bees
And her geese sitting;
A pair of mattrass beds,
And a bag full of shreds.
And yet for all this guedes
   Phillada flouts me.

She hath a clout of mine,
Wrought with good Coventry:
Which she keeps for a sign
Of my fidelity.
But i' faith, if she flinch,
She shall not wear it:
To Tibb my t'other wench
I mean to bear it.
And yet it grieves my heart,
So soon from her to part;
Death strikes me with his dart.
   Phillada flouts me.

Fair maiden! have a care
And in time take me
I can have those as fair,
If you forsake me.
For *Doll* the dairymaid
Laugh'd on me lately,
And wanton *Winifred*
Favours me greatly.
One throws milk on my clothes;
T'other plays with my nose.
What wanton signs are those!
   Phillada flouts me.

I cannot work and sleep
All at a season
Love wounds my heart so deep,
Without all reason.

I 'gin to pine away
With grief and sorrow;
Like to a fatted beast
Penned in a meadow.
I shall be dead, I fear,
Within this thousand year;
And all for very fear
    Phillada flouts me.

about 1630   ANONYMOUS

78. Sonnet

OH, for some honest Lover's ghost,
    Some kind unbodied post
    Sent from the shades below.
    I strangely long to know
Whether the noble Chaplets wear
Those that their mistresse scorn did bear
    Or those that were us'd kindly.

For whatsoe're they tell us here
    To make those sufferings dear,
    'Twill there, I fear, be found
    That to the being crown'd
T' have lov'd alone will not suffice,
Unlesse we also have been wise
    And have our Loves enjoy'd.

What posture can we think him in
    That here unlov'd, agen
    Departs, and's thither gone
    Where each sits by his own?
Or, how can that *Elizium* be
Where I my Mistresse still must see
    Circled in other's Arms?

For there the Judges all are just,
    And *Sophonisba* must
    Be his whom she held dear,
    Not his who lov'd her here.

The sweet *Philoclea*, since she dy'de,
Lies by her *Pirocles* his side
 Not by *Amphialus*.

Some Bayes (perchance), or Myrtle bough
 For difference crowns the brow
 Of those kind souls that were
 The noble Martyrs here.
And if that be the onely odds,
(As who can tell) ye kinder Gods
 Give me the Woman here.

about 1635   JOHN SUCKLING

79. Song

IF you refuse me once, and think again,
 I will complain
You are deceived, Love is no work of Art,
 It must be Got and Born,
 Not made and worn
By every one that hath a Heart.

Or do you think they more than once can dye
 Whom you deny,
Who tell you of a thousand Deaths a Day,
 Like the old Poets feign
 And tell the pain
They met, but in the common way.

Or do you think 't too soon to yield,
 And quit the Field.
Nor is that right they yield that first intreat:
 Once one may crave for Love,
 But more would prove
This Heart too little, that too great.

Oh that I were all Soul, that I might prove
      For you as fit a Love
As you are for an Angel; for I know
None but pure Spirits are fit Loves for you.

You are all Etherial, there's in you no dross,
      Nor any part that's gross,
Your coarsest part is like a curious Lawn,
The Vestal Relicks for a covering drawn.

Your other parts, part of the purest fire,
      That e're Heaven did inspire;
Makes every thought that is refin'd by it,
      A quintessence of goodness and of wit.

Thus have your Raptures reach'd to that degree
      In Love's Philosophy,
That you can figure to yourself a Fire
Void of all heat, a Love without desire.

Nor in Divinity do you go less,
      You think, and you profess,
That Souls may have a plenitude of Joy
Although their Bodies meet not to employ.

But I must needs confess, I do not find
      The motions of my mind
So purified as yet, but at the best
My body claims in them an interest.

I hold that perfect joy makes all our parts
      As joyful as our hearts.
Our senses tell us, if we please not them,
Our Love is but a Dotage or a Dream.

How shall we then agree; you may descend,
      But will not, to my end.
I fain would tune my fancy to your Key,
But cannot reach to that obstructed way.

The Sacred Fire

There rests but this, that whilst we sorrow here,
  Our Bodies may draw near:
And when no more their joys they can extend,
Then let our Souls begin where they did end.

about 1635   JOHN SUCKLING

80. Song

WHEN, Dearest, I but think of thee,
Methinks all things that lovely be
Are present, and my Soul delighted:
For Beauties that from worth arise,
Are like the grace of Deities,
Still present with us, though unsighted.

Thus whilst I sit, and sigh the Day
With all his borrowed Lights away,
Till Night's black Wings do overtake me,
Thinking on thee, thy Beauties then,
As sudden Lights do sleepy Men,
So they by their bright Rays awake me.

Thus absence dies, and dying proves
No absence can subsist with Loves
That do partake of fair perfection;
Since in the darkest Night they may
By Love's quick motion find a way
To see each other by reflection.

The waving Sea can with each Flood
Bath some high Promont that hath stood
Far from the Main up in the River:
Oh think not then but Love can do
As much, for that's an Ocean too,
Which flows not every day, but ever.

about 1635   JOHN SUCKLING

81. Song

CLORIS, it is not thy disdaine
   Can ever cover with dispaire
   Or in cold ashes hide that care
Which I have fedd with soe long paine.
I may perhaps myne eyes refraine
And fruiteless words noe more impart
But yet still serve, still serve thee in my hearte.

What though I spend my haplesse dayes,
   In finding entertainements out
   Carelesse of what I goe about,
Or seeke my peace in skillfull wayes
Applying to my Eyes new rays
Of Beauty, and another flame
Unto my Heart, my Heart is still the same.

'Tis true that I could love noe face
   Inhabited by cold disdayne
   Taking delight in others paine.
Thy lookes are full of native grace,
Since then by chance scorne there hath place
'Tis to be hop'd I may remove
This scorne one day, one day by endless love.

about 1635   SIDNEY GODOLPHIN

82. Hymn

LORD when the wise men came from farr,
Ledd to thy Cradle by a Starr,
Then did the shepheards too rejoyce,
Instructed by thy Angells voyce:
Blest were the wise men in their skill,
And shepheards in their harmelesse will.

The Sacred Fire

Wise men in tracing Nature's lawes
Ascend unto the highest Cause;
Shepheards with humble fearefulnesse
Walk safely, though their light be lesse:
Though wise men better know the way,
It seems noe honest heart can stray.

There is noe meritt in the wise
But love (the shepherds' sacrifice);
Wise men all wayes of knowledge past,
To th' shepheards wonder come at last;
To know, can only wonder breede,
And not to know, is wonders seede.

A wise man at the Alter bowes
And offers up his studied vowes,
And is received: may not the teares,
Which spring too from a shepheards feares,
And sighs upon his fraylty spent,
Though not distinct, be eloquent?

'Tis true, the object sanctifies
All passions which within us rise,
But since noe creature comprehends
The Cause of causes, end of ends,
Hee who himself vouchsafes to know
Best pleases his creator soe.

When, then, our sorrowes wee applye
To our owne wantes and poverty,
When wee look up in all distresse
And our owne misery confesse,
Sending both thankes and prayers above
Then though wee doe not know, we love.

about 1635   SIDNEY GODOLPHIN

83. Song:
Perswasions to enjoy

IF the quick spirits in your eye
 Now languish, and anon must dye;
If every sweet, and every grace,
Must fly from that forsaken face:
 Then, *Celia*, let us reape our joyes
 E're time such goodly fruit destroyes.

Or, if that golden fleece must grow
For ever free, from aged snow;
If those bright Suns must know no shade,
Nor your fresh beauties ever fade;
Then fear not, *Celia*, to bestow,
What, still being gather'd, still must grow.
 Thus, either *Time* his Sickle brings
 In vaine, or else in vaine his wings.

about 1640   THOMAS CAREW

84. Song:
To my inconstant Mistress

WHEN thou, poore excommunicate
 From all the joyes of love, shalt see
The full reward, and glorious fate,
 Which my strong faith shall purchase me,
 Then curse thine owne inconstancy.

A fayrer hand then thine, shall cure
 That heart, which thy false oathes did wound;
And to my soule, a soule more pure
 Then thine, shall by Loves hand be bound,
 And both with equall glory crown'd.

Then shalt thou weepe, entreat, complaine
  To Love, as I did once to thee;
When all thy teares shall be as vaine
  As mine were then, for thou shalt bee
  Damn'd for thy false Apostasie.

about 1640   THOMAS CAREW

85. To his Coy Mistress

HAD we but World enough, and Time,
This coyness Lady were no crime.
We would sit down, and think which way
To walk, and pass our long Loves Day.
Thou by the *Indian Ganges* side
Should'st Rubies find: I by the Tide
Of *Humber* would complain.   I would
Love you ten years before the Flood,
And you should if you please refuse
Till the Conversion of the *Jews*.
My vegetable Love should grow
Vaster than Empires and more slow,
An hundred years should go to praise
Thine Eyes and on thy Forehead Gaze;
Two hundred to adore each Breast,
But thirty thousand to the rest.
An Age at least to every part,
And the last Age should show your Heart.
For Lady, you deserve this State,
Nor would I love at lower rate.
  But at my back I alwaies hear
Times winged Charriot hurrying near:
And yonder all before us lye
Desarts of vast Eternity.
Thy Beauty shall no more be found,
Nor in thy marble Vault shall sound
My ecchoing Song; then Worms shall try
That long preserv'd Virginity:

And your quaint Honour turn to dust,
And into ashes all my Lust.
The Grave's a fine and private place,
But none, I think, do there embrace.
   Now therefore, while the youthful hew
Sits on thy skin like morning dew
And while thy willing Soul transpires
At every pore with instant Fires
Now let us sport us while we may;
And now like am'rous birds of prey,
Rather at once our Time devour,
Than languish in his slow chapt pow'r.
Let us roll all our Strength, and all
Our Sweetness, up into one Ball;
And tear our Pleasures with rough strife
Thorough the iron gates of Life.
Thus, though we cannot make our Sun
Stand still, yet we will make him run.

about 1650   ANDREW MARVELL

86. Bermudas

WHERE the remote *Bermudas* ride
In th' ocean's bosome unespy'd
From a small Boat that row'd along,
The listening Winds received this Song:
   What should we do but sing his Praise
That led us through the watry Maze,
Unto an Isle so long unknown,
And yet far kinder than our own?
Where he the huge Sea-Monsters wracks
That lift the Deep upon their Backs,
He lands us on a grassy Stage,
Safe from the Storms, and prelat's rage.
He gave us this eternal Spring,
Which here enamells every thing,
And sends the Fowls to us in care,
On daily Visits through the Air;

He hangs in shades the Orange bright,
Like golden lamps in a green night,
And does in the Pomgranates close
Jewels more rich than *Ormus* shows;
He makes the Figs our mouths to meet,
And throws the Melons at our feet;
But Apples plants of such a price,
No Tree could ever bear them twice.
With Cedars, chosen by His hand,
From *Lebanon*, he stores the Land,
And makes the hollow Seas, that roar,
Proclaim the Ambergris on shore;
He cast (of which we rather boast)
The Gospel's Pearl upon our Coast,
And in these Rocks for us did frame
A Temple where to sound his Name.
Oh let our Voice his Praise exalt,
Till it arrive at Heaven's Vault:
Which thence (perhaps) rebounding, may
Eccho beyond the *Mexique Bay*.
   Thus sung they, in the *English* boat,
An holy and a chearful Note,
And all the way, to guide their Chime
With falling Oars they kept the time.

about 1653   ANDREW MARVELL

87. The Nymph complaining for the death of
her Faun

THE wanton Troopers riding by
Have shot my Faun, and it will dye.
Ungentle men!   They cannot thrive
To kill thee.   Thou neer didst, alive,
Them any harm: alas nor could
Thy death yet do them any good.
I'm sure I never wished them ill,
Nor do I for all this; nor will:

But if my simple Pray'rs may yet
Prevail with Heaven to forget
Thy murder, I will joyn my Tears
Rather than fail.   But, O my fears!
It cannot dye so.   Heavens King
Keeps register of every thing,
And nothing may we use in vain:
Ev'n beasts must be with justice slain
Else men are made their *Deodands*.
Though they should wash their guilty hands
In this warm life-blood which doth part
From thine and wound me to the Heart,
Yet could they not be clean; their Stain
Is dyed in such a Purple Grain.
There is not such another in
The World, to offer for their Sin.

   Unconstant *Sylvio*, when yet
I had not found him counterfeit,
One morning (I remember well),
Ty'd in this silver Chain and Bell,
Gave it to me: nay and I know
What he said then; I'm sure I do.
Said He, Look how your huntsman here
Hath taught a Faun to hunt his *Dear*.
But *Sylvio* soon had me beguil'd:
This waxed tame, while he grew wild,
And quite regardless of my Smart,
Left me his Faun but took his Heart.

   Thenceforth I set myself to play
My solitary time away,
With this: and very well content,
Could so mine idle Life have spent.
For it was full of sport; and light
Of foot and heart; and did invite
Me to its game: it seem'd to bless
Itself in me.   How could I less
Than love it?   O I cannot be
Unkind to a Beast that loveth me.

   Had it liv'd long, I do not know

The Sacred Fire

Whether it too might have done so
As *Sylvio* did: his gifts might be
Perhaps as false or more than he.
But I am sure, for aught that I
Could in so short a time espie,
Thy Love was far more better then
The love of false and cruel men.

  With sweetest milk and sugar, first
I it at mine own fingers nurst;
And as it grew, so every day
It wax'd more white and sweet than they.
It had so sweet a Breath! and oft
I blusht to see its foot more soft,
And white (shall I say) than my hand?
Nay, any Lady's of the Land!

  It is a wond'rous thing, how fleet
'Twas on those little silver feet;
With what a pretty skipping grace
It oft would challenge me the Race;
And when 't had left me far away,
'T would stay, and run again, and stay.
For it was nimbler much than Hindes;
And trod as if on the four Winds.

  I have a Garden of my own
But so with Roses over grown
And Lillies, that you would it guess
To be a little Wilderness;
And all the Spring time of the year
It only lovèd to be there.
Among the beds of Lillies, I
Have sought it oft, where it should lye;
Yet could not, till it self would rise,
Find it, although before mine Eyes—
For in the flaxen Lillies shade,
It like a bank of Lillies laid.
Upon the Roses it would feed,
Until its lips ev'n seemed to bleed:
And then to me 'twould boldly trip,
And print those Roses on my Lip.

But all its chief delight was still
On Roses thus it self to fill:
And its pure virgin Limbs to fold
In whitest sheets of Lillies cold.
Had it liv'd long, it would have been
Lillies without, Roses within.

    O help! O help! I see it faint
And die as calmely as a Saint!
See how it weeps! The Tears do come
Sad, slowly dropping like a Gumme.
So weeps the wounded Balsome; so
The holy Frankincense doth flow.
The brotherless *Heliades*
Melt in such Amber Tears as these.

    I in a golden Vial will
Keep these two crystal Tears; and fill
It till it do o'reflow with mine,
Then place it in *Diana's* shrine.

    Now my sweet Faun is vanished to
Whither the swans and turtles go;
In fair *Elizium* to endure
With milk-white Lambs and Ermins pure.
O do not run too fast, for I
Will but bespeak thy Grave, and dye.

    First, my unhappy Statue shall
Be cut in Marble; and withal,
Let it be weeping too: but there
Th' Engraver sure his Art may spare;
For I so truly thee bemoane,
That I shall weep though I be Stone,
Until my Tears, still dropping, wear
My breast, themselves engraving there.
There at my feet shalt thou be laid,
Of purest Alabaster made;
For I would have thine Image be
White as I can, though not as thee.

about 1650   ANDREW MARVELL

88. The Mower to the Glo-worms

Ye living Lamps by whose dear light
The Nightingale does sit so late,
And studying all the Summer-night,
Her matchless Songs does meditate;

Ye Country Comets, that portend
No War, nor Princes funeral,
Shining unto no higher end
Than to presage the Grasses fall;

Ye glo-worms, whose officious Flame
To wandering Mowers shows the way,
That in the Night have lost their aim,
And after foolish Fires do stray;

Your courteous Lights in vain you wast,
Since *Juliana* here is come,
For She my mind hath so displac'd,
That I shall never find my home.

about 1650   ANDREW MARVELL

89. The Garden

I

How vainly men themselves amaze
To win the Palm, the Oke, or Bayes;
And their uncessant Labours see
Crown'd from some single Herb or Tree,
Whose short and narrow verged Shade
Does prudently their Toyles upbraid;
While all Flow'rs and all Trees do close,
To weave the Garlands of repose.

II

Fair quiet, have I found thee here,
And Innocence, thy Sister dear!
Mistaken long, I sought you then
In busy Companies of Men.
Your sacred Plants, if here below,
Only among the Plants will grow;
Society is all but rude
To this delicious Solitude.

III

No white nor red was ever seen
So am'rous as this lovely green.
Fond Lovers, cruel as their Flame,
Cut in these Trees their Mistress name.
Little, Alas, they know, or heed,
How far these Beauties Hers exceed!
Fair Trees! wheres'e'er your barkes I wound,
No Name shall but your own be found.

IV

When we have run our Passion's heat,
Love hither makes his best retreat.
The *Gods*, that mortal Beauty chase,
Still in a Tree did end their race;
Apollo hunted *Daphne* so,
Only that She might Laurel grow
And *Pan* did after *Syrinx* speed,
Not as a Nymph, but for a Reed.

V

What wond'rous Life is this I lead!
Ripe Apples drop about my head;
The Luscious Clusters of the Vine
Upon my Mouth do crush their Wine;
The Nectaren and curious Peach,
Into my hands themselves do reach;
Stumbling on Melons, as I pass
Insnared with Flow'rs, I fall on Grass.

The Sacred Fire

VI

Meanwhile the Mind, from pleasure less,
Withdraws into its happiness;
The Mind, that Ocean where each kind
Does streight its own resemblance find;
Yet it creates, transcending these,
Far other Worlds, and other Seas,
Annihilating all that's made
To a green Thought in a green Shade.

VII

Here at the Fountains sliding foot,
Or at some Fruit-trees mossy root,
Casting the Bodies Vest aside,
My Soul into the boughs does glide:
There like a Bird, it sits and sings,
Then whets, and combs its silver Wings,
And, till prepar'd for longer flight,
Waves in its Plumes the various Light.

VIII

Such was that happy Garden-state,
While Man there walk'd without a Mate:
After a Place so pure and sweet,
What other Help could yet be meet!
But 'twas beyond a Mortal's share
To wander solitary there:
Two Paradises 'twere in one,
To live in Paradise alone.

IX

How well the skilful Gardner drew
Of flow'rs and herbes this Dial new;
Where from above the milder Sun
Does through a fragrant Zodiack run;

And, as it works, the industrious Bee
Computes its time as well as we.
How could such sweet and wholsome Hours
Be reckon'd but with herbs and flow'rs.

about 1650   ANDREW MARVELL

90. An Horatian Ode upon Cromwell's return
from Ireland

THE forward youth that would appeare,
Must now forsake his Muses deare,
      Nor in the shadows sing
      His numbers languishing:

'Tis time to leave the books in dust,
And oyle th' unused armour's rust;
      Removing from the wall
      The corselett of the hall.

So restlesse Cromwell could not cease
In the inglorious arts of peace,
      But through adventurous warre
      Urged his active starre;

And, like the three-fork'd lightning, first
Breaking the clouds where it was nurst,
      Did thorough his own Side
      His fiery way divide:

(For 'tis all one to courage high,
The emulous, or enemy;
      And with such, to enclose,
      Is more than to oppose;)

Then burning through the aire he went,
And palaces and temples rent;
      And Caesar's head at last
      Did through his laurels blast.

The Sacred Fire

'Tis madness to resist or blame
The force of angry heaven's flame;
    And if we would speak true,
    Much to the man is due,

Who, from his private gardens, where
He lived reserved and austere,
    (As if his highest plott
    To plant the bergamott:)

Could by industrious valour climb
To ruin the great work of Time,
    And cast the kingdoms old,
    Into another mold;

Though Justice against Fate complaine,
And plead the antient rights in vaine.
    But those do hold or breake,
    As men are strong or weake;

Nature, that hateth emptinesse,
Allows of penetration lesse,
    And therefore must make room
    Where greater spirits come.

What field of all the Civil Warre
Where his were not the deepest scarre?
    And Hampton shows what part
    He had of wiser art,

Where, twining subtile fears with hope,
He wove a net of such a scope
    That Charles himself might chase
    To Caresbrook's narrow case,

That thence the royal actor borne,
The tragic scaffold might adorne;
    While round the armed bands
    Did clap their bludy hands.

He nothing common did or mean,
Upon that memorable scene,
    But with his keener eye
    The axe's edge did trye;

Nor called the gods with vulgar spight
To vindicate his helplesse right;
    But bowed his comely head
    Downe, as upon a bed.

This was that memorable houre,
Which first assur'd the forced power:
    So, when they did designe
    The capitol's first line,

A Bleeding Head, where they begun,
Did fright the architects to run;
    And yet in that the State
    Foresaw its happy fate!

And now the Irish are asham'd,
To see themselves in one year tam'd:
    So much one man can doe
    That does both act and know.

They can affirme his praises best,
And have, though overcome, confest
    How good he is, how just,
    And fit for highest trust.

Not yet grown stiffer with command,
But still in the Republick's hand—
    How fit he is to sway,
    That can so well obey!

He to the Commons' feet presents
A kingdom for his first year's rents;
    And (what he may) forbears
    His fame, to make it theirs:

The Sacred Fire

And has his sword and spoyls ungirt,
To lay them at the Publick's skirt:
    So, when the falcon high
    Falls heavy from the skigh,

She, having killed, no more doth search
But on the next green bough to perch,
    Where, when he first does lure,
    The faulkner has her sure.

—What may not then our Isle presume,
While victory his crest does plume?
    What may not others feare,
    If thus he crowns each year?

As Caesar, he, ere long to Gaul,
To Italy an Hannibal,
    And to all States not free,
    Shall clymacterick be.

The Pict no shelter now shall find
Within his party-colour'd mind,
    But, from this valour sad,
    Shrink underneath the plad—

Happy, if, in the tufted brake,
The English hunter him mistake,
    Nor lay his hounds in neere
    The Caledonian deer.

But thou, the Warr's and Fortune's sonne,
March indefatigably on;
    And for the last effect,
    Still keep the sword erect:

Besides the force it has to fright
The spirits of the shady night,
    The same arts that did gain
    A pow'r, must it maintain.

about 1650   ANDREW MARVELL

XI

from Paradise Lost

from Samson Agonistes

The Sacred Fire

91. *from* Paradise Lost

HAIL holy light, ofspring of Heav'n first-born,
Or of th' Eternal Coeternal beam
May I express thee unblam'd? since God is light,
And never but in unapproached light
Dwelt from Eternitie, dwelt then in thee,
Bright effluence of bright essence increate.
Or hear'st thou rather pure Ethereal stream,
Whose fountain who shall tell? before the Sun,
Before the Heavens thou wert, and at the voice
Of God, as with a mantle didst invest
The rising world of waters dark and deep,
Won from the void and formless infinite.
Thee I re-visit now with bolder wing,
Escap't the *Stygian* Pool, though long detain'd
In that obscure sojourn, while in my flight
Through utter and through middle darkness borne
With other notes then to th' *Orphean* Lyre
I sung of *Chaos* and *Eternal Night*,
Taught by the heav'nly Muse to venture down
The dark descent, and up to reascend,
Though hard and rare: thee I revisit safe,
And feel thy sovran vital Lamp; but thou
Revisit'st not these eyes, that rowle in vain
To find thy piercing ray, and find no dawn;
So thick a drop serene hath quencht thir Orbs,
Or dim suffusion veild.   Yet not the more
Cease I to wander where the Muses haunt
Clear Spring, or shadie Grove, or Sunnie Hill,
Smit with the love of sacred song; but chief
Thee *Sion* and the flowerie Brooks beneath
That wash thy hallowd feet, and warbling flow,
Nightly I visit: nor sometimes forget
Those other two equal'd with me in Fate,
So were I equal'd with them in renown,
Blind *Thamyris* and blind *Mæonides*,
And *Tiresias* and *Phineus* Prophets old.
Then feed on thoughts, that voluntarie move

The Sacred Fire

Harmonious numbers; as the wakeful Bird
Sings darkling, and in shadiest Covert hid
Tunes her nocturnal Note.   Thus with the Year
Seasons return, but not to me returns
Day, or the sweet approach of Ev'n or Morn,
Or sight of vernal bloom or Summers Rose,
Or flocks, or herds, or human face divine;
But cloud in stead, and ever-during dark
Surrounds me, from the chearful waies of men
Cut off, and for a Book of knowledg fair
Presented with a Universal blanc
Of Natures works to mee expung'd and ras'd,
And wisdom at one entrance quite shut out.
So much the rather thou Celestial light
Shine inward, and the mind through all her powers
Irradiate, there plant eyes, all mist from thence
Purge and disperse, that I may see and tell
Of things invisible to mortal sight.

      *   *   *   *   *

            At last his Sail-broad Vannes
He spreads for flight, and in the surging smoak
Uplifted spurns the ground, thence many a League
As in a cloudy Chair ascending rides
Audacious, but that seat soon failing, meets
A vast vacuitie: all unawares
Fluttring his pennons vain plumb down he drops
Ten thousand fadom deep, and to this hour
Down had been falling, had not by ill chance
The strong rebuff of some tumultuous cloud
Instinct with Fire and Nitre hurried him
As many miles aloft: that furie stay'd,
Quenched in a Boggie *Syrtis*, neither Sea,
Nor good dry Land: nigh foundered on he fares,
Treading the crude consistence, half on foot,
Half flying; behoves him now both Oare and Saile.
As when a Gryfon through the Wilderness
With winged course ore Hill or moarie Dale,
Pursues the *Arimaspian*, who by stelth

Had from his wakeful custody purloind
The guarded Gold: so eagerly the fiend
Ore bog or steep, through strait, rough, dense, or rare,
With head, hands, wings, or feet pursues his way,
And swims or sinks, or wades, or creeps, or flies:
At length a universal hubbub wilde
Of stunning sounds and voices all confus'd
Born through the hollow dark assaults his care
With loudest vehemence: thither he plyes,
Undaunted to meet there what ever power
Or spirit of the nethermost Abyss
Might in that noise reside, of whom to ask
Which way the neerest coast of darkness lyes
Bordering on light; when strait behold the Throne
Of *Chaos* and his dark Pavilion spread
Wide on the wasteful Deep; with him Enthron'd
Sat Sable-vested Night, eldest of things
The Consort of his Reign; and by them stood
Orcus and *Ades*, and the dreaded name
Of *Demogorgon*; Rumour next and Chance,
And Tumult and Confusion all imbroild
And Discord with a thousand various mouths.

*   *   *   *   *

But now at last the sacred influence
Of light appears, and from the walls of Heav'n
Shoots farr into the bosom of dim Night
A glimmering dawn; here Nature first begins
Her fardest verge and *Chaos* to retire
As from her outmost works a brok'n foe
With tumult less and with less hostile din,
That *Satan* with less toil, and now with ease
Wafts on the calmer wave by dubious light
And like a weather-beaten Vessel holds
Gladly the Port, though Shrouds and Tackle torn;
Or in the emptier waste, resembling Air,
Weighs his spread wings, at leasure to behold
Farr off th' Empyreal Heav'n, extended wide
In circuit, undetermind square or round,

The Sacred Fire

With Opal Towrs and Battlements adorn'd
Of living Saphire, once his native Seat;
And fast by hanging in a golden Chain
This pendant world, in bigness as a Starr
Of smallest Magnitude close by the Moon.
Thither full fraught with mischievous revenge,
Accurst, and in a cursed hour he hies.

*   *   *   *   *

       . . . and *Uriel* to his charge
Returnd on that bright beam, whose point now raisd
Bore him slope downward to the Sun now fall'n
Beneath th' *Azores*; whither the prime Orb,
Incredible how swift, had thither rowl'd
Diurnal, or this less volubil Earth
By shorter flight to th' East, had left him there
Arraying with reflected Purple and Gold
The Clouds that on his Western Throne attend:
Now came still Eevning on, and Twilight gray
Had in her sober Liverie all things clad;
Silence accompanied, for Beast and Bird,
They to their grassie Couch, these to thir Nests
Were slunk, all but the wakeful Nightingale;
She all night long her amorous descant sung;
Silence was pleas'd: now glow'd the Firmament
With living Saphirs: *Hesperus* that led
The starrie Host rode brightest, till the Moon
Rising in clouded Majestie, at length
Apparent Queen unvaild her peerless light,
And ore the dark her Silver mantle threw.

*   *   *   *   *

Satan from hence now on the lower stair
That scal'd by steps of Gold to Heaven Gate
Looks down with wonder at the sudden view
Of all this World at once. As when a scout
Through dark and desert wayes with peril gone
All night; at last by break of chearful dawne
Obtains the brow of some high-climbing Hill,

Which to his eye discovers unaware
The goodly prospect of some forein land
First seen, or some renownd Metropolis
With glistering Spires and Pinnacles adornd,
Which now the Rising Sun guilds with his beams.
Such wonder seis'd, though after Heaven seen,
The Spirit maligne, but much more envy seis'd
At sight of all this World beheld so faire.
Round he surveys, and well might, where he stood
So high above the circling Canopie
Of Night's extended shade; from Eastern Point
Of *Libra* to the fleecy Starr that bears
Andromeda farr off *Atlantick* Seas
Beyond th' *Horizon*; then from Pole to Pole
He views in bredth, and without longer pause
Down right into the Worlds first Region throws
His flight precipitant, and windes with ease
Through the pure marble Air his oblique way
Amongst innumerable Starrs, that shon
Stars distant, but nigh hand seemd other Worlds,
Or other Worlds they seemd, or happy Iles,
Like those *Hesperian* Gardens fam'd of old,
Fortunate Fields, and Groves and flourie Vales,
Thrice happy Iles, but who dwelt happy there
He stayd not to enquire.

 *   *   *   *   *

So threaten'd hee, but *Satan* to no threats
Gave heed, but waxing more in rage repli'd.
 Then when I am thy captive talk of chaines,
Proud limitarie Cherube, but ere then
Farr heavier load thy self expect to feel
From my prevailing arme, though Heavens King
Ride on thy wings, and thou with thy Compeers,
Us'd to the yoak, draw'st his triumphant wheels
In progress through the rode of Heav'n Star-pav'd.
 While thus he spake, th' Angelic Squadron bright
Turnd fierie red, sharpning in mooned hornes
Thir Phalanx, and begann to hemm him round

The Sacred Fire

With ported Spears, as thick as when a field
Of *Ceres* ripe for harvest waving bends
Her bearded Grove of ears, which way the wind
Swayes them; the careful Plowman doubting stands
Least on the threshing floore his hopeful sheaves
Prove chaff.   On th' other side *Satan* allarm'd
Collecting all his might dilated stood,
Like *Teneriff* or *Atlas* unremov'd:
His stature reacht the Skie, and on his Crest
Sat horror Plum'd; nor wanted in his graspe
What seemd both Spear and Shield: now dreadful deeds
Might have ensu'd, nor onely Paradise
In this commotion, but the Starrie Cope
Of Heav'n perhaps, or all the Elements
At least had gon to rack, disturbd and torne
With violence of this conflict, had not soon
Th' Eternal to prevent such horrid fray
Hung forth in Heav'n his golden Scales, yet seen
Betwixt *Astrea* and the *Scorpion* signe,
Wherein all things created first he weighd
The pendulous round Earth with ballanc't Aire
In counterpoise, now ponders all events,
Battels and Realms: in these he put two weights
The sequel each of parting and of fight;
The latter quick up flew and kickt the beam;
Which *Gabriel* spying, thus bespake the Fiend.

   Satan, I know thy strength and thou knowst mine
Neither our own but giv'n; what follie then
To boast what Arms can doe, since thine no more
Then Heav'n permits, nor mine, though doubld now
To trample thee as mire: for proof look up,
And read thy Lot in yon celestial Sign
Where thou art weigh'd, & shown how light, how weak,
If thou resist.   The Fiend lookt up and knew
His mounted scale aloft: nor more; but fled
Murmuring, and with him fled the shades of night.

*   *   *   *   *

Descend from Heav'n *Urania*, by that name

If rightly thou art call'd, whose Voice divine
Following, above th' *Olympian* Hill I soare,
Above the flight of *Pegasean* wing.
The meaning, not the Name I call: for thou
Nor of the Muses nine, nor on the top
Of old *Olympus* dwell'st, but Heav'nlie borne,
Before the Hills appeerd, or Fountain flow'd,
Thou with Eternal wisdom didst converse,
Wisdom thy Sister, and with her didst play
In presence of th' Almightie Father, pleas'd
With thy Celestial Song.   Up led by thee
Into the Heav'n of Heav'ns I have presum'd,
An Earthlie Guest, and drawn Empyreal Aire,
Thy tempring; with like safetie guided down
Return me to my Native Element:
Least from this flying Steed unrein'd (as once
Bellerophon, though from a lower Clime)
Dismounted, on th' *Aleian* Field I fall
Erroneous, there to wander and forlorne.
Half yet remains unsung, but narrower bound
Within the visible Diurnal Spheare;
Standing on Earth, not rapt above the Pole,
More safe I Sing with mortal voice, unchang'd
To hoarce or mute, though fall'n on evil dayes,
On evil dayes though fall'n, and evil tongues;
In darkness, and with dangers compast round,
And solitude; yet not alone, while thou
Visit'st my slumbers Nightly, or when Morn
Purples the East: still govern thou my Song,
Urania, and fit audience find, though few.
But drive farr off the barbarous dissonance
Of *Bacchus* and his Revellers, the Race
Of that wilde Rout that tore the *Thracian* Bard
In *Rhodope*, where Woods and Rocks had Eares
To rapture, till the savage clamor dround
Both Harp and Voice; nor could the Muse defend
Her Son.   So fail not thou, who thee implores:
For thou art Heav'nlie, shee an empty dreame.

*   *   *   *   *

The Sacred Fire

These are thy glorious works Parent of good,
Almightie, thine this universal Frame,
Thus wondrous fair; thy self how wondrous then!
Unspeakable, who sitst above these Heavens
To us invisible or dimly seen
In these thy lowest works, yet these declare
Thy goodness beyond thought, and Power Divine:
Speak yee who best can tell, ye Sons of light,
Angels, for yee behold him, and with songs
And choral symphonies, Day without Night,
Circle his throne rejoycing, yee in Heav'n,
On earth joyn all yee Creatures to extoll
Him first, him last, him midst, and without end.
Fairest of Starrs, last in the train of Night,
If better thou belong not to the dawn,
Sure pledge of day, that crownst the smiling Morn
With thy bright Circlet, praise him in thy Spheare
While day arises, that sweet hour of Prime.
Thou Sun, of this great World both Eye and Soule,
Acknowledge him thy Greater, sound his praise
In thy Eternal course, both when thou climb'st,
And when high Noon hast gaind, and when thou fallst.
Moon, that now meetst the orient Sun, now fl'st
With the fixt Starrs, fixt in thir Orb that flies,
And yee five other wandring Fires that move
In mystic Dance not without Song, resound
His praise, who out of Darkness call'd up Light.
Aire, and ye Elements the eldest birth
Of Natures Womb, that in quaternion run
Perpetual Circle, multiform; and mix
And nourish all things, let your ceaseless change
Varie to our great Maker still new praise.
Ye Mists and Exhalations that now rise
From Hill and steaming Lake, duskie or grey,
Till the Sun paint your fleecie skirts with Gold,
In honour to the Worlds great Author rise,
Whether to deck with Clouds the uncolour'd skie,
Or wet the thirstie Earth with falling showers,
Rising or falling still advance his praise.

His praise ye Winds, that from four Quarters blow,
Breath soft or loud; and wave your tops, ye Pines,
With every Plant, in sign of Worship wave.
Fountains and yee, that warble, as ye flow,
Melodious murmurs, warbling tune his praise.
Joyn voices all ye living Souls, ye Birds,
That singing up to Heaven Gate ascend,
Bear on your wings and in your notes his praise.
Yee that in Waters glide, and yee that walk
The Earth, and stately tread, or lowly creep;
Witness if I be silent, Morn or Eevn,
To Hill, or Valley, Fountain, or fresh shade.
Made vocal by my Song, and taught his praise.
Hail universal Lord, be bounteous still
To give us onely good; and if the night
Have gathered aught of evil or conceald,
Disperse it, as now light dispels the dark.

＊   ＊   ＊   ＊   ＊

With thee conversing I forget all time,
All seasons and thir change, all please alike.
Sweet is the breath of morn, her rising sweet,
With charm of earliest Birds; pleasant the Sun
When first on this delightful Land he spreads
His orient Beams, on herb, tree, fruit, and flour,
Glistring with dew; fragrant the fertil earth
After soft showers; and sweet the coming on
Of grateful Eevning milde, then silent Night
With this her solemn Bird and this fair Moon,
And these the Gemms of Heav'n, her starrie train:
But neither breath of Morn when she ascends
With charm of earliest Birds, nor rising Sun
On this delightful land, nor herb, fruit, floure,
Glistring with dew, nor fragrance after showers,
Nor grateful Evening mild, nor silent Night
With this her solemn Bird, nor walk by Moon
Or glittering Starr-light without thee is sweet.

＊   ＊   ＊   ＊   ＊

The Sacred Fire

For now, and since first break of dawne the Fiend
Meer Serpent in appearance, forth was come,
And on his Quest, where likeliest he might finde
The only two of Mankinde, but in them
The whole included Race, his purposd prey.
In Bowre and Field he sought, where any tuft
Of Grove or Garden-Plot more pleasant lay,
Thir tendance or Plantation for delight,
By Fountain or by Shadie Rivulet
He sought them both, but wish'd his hap might find
Eve separate, he wish'd, but not with hope
Of what so seldom chanc'd, when to his wish,
Beyond his hope, *Eve* separate he spies,
Veil'd in a Cloud of Fragrance, where she stood,
Half spi'd, so thick the Roses bushing round
About her glowd, oft stooping to support
Each Flour of slender stalk, whose head though gay
Carnation, Purple, Azure, or spect with Gold,
Hung drooping unsustained, them she upstaies
Gently with Mirtle band, mindless the while,
Her self, though fairest unsupported Flour,
From her best prop so farr and storm so nigh.

*   *   *   *   *

                    ... for now too nigh
Th' Archangel stood, and from the other Hill
To thir fixt Station, all in bright array
The Cherubim descended; on the ground
Gliding meteorous, as Ev'ning Mist
Ris'n from a River o're the marish glides,
And gathers ground fast at the Labourers heel
Homeward returning.   High in front advanc't,
The brandisht Sword of God before them blaz'd
Fierce as a Comet; which with torrid heat,
And vapour as the *Libyan* Air adust,
Began to parch that temperate Clime; whereat
In either hand the hastning Angel caught
Our lingring Parents, and to th' Eastern Gate
Led them direct, and down the Cliff as fast

To the subjected Plaine; then disappeer'd.
They looking back, all th' Eastern side beheld
Of Paradise, so late thir happie seat,
Wav'd over by that flaming Brand, the Gate
With dreadful Faces throng'd and fierie Armes:
Som natural tears they drop'd, but wip'd them soon;
The World was all before them, where to choose
Thir place of rest, and Providence thir guide:
They hand in hand with wandring steps and slow,
Through *Eden* took thir solitarie way.

about 1665   JOHN MILTON

92. *from* Samson Agonistes

A LITTLE onward lend thy guiding hand
To these dark steps, a little further on;
For yonder bank hath choice of Sun or shade,
There I am wont to sit, when any chance
Relieves me from my task of servile toyl,
Daily in the common Prison else enjoyn'd me,
Where I a Prisoner chain'd, scarce freely draw
The air imprison'd also, close and damp,
Unwholsom draught; but here I feel amends,
The breath of Heav'n fresh-blowing, pure and sweet,
With day-spring born; here leave me to respire.
This day a solemn Feast the people hold
To *Dagon* thir Sea-Idol, and forbid
Laborious works, unwillingly this rest
Thir Superstition yields me; hence with leave
Retiring from the popular noise, I seek
This unfrequented place to find some ease,
Ease to the body some, none to the mind
From restless thoughts, that like a deadly swarm
Of Hornets arm'd, no sooner found alone,
But rush upon me thronging, and present
Times past, what once I was, and what am now.
O wherefore was my birth from Heaven foretold

The Sacred Fire

Twice by an angel, who at last in sight
Of both my Parents all in flames ascended
From off the Altar, where an Off'ring burn'd,
As in a fiery column charioting
His Godlike presence, and from some great act
Or benefit reveal'd to *Abraham's* race?
Why was my breeding order'd and prescrib'd
As of a person separate to God,
Design'd for great exploits; if I must dye
Betray'd, Captiv'd, and both my Eyes put out,
Made of my Enemies the scorn and gaze;
To grind in Brazen Fetters under task
With this Heav'n-gifted strength?   O glorious strength
Put to the labour of a Beast, debas't
Lower then bondslave!   Promise was that I
Should *Israel* from *Philistian* yoke deliver;
Ask for this great Deliverer now, and find him
Eyeless in *Gaza* at the Mill with slaves,
Himself in bonds under *Philistian* yoke;
Yet stay, let me not rashly call in doubt
Divine Prediction; what if all foretold
Had been fulfilld but through mine own default,
Whom have I to complain of but my self?
Who this high gift of strength committed to me,
In what part lodg'd, how easily bereft me,
Under the Seal of silence could not keep,
But weakly to a woman must reveal it
O're come with importunity and tears.
O impotence of mind, in body strong!
But what is strength, without a double share
Of wisdom, vast, unwieldy, burdensom,
Proudly secure, yet liable to fall
By weakest subtleties, not made to rule,
But to subserve where wisdom bears command.
God, when he gave me strength, to show withal
How slight the gift was, hung it in my Hair.
But peace, I must not quarrel with the will
Of highest dispensation, which herein
Happ'ly had ends above my reach to know:

Suffices that to me strength is my bane,
And proves the sourse of all my miseries;
So many, and so huge, that each apart
Would ask a life to wail, but chief of all,
O loss of sight, of thee I most complain!
Blind among enemies, O worse then chains,
Dungeon, or beggery, or decrepit age!
Light the prime work of God to me is extinct,
And all her various objects of delight
Annull'd, which might in part my grief have eas'd,
Inferiour to the vilest now become
Of man or worm; the vilest here excel me,
They creep, yet see, I dark in light expos'd
To daily fraud, contempt, abuse and wrong,
Within doors, without, still as a fool,
In power of others, never in my own;
Scarce half I seem to live, dead more then half.
O dark, dark, dark, amid the blaze of noon,
Irrecoverably dark, total Eclipse
Without all hope of day!
O first created Beam, and thou great Word,
Let there be light, and light was over all;
Why am I thus bereav'd thy prime decree?
The Sun to me is dark
And silent as the Moon,
When she deserts the night
Hid in her vacant interlunar cave.
Since light so necessary is to life,
And almost life itself, if it be true
That light is in the Soul,
She all in every part; why was the sight
To such a tender ball as th' eye confin'd?
So obvious and so easie to be quench't,
And not as feeling through all parts diffus'd,
That she might look at will through every pore?
Then had I not been thus exil'd from light,
As in the land of darkness yet in light;
To live a life half dead, a living death,
And buried; but O yet more miserable!

The Sacred Fire

Myself, my Sepulcher, a moving Grave,
Buried, yet not exempt
By priviledge of death and burial
From worst of other evils, pains and wrongs,
But made hereby obnoxious more
To all the miseries of life,
Life in captivity
Among inhuman foes.

*   *   *   *   *

O that torment should not be confin'd
To the bodies wounds and sores
With maladies innumerable
In heart, head, brest and reins;
But must secret passage find
To th' inmost mind,
There exercise all his fierce accidents,
And on her purest spirits prey,
As on entrails, joints, and limbs,
With answerable pains, but more intense,
Though void of corporal sense.
My griefs not only pain me
As a lingring disease,
But finding no redress, ferment and rage,
Nor less then wounds immedicable
Rancle, and fester, and gangrene,
To black mortification.
Thoughts my Tormenters arm'd with deadly stings
Mangle my apprehensive tenderest parts,
Exasperate, exulcerate, and raise
Dire inflammation which no cooling herb
Or medcinal liquor can asswage,
Nor breath of Vernal air from snowy *Alp*.
Sleep hath forsook and giv'n me o're
To deaths benumming Opium as my only cure,
Thence faintings, swounings of despair,
And sense of Heav'ns desertion.
I was his nursling once and choice delight,
His destin'd from the womb,

Promisd by Heavenly message twice descending.
Under his special eie
Abstemious I grew up and thriv'd amain;
He led me on to mightiest deeds
Above the nerve of mortal arm
Against the uncircumcis'd, our enemies.
But now hath cast me off as never known,
And to those cruel enemies,
Whom I by his appointment had provok't,
Left me all helpless with th' irreparable loss
Of sight, reserv'd alive to be repeated
The subject of thir cruelty, or scorn.
Nor am I in the list of them that hope;
Hopeless are all my evils, all remediless;
This one prayer yet remains, might I be heard,
No long petition, speedy death,
The close of all my miseries, and the balm.

about 1670   JOHN MILTON

XII

93. The Chronicle: a Ballad

I

Margarita first possest,
   If I remember well, my brest;
   Margarita, first of all;
But when a while the wanton Maid,
With my restless Heart had plaid,
   Martha took the flying Ball.

II

Martha soon did it resign
   To the beauteous *Catharine*:
   Beauteous *Catharine* gave place
('Though loth and angry she to part
With the possession of my Heart)
   To *Eliza's* conquering face.

III

Eliza till this hour might reign,
   Had she not *Evil Counsels* ta'en.
   Fundamental laws she broke,
And still new *Favorites* chose,
Till up in *Arms* my *Passions* rose,
   And cast away her yoke.

IV

Mary then, and gentle *Ann*
   Both to reign at once began:
   Alternately they sway'd,
And sometimes *Mary Fair*
And sometimes *Anne* the *Crown* did wear,
   Sometimes I *Both* obeyed.

The Sacred Fire

V

Another *Mary* then arose,
  And did rigorous Laws impose.
  A mighty *Tyrant* she!
Long, alas, should I have been
Under that *Iron-Sceptr'd Queen*,
  Had not *Rebecca* set me free.

VI

When fair *Rebecca* set me free,
  'Twas then a *golden Time* with me,
  But soon those pleasures fled,
For the gracious Princess dy'd,
In her Youth and Beauties pride:
  And *Judith* reigned in her sted.

VII

One Month, three Days, and half an Hour,
  Judith held the *Soverain Power*.
  Wondrous beautiful her Face,
But so weak and small her Wit,
That she to govern was unfit,
  And so *Susanna* took her place.

VIII

But when *Isabella* came,
  Arm'd with a resistless flame
  And th' Artillery of her Eye;
Whilst she proudly marcht about,
Greater Conquests to find out,
  She beat out *Susan* by the By.

IX

But in her place, I then obey'd
  Black-eyed *Besse* her *Viceroy-Maid*:
  To whom ensu'd a *Vacancy*.
Thousand worse *Passions* then possesst
The *Interregnum* of my breast.
  Bless me from such an *Anarchy*!

X

Gentle *Henriette* than,
  And a third *Mary* next began,
  Then *Jone*, and *Jane*, and *Audria*;
And then a pretty *Thomasine*
And then another *Katharine*,
  And then a *long Et cætera*.

XI

But should I now to you relate,
  The strength and riches of their *state*,
  The *Powder*, *Patches*, and the *Pins*,
The *Ribbans*, *Jewels*, and the *Rings*,
The *Lace*, the *Paint* and *warlike things*,
  That make up all their *Magazins*!

XII

If I should tell their politick Arts
  To take, and keep, men's hearts,
  The Letters, Embassies, and Spies,
The Frowns, and Smiles, and Flatteries,
The Quarrels, Tears, and Perjuries,
  Numberless, nameless Mysteries!

XIII

And all the *Little-Lime-twigs* laid
  By *Machiavel*, the *Waiting maid*;
  'T, more voluminous should grow,
(Chiefly if I like them should tell
All Change of *Weathers* that befel)
  Than *Holinshead* or *Stow*.

XIV

But I will briefer with them be;
  Since few of them were long with Me.
  A higher and a nobler strain
My present *Emperess* does claim;
Heleonora, First o' the name;
  Whom, *God grant long to reign*!

1669   ABRAHAM COWLEY

94. Winter

HARK, hark, I hear the *North* Wind roar,
See how he riots on the Shoar;
And, with expanded Wings outstretch,
Ruffels the Billows on the Beach.

Hark, how the routed Waves complain,
And call for Succor to the Main,
Flying the Storm as if they meant
To creep into the Continent.

Surely all *Æoll's* huffing Brood
Are met to War against the Flood,
Which seem surpriz'd, and have not yet
Had time his Levies to compleat.

The beaten Bark her Rudder lost,
Is on the rowling Billows tost;
Her Keel now Plows the *Ouse*, and soon
Her Top-Mast tilts against the Moon.

'Tis strange! the Pilot keeps his seat;
His bounding Ship does so curvet,
Whilst the poor Passengers are found,
In their own fears already drown'd.

Now Fins do serve for Wings, and bear
Their Scaly Squadrons through the Air;
Whilst the Air's Inhabitants do stain
Their gaudy Plumage in the Main.

Now Stars conceal'd in Clouds do peep
Into the Secrets of the Deep;
And Lobsters spued from the brine
With *Cancer* constellations shine.

Sure *Neptune's* Watery Kingdoms yet
Since first their Corral Graves were wet,
Were ne're disturbed with such alarms,
Nor had such trial of their Arms.

See where a Liquid Mountain rides,
Made up of innumerable Tides,
And tumbles headlong to the Strand,
As if the Sea would come to Land.

A Sail, a Sail, I plainly spy
Betwixt the Ocean and the Sky,
An *Argosy*, a tall built Ship,
With all her Pregnant Sails a-trip.

Nearer, and nearer, she makes way,
With Canvis Wings into the Bay;
And now upon the Deck appears
A crowd of busy Mariners.

Methinks I hear the Cordage crack,
With furrowing *Neptune's* foaming Back,
Who wounded, and revengeful roars
His Fury to the neighb'ring Shoars.

With massy trident high, he heaves
Her sliding Keel above the Waves,
Opening his Liquid Arms to take
The bold invader in his wrack.

See how she dives into his Chest,
Whilst raising up his floating Brest
To clasp her in, he makes her rise
Out of the reach of his surprize.

Nearer she comes, and still doth sweep
The Azure Surface of the deep,
And now at last the Waves have thrown
The Rider on our *Albion*.

Under the Black cliff's spumy base
The Sea-sick Hulk her fraight displays,
And as she walloweth on the Sand
Vomits her burthen to the Land.

The Sacred Fire

With Heads erect, and plying Oar,
The ship-wracked Mates make to the Shoar;
And dreadless of their danger, climb
The floating Mountains of the brine.

Hark, hark, the noise their Eccho make
The Islands Silver Waves to shake;
Sure with these throws, the lab'ring Main
'S delivered of a Hurricane.

And see the Sea's becalm'd behind,
Not crispt with any breeze of Wind;
The Tempest has forsook the Waves,
And on the Land begins his braves.

Hark, hark their Voices higher rise,
They tear the Welkin with their Cries;
The very Rocks their fury feel,
And like Sick Drunkards nod, and reel.

Louder, and louder, still they come,
Nile's Cataracts to these are dumb;
The *Cyclope* to these Blades are still,
Whose Anvils shake the burning Hill.

Were all the Stars enlight'ned Skies,
As full of Ears as sparkling Eyes;
This rattle on the *Chrystal* Hall
Would be enough to deaf them all.

What monstrous Race is hither tost
Thus to Alarm our *British* Coast;
With Outcries such as never yet
War, or Confusion could beget.

Oh! now I know them Let us home:
Our Mortal Enemy is come,
Winter and all his blust'ring train
Have made a voyage o'er the Main.

Vanisht the Countrys of the Sun,
The Fugitive is hither run,
To ravish from our fruitful Fields
All that the teeming Season Yields.

Like an Invader, not a Guest,
He comes to Riot, not to Feast;
And in wild fury overthrows
Whatever does his march oppose.

With bleak and with congealing Winds,
The Earth in shining Chains he binds;
And still as he doth farther pass,
Quarries his way with Liquid Glass.

Hark! how the Blusterers of the Bear,
Their Gibbouse Cheeks in triumph tear,
And with continued Shouts do ring
The entry of their Palsy'd King.

The Squadron nearest to your Eye
Is his Forlorn of Infantry,
Bow-men of unrelenting Minds,
Whose Shafts are Feathered with the Winds.

Now you may see his Van-guard rise
Above the Earthy Precipice,
Bold Horse on bleakest Mountains bred,
With Hail instead of Provend fed.

Their Launces are the pointed Locks]
Torn from the Brows of Frozen Rocks,
Their Shields are Chrystals as their Swords,
The steel the rusted Rock affords.

See the main Body now appears,
And hark the *Aeolian* Trumpetters
By their Hoarse Levets do declare
That the bold General rides there.

The Sacred Fire

And look when Mantled up in white,
He steads it like the *Muscovite*:
I know him by the Port he bears
And his Life-guard of Mountaineers.

Their Caps are Fur'd with Hoary Frost,
Their Brav'ry their Cold Kingdom boasts:
Their spungy Plads are Milk-white Frieze,
Spun from the Snowy Mountain's Fleece.

Their Partizans are fine carved Glass
Fringed with the Mornings spangled Grass;
And, Pendant by their brawny Thighs,
Hang Cimetars of burnisht Ice.

See, see, the Reerward now has won
The *Promontories* trembling Crown,
Whilst at their numerous Spurs, the ground
Groans out a hollow murmering Sound.

The Forlorn now halts for the Van;
The Reer-guard draws up to the Main;
And now they altogether crowd
Their Troops into a threatning Cloud.

Fly, Fly; the foe advances fast—
Into our Fortress, let us hast
Where all the Roarers of the North
Can neither Storm, nor Starve us forth.

There under Ground a Magazine
Of Sovereign juice is collard in,
Liquor that will the Seige maintain
Shou'd *Phoebus* ne'er return again.

Till that, that gives the Poet rage,
And thaws the gelly'd Blood of Age;
Matures the Young, restores the Old,
And makes the fainting Coward bold.

It lays the careful Head to rest,
Calms Palpitations in the Breast,
Renders our Lives misfortune Sweet,
And Venus frolick in the Sheet.

Then let the chill Sciorocco blow,
And gird us round with Hills of Snow;
Or else go whistle to the Shoar,
And make the hollow Mountains roar.

Whilst we together jovial sit
Careless, and Crown'd with Mirth and Wit;
Where, though bleak Winds confine us Home,
Our fancies round the World shall roam.

We'll think of all the Friends we know,
And Drink to all worth Drinking to:
When having Drunk all thine and mine,
We rather shall want Health than Wine.

But where Friends fail us, we'll supply
Our friendships with our Charity:
Men that remote in Sorrows live,
Shall by our lusty Brimmers thrive.

We'll Drink the Wanting into Wealth,
And those that Languish into Health,
The Afflicted into Joy, th' Opprest
Into Security and Rest.

The Worthy in Disgrace shall find
Favour return again more kind,
And in restraint who stifled lye
Shall taste the Air of Liberty.

The Brave shall triumph in Success,
The Lovers shall have Mistresses,
Poor unreguarded Virtue Praise,
And the Neglected Poet Baies.

Thus shall our Healths do others good,
Whilst we our selves do all we wou'd;
For, freed from Envy and from Care,
What would we be but what we are?

'Tis the plump Grapes Immortal Juice
That does this happiness produce,
And will preserve us free together,
Maugre mischance, or Wind or Weather.

Then let Old Winter take his course,
And roar abroad till he be hoarse,
And his Lungs crack with Ruthless Ire,
It shall but serve to blow our Fire.

Let him our little Castle ply
With all his loud Artillery,
Whilst Sack and Claret Man the Fort,
His Fury shall become our Sport.

Or, let him *Scotland* take, and there
Confine the plotting Presbyter;
His Zeal may Freeze, whilst we, kept warm
With Love and Wine, can know no harm.

about 1675   CHARLES COTTON

95. A Sonnet

Chloris, whil'st thou and I were free,
Wedded to nought but Liberty,
How sweetly happy did we live?
How free to promise, free to give?

Then *Monarchs* of our selves, we might
Love here, or there, to change delight,
And, ty'd to none, with all dispence,
Paying each love its recompence.

But in that happy freedom we
Were so improvidently free,
    To give away our Liberties;

And now in fruitless Sorrow pine
At what we are, what might have been,
    Had thou, or I, or both been wise.

about 1670   CHARLES COTTON

96. Song

PHILLIS, for shame, let us improve
A thousand different ways
Those few short moments snatched by love
From many tedious days.

If you want courage to despise
The censure of the grave,
Though love's a tyrant in your eyes
Your heart is but a slave.

My love is full of noble pride,
Nor can it e'er submit
To let that fop, Discretion, ride
In triumph over it.

False friends I have, as well as you,
Who daily counsel me
Fame and ambition to pursue,
And leave off loving thee.

But when the least regard I show
To fools who thus advise,
May I be dull enough to grow
Most miserably wise.

about 1670   CHARLES SACKVILLE, EARL OF DORSET

97. To a Lady

Asking how long he would love Her

It is not, Celia, in our power
    To say how long our love will last;
It may be we within this hour
    May lose those joys we now do taste:
The blessed, that immortal be,
From change in love are only free.

Then since we mortal lovers are,
    Ask not how long our love may last;
But while it does, let us take care
    Each minute be with pleasure pass'd:
Were it not madness to deny
To live because we're sure to die?

about 1670   GEORGE ETHEREGE

98. To a very young lady

Sweetest Bud of Beauty! may
No untimely frost decay
The early glories, which we trace
Blooming in thy matchless face.
Fresh beauties, every day disclose;
Such as by Nature are not shown
In all the blossoms she has blown:
And then, what conquest shall you make;
Who hearts already daily take!
Scorch'd, in the morning with thy beams,
How shall we bear those sad extremes
Which must attend thy threatening eyes,
When thou shalt to thy noon arise?

about 1670   GEORGE ETHEREGE

99. Song

Oh love! that stronger art than Wine,
Pleasing Delusion, Witchery divine,
Wont to be priz'd above all Wealth,
Disease that has more Joys than Health;
Though we blaspheme thee in our Pain,
And of thy Tyranny complain,
We are all better'd by thy Reign.

What Reason never can bestow,
We to this useful Passion owe:
Love wakes the dull from sluggish Ease,
And learns a Clown the Art to please:
Humbles the Vain, kindles the Cold,
Makes Misers free, and Cowards bold;
And teaches airy Fops to think.

When full brute Appetite is fed,
And choakd the Glutton lies and dead;
Thou new Spirits dost dispense,
And fine'st the gross Delights of Sense.

Virtue's unconquerable Aid
That against Nature can persuade;
And makes a roving Mind retire
Within the Bounds of just Desire.
Chearer of Age, Youth's kind Unrest,
And half the Heaven of the blest!

about 1685   APHRA BEHN

100. Song

You charm'd me not with that fair face,
    Though it was all Divine:
To be anothers is the Grace
    That makes me wish you mine.

The Sacred Fire

The Gods and Fortune take their part
    Who, like young Monarchs, fight;
And boldly dare invade that Heart
    Which is another's right.
First mad with hope we undertake
    To pull up ev'ry Bar;
But once possessed we faintly make
    A dull defensive War.
Now, ev'ry friend is turned a foe,
    In hope to get our store:
And passion makes us Cowards grow,
    Which made us brave before.

about 1670   JOHN DRYDEN

101. Song

FAIR, sweet and young, receive a prize
Reserved for your victorious eyes:
From crowds, whom at your feet you see,
O pity, and distinguish me!
As I from thousand beauties more
Distinguish you, and only you adore.

Your face for conquest was designed,
Your every motion charms my mind;
Angels, when you your silence break,
Forget their hymns, to hear you speak;
But when at once they hear and view,
Are loth to mount, and long to stay with you.

No graces can your form improve,
But all are lost unless you love;
While that sweet passion you disdain,
Your veil and beauty are in vain;
In pity then prevent my fate,
For after dying all reprieve's too late.

about 1700   JOHN DRYDEN

102. Ode

To the Pious Memory of the accomplisht young lady, Mrs. Anne Killigrew, excellent in the two sister-arts of Poesie and Painting

THOU youngest Virgin Daughter of the Skies,
     Made in the last Promotion of the *Blest*;
Whose Palms, new-plucked from Paradise,
In spreading *Branches* more sublimely rise,
     Rich with Immortal Green, above the rest:
Whether, adopted to some Neighbouring Star,
Thou roll'st above us in thy wand'ring Race,
     Or, in procession fixt and regular
Mov'd with the Heavens Majestick pace,
     Or, called to more Superiour *Bliss*,
Thou tread'st with Seraphims the vast *Abyss*:
Whatever happy region be thy place,
Cease thy Celestial Song a little space;
(Thou wilt have time enough for Hymns Divine,
Since Heaven's Eternal Year is thine.)
Hear then a Mortal Muse thy praise rehearse,
     In no ignoble Verse,
But such as thy own voice did practise here,
When thy first Fruits of Poesie were given,
To make thyself a welcome Inmate there;
     While yet a young Probationer
     And Candidate of Heaven.

If by Traduction came thy Mind,
     Our Wonder is the less to find
A Soul so charming from a Stock so good;
Thy Father was transfus'd into thy *Blood*:
So wert thou born into the tuneful strain
(An early, rich and inexhausted Vein).
     But if thy Præ-existing Soul
Was form'd, at first, with Myriads more,
     It did through all the Mighty Poets roul
Who *Greek* or *Latine* Laurels wore,

The Sacred Fire

And was that *Sappho* last, which once it was before;
  If so, then cease thy flight, *O Heav'n-born Mind*!
Thou hast no *Dross* to purge from thy rich ore:
    Nor can thy Soul a fairer Mansion find
    Than was the *Beauteous* Frame she left behind:
Return, to fill or mend the Quire of thy Celestial kind.

  May we presume to say, that at thy *Birth*,
New joy was sprung in Heav'n as well as here on *Earth*?
For sure the Milder Planets did combine
On thy *Auspicious* Horoscope to shine,
And ev'n the most Malicious were in Trine.
Thy *Brother-Angels* at thy *Birth*
  Strung each his Lyre, and tun'd it high,
    That all the People of the Skie
Might know a Poetess was born on Earth;
    And then if ever Mortal Ears
    Had heard the Musick of the Spheres!
  And if no clust'ring Swarm of *Bees*
On thy sweet Mouth distill'd their golden Dew,
    'Twas that such vulgar Miracles
    Heav'n had no Leasure to renew:
  For all the Blest Fraternity of Love
Solemniz'd there thy *Birth*, and kept thy Holyday above.

    O gracious God! how far have we
Prophan'd thy Heav'nly Gift of Poesy!
Made prostitute and profligate the Muse,
Debas'd to each obscene and impious use,
Whose Harmony was first ordained above,
For tongues of angels and for hymns of love!
O wretched we! why were we hurried down
    This lubrique and adult'rate age
  (Nay, added fat Pollutions of our own)
    T' increase the steaming Ordures of the Stage?
What can we say t' excuse our *Second Fall*?
Let this thy *Vestal*, Heav'n, atone for all:
Her *Arethusian* Stream remains unsoiled,
Unmixed with foreign filth and undefiled;
Her Wit was more than Man, her Innocence a Child.

Art she had none, yet wanted none,
  For Nature did that Want supply:
So rich in Treasures of her Own,
  She might our boasted Stores defy:
Such Noble Vigour did her Verse adorn,
That it seem'd borrow'd, where 'twas only born.
Her Morals too were in her *Bosom* bred
  By great Examples daily fed,
What in the best of *Books*, her Father's Life, she read.
  And to be read herself she need not fear;
  Each Test and ev'ry Light her Muse will bear,
  Though *Epictetus* with his Lamp were there.
  Ev'n Love (for Love sometimes her Muse expresst),
Was but a Lambent-flame which play'd about her *Breast*,
    Light as the Vapours of a Morning Dream;
So cold herself, while she such Warmth expressed,
'Twas *Cupid* bathing in *Diana's* stream.

Born to the spacious Empire of the Nine,
One wou'd have thought, she should have been content
To manage well that Mighty Government;
But what can young ambitious Souls confine?
    To the next-Realm she stretch'd her sway,
    For *Painture* near adjoyning lay,
A plenteous province, and alluring Prey.
  A *Chamber of Dependences* was fram'd
(As conquerors will never want Pretence,
  When arm'd, to justifie th' Offence)
And the whole Fief, in right of Poetry, she claim'd.
The Country open lay without Defence:
For Poets frequent Inrodes there had made,
    And perfectly cou'd represent
    The Shape, the Face, with ev'ry Lineament;
And all the large Demains which the Dumb-Sister sway'd,
    All bow'd beneath her Government,
    Receiv'd in Triumph wheresoe're she went.
Her Pencil drew, whate're her soul design'd,
And oft the *happy Draught* surpass'd the *Image* in her *Mind*,
    The *Sylvan* Scenes of Herds and Flocks,

And fruitful Plains and barren Rocks,
Of shallow *Brooks* that flow'd so clear,
The bottom did the top appear;
Of deeper too and ampler floods,
Which as in Mirrours, shew'd the Woods;
Of lofty Trees, with Sacred Shades,
And Perspectives of pleasant Glades,
Where Nymphs of brightest Form appear,
And shaggy Satyrs standing near,
Which them at once admire and fear.
The Ruines too of some Majestick Piece,
Boasting the Pow'r of ancient *Rome* or *Greece*,
Whose Statues, Freezes, Columns, broken lie,
And, tho' defac'd, the Wonder of the Eye;
What *Nature, Art,* bold *Fiction* e're durst frame,
Her forming Hand gave feature to the Name.
So strange a Concourse ne're was seen before,
But when the peopl'd *Ark* the whole Creation bore.

The Scene then chang'd; with bold Erected Look
Our Martial King the sight with Rev'rence strook:
For, not content t' express his Outward Part,
Her hand call'd out the Image of his Heart,
His Warlike Mind, his Soul devoid of Fear,
His High-designing *Thoughts* were figur'd there,
As when, by Magick, Ghosts are made appear.
Our Phenix queen was pourtray'd too so bright,
Beauty alone could *beauty* take so right:
Her Dress, her Shape, her matchless Grace,
Were all observ'd, as well as heavenly Face.
With such a Peerless Majesty she stands,
As in that Day she took the Crown from Sacred hands;
Before a Train of heroins was seen,
In *Beauty* foremost, as in Rank, the Queen.
Thus nothing to her Genius was deny'd,
But like a *Ball* of Fire the farther thrown,
Still with a greater *Blaze* she shone,
And her bright Soul broke out on ev'ry side.
What next she had design'd, heaven only knows

To such Immod'rate Growth her Conquest rose,
That Fate alone its Progress cou'd oppose.

    Now all those Charms, that blooming Grace,
The well-proportion'd Shape, and beauteous Face,
Shall never more be seen by Mortal Eyes;
In Earth the much-lamented Virgin lies!
    Not Wit, nor Piety cou'd Fate prevent;
    Nor was the cruel *Destiny* content
    To finish all the Murder at a blow,
    To sweep at once her *Life*, and *Beauty* too;
But like a hardn'd Fellon, took a pride
      To work more Mischievously slow,
      And plunder'd first, and then destroy'd.
O double Sacrilege on things Divine,
To rob the Relique, and deface the Shrine!
      But thus *Orinda* dy'd:
    Heaven, by the same Disease, did both translate;
As equal were their Souls, so equal was their fate.

    Mean-time her *Warlike Brother* on the Seas
His waving Streamers to the Winds displays,
And vows for his Return, with vain Devotion, pays.
      Ah, generous Youth! that Wish forbear,
      The Winds too soon will waft thee here!
    Slack all thy Sails, and fear to come,
Alas, thou know'st not, thou art wreck'd at home!
No more shalt thou behold thy Sister's Face,
Thou hast already had her last Embrace.
But look aloft, and if thou ken'st from far
Among the *Pleiads*, a New-kindled star,
If any sparkles, than the rest, more bright,
'Tis she that shines in that propitious Light.

    When in mid-Air the Golden Trump shall sound,
      To raise the Nations under ground;
      When in the Valley of *Jehosophat*,
The Judging God shall close the book of Fate;
      And there the last Assizes keep,
      For those who Wake, and those who Sleep;

The Sacred Fire

When rattling *Bones* together fly,
  From the four Corners of the Skie,
When Sinews o're the Skeletons are spread,
Those cloath'd with Flesh, and Life inspires the Dead;
The Sacred Poets first shall hear the Sound,
And formost from the Tomb shall bound:
For they are cover'd with the lightest ground;
And straight with in-born Vigour, on the wing,
Like mounting larks, to the New Morning sing.
There *Thou*, sweet saint, before the Quire shall go,
As Harbinger of Heav'n, the Way to show,
The Way which thou so well hast learn'd below.

1685

JOHN DRYDEN

103. *from* Absalom and Achitophel

In pious times, e'er Priest-craft did begin,
Before *Polygamy* was made a Sin;
When Man on many multiplied his kind,
E'r one to one was, cursedly, confin'd,
When Nature prompted and no Law deni'd
Promiscuous use of Concubine and Bride;
Then *Israel's* Monarch, after Heavens own heart,
His vigorous warmth did, variously, impart
To Wives and Slaves: And, wide as his Command,
Scatter'd his Maker's Image through the Land.
Michal, of Royal Blood, the Crown did wear,
A soil ungrateful to the Tiller's care:
Not so the rest; for several Mothers bore
To God-like *David* several sons before.
But since like Slaves his Bed they did ascend,
No True Succession could their Seed attend.
Of all this Numerous Progeny was none
So beautiful so Brave as Absalon:
Whether, inspird by some diviner Lust,
His father got him with a greater Gust,
Or that his Conscious Destiny made way
By manly Beauty to Imperial Sway

Early in Foreign Fields he won Renown
With Kings and States allied to *Israel's* Crown:
In Peace the thoughts of War he coud remove
And seem'd as he were onely born for Love.
What e'er he did was done with so much ease,
In him alone, 'twas Natural to please;
His motions all accompanied with grace;
And *Paradise* was open'd in his face.
With secret Joy, indulgent *David* view'd
His Youthful Image in his Son renew'd;
To all his wishes Nothing he deni'd
And made the charming *Annabel* his Bride.
What faults he had (for who from faults is free?)
His father coud not or he woud not see.
Some warm excesses, which the Law forebore,
Were constru'd Youth that purg'd by boiling o'r:
And *Amnon's* Murther, by a specious Name,
Was call'd a Just Revenge for injur'd Fame.
Thus Prais'd and Lov'd, the Noble Youth remain'd,
While *David*, undisturbed, in *Sion* reign'd.
But Life can never be sincerely blest:
Heav'n punishes the bad, and proves the best.
The *Jews*, a Headstrong, Moody, Murm'ring race
As ever tri'd th' extent and stretch of grace;
God's pamper'd People, whom, debauch'd with ease,
No King could govern nor no God could please;
(Gods they had tri'd of every shape and size
That God-smiths could produce or Priests devise:)
These *Adam*-wits, too fortunately free,
Began to dream, they wanted liberty;
And when no rule, no president was found
Of men, by Laws less circumscrib'd and bound;
They led their wild desires to Woods and Caves;
And thought that all but Savages were Slaves. . . .

*   *   *   *   *

How happy had he been, if Destiny
Had higher placed his Birth, or not so high!
His Kingly Vertues might have claim'd a Throne

And blest all other Countries but his own:
But charming Greatness, since so few refuse;
'Tis Juster to Lament him, than Accuse.
Strong were his hopes a Rival to remove,
With blandishments to gain the publick Love;
To Head the Faction while their Zeal was hot,
And Popularly Prosecute the Plot.
To farther this, *Achitophel* Unites
The Malecontents of all the Israelites:
Whose differing Parties he could wisely Join
For several Ends, to serve the same Design.
The Best, and of the Princes some were such,
Who thought the pow'r of Monarchy too much:
Mistaken Men, and Patriots in their Hearts;
Not Wicked, but seduc'd by Impious Arts.
By these the Springs of Property were bent,
And wound so high, they Crack'd the Government.
The next for Interest sought t' embroil the State,
And sell their Duty at a dearer rate;
And make their *Jewish* Markets of the Throne;
Pretending Publick Good, to serve their own.
Others thought Kings an useless heavy Load,
Who Cost too much, and did too little Good.
These were for laying Honest *David* by
On Principles of pure good Husbandry.
With them Joyn'd all th' Haranguers of the Throng
That thought to get Preferment by the Tongue.
Who follow next, a double danger bring,
Not only hating *David*, but the King;
The *Solymæan* Rout; well Vers'd of old
In Godly Faction, and in Treason bold;
Cowring and Quaking at a Conqu'ror's Sword,
But Lofty to a Lawful Prince Restored;
Saw with Disdain an *Ethnick* Plot begun
And Scorned by *Jebusites* to be Out-done.
Hot *Levites* Headed these; who pul'd before
From th' *Ark*, which in the Judges days they bore,
Resum'd their Cant, and with a Zealous Crie
Pursu'd their old belov'd Theocracie.

Where Sanhedrin and Priest enslav'd the Nation
And justifi'd their Spoils by Inspiration:
For who so fit for Reign as *Aaron's* Race,
If once Dominion they could found in Grace?
These led the Pack; though not by surest scent,
Yet deepest mouth'd against the Government.
A numerous Host of dreaming Saints succeed;
Of the true old Enthusiastick Breed:
'Gainst Form and Order they their Pow'r imploy.
Nothing to Build and all things to Destroy.
But far more numerous was the Herd of such,
Who think too little, and who talk too much.
These, out of meer instinct, they knew not why,
Adored their Father's God and Property:
And by the same blind Benefit of Fate,
The Devil and the *Jebusite* did hate:
Born to be sav'd, even in their own despight;
Because they could not help believing right.
Such were the Tools; but a whole Hydra more
Remains, of sprouting heads too long to score.
Some of their Chiefs were Princes of the Land;
In the first Rank of these did *Zimri* stand:
A man so various, that he seem'd to be
Not one, but all Mankind's Epitome.
Stiff in opinions, always in the wrong;
Was Everything by starts, and Nothing long:
But, in the course of one revolving Moon,
Was Chymist, Fidler, States-man, and Buffoon;
Then all for Women, Painting, Rhyming, Drinking,
Besides ten thousand Freaks that died in thinking.
Blest Madman, who coud every hour employ,
With something New to wish, or to enjoy!
Railing and praising were his usual Theams;
And both (to show his Judgment) in Extreams:
So over Violent, or over Civill,
That every man, with him, was God or Devil.
In squandering Wealth was his peculiar Art:
Nothing went unrewarded, but Desert.
Begger'd by fools, whom still he found too late:

He had his Jest, and they had his Estate.
He laugh'd himself from Court; then sought Relie
By forming Parties, but could ne'er be Chief:
For, spight of him, the weight of Business fell
On *Absalom* and wise *Achitophel*:
Thus wicked but in Will, of Means bereft,
He left not Faction, but of that was left.

about 1680   JOHN DRYDEN

104. Alexander's Feast or, the Power of Musique
an Ode
in honour of St. Cecilia's Day

I

'TWAS at the Royal Feast, for *Persia* won,
        By *Philip's* Warlike Son:
        Aloft in awful State
        The God-like Heroe sate
        On his Imperial Throne:
    His valiant Peers were plac'd around;
Their Brows with Roses and with Myrtles bound.
    (So should Desert in Arms be Crown'd:)
The Lovely *Thais* by his side,
Sate like a blooming *Eastern* Bride
In Flow'r of Youth and Beauty's Pride.
        Happy, happy, happy Pair!
        None but the Brave
        None but the Brave
        None but the Brave deserves the Fair

CHORUS

Happy, happy, happy Pair!
None but the Brave
None but the Brave
None but the Brave deserves the Fair.

II

Timotheus plac'd on high
  Amid the tuneful Quire,
  With flying Fingers touch'd the Lyre:
The trembling Notes ascend the Sky,
    And Heav'nly Joys inspire.
The Song began from *Jove*;
Who left his blissful Seats above,
(Such is the pow'r of mighty Love.)
A Dragon's fiery form bely'd the God:
Sublime on Radiant Spires He rode,
   When He to fair *Olympia* press'd:
   And while He sought her snowy Breast:
Then, round her slender Waste he curl'd,
And stamp'd an Image of himself, a Sov'raign of the World.
The list'ning Crowd admire the lofty Sound,
A present Deity, they shout around:
A present Deity the vaulted Roofs rebound.
   With ravish'd Ears
   The Monarch hears,
   Assumes the God,
   Affects to nod,
  And seems to shake the Spheres.

CHORUS

  With ravish'd Ears
  The Monarch hears,
  Assumes the God,
  Affects to nod,
And seems to shake the Spheres.

III

The Praise of *Bacchus* then, the sweet Musician sung;
  Of *Bacchus* ever Fair, and ever Young:
   The jolly God in Triumph comes;
   Sound the Trumpets; beat the Drums;
    Flush'd with a purple Grace
    He shews his honest Face:
Now give the Hautboys breath; He comes, He comes.

Bacchus ever Fair and Young,
  Drinking Joys did first ordain:
Bacchus Blessings are a Treasure;
Drinking is the Soldier's Pleasure;
    Rich the Treasure,
    Sweet the Pleasure;
  Sweet is Pleasure after Pain.

CHORUS

  Bacchus *Blessings are a Treasure;*
  Drinking is the Soldier's Pleasure;
    Rich the Treasure,
    Sweet the Pleasure;
  Sweet is Pleasure after Pain.

IV

Sooth'd with the Sound the King grew vain;
  Fought all his Battails o'er again;
And thrice He routed all his Foes; and thrice He slew the slain.
    The Master saw the Madness rise;
    His glowing Cheeks, his ardent Eyes;
    And while He Heav'n and Earth defy'd,
    Chang'd his hand, and check'd his Pride.
      He chose a Mournful Muse
      Soft Pity to infuse:
    He sung *Darius* Great and Good,
      By too severe a Fate,
    Fallen, fallen, fallen, fallen,
      Fallen from his high Estate
        And weltering in his Blood:
Deserted at his utmost Need,
By those his former Bounty fed:
On the bare Earth expos'd He lyes,
With not a Friend to close his Eyes.

  With down-cast Looks the joyless Victor sate,
    Revolveing in his alter'd Soul
      The various Turns of Chance below;
    And, now and then, a Sigh he stole;
      And Tears began to flow.

CHORUS

Revolveing in his alter'd Soul
The various Turns of Chance below;
And, now and then, a Sigh he stole;
And Tears began to flow.

v

The Mighty Master smil'd to see
That Love was in the next Degree:
'Twas but a Kindred-Sound to move;
For Pity melts the Mind to Love.
    Softly sweet, in *Lydian* Measures,
    Soon He sooth'd his Soul to Pleasures.
    War, he sung, is Toil and Trouble;
    Honour but an empty Bubble.
        Never ending, still beginning,
        Fighting still, and still destroying,
            If the World be worth thy Winning,
            Think, O think, it worth Enjoying.
        Lovely *Thais* sits beside thee,
        Take the Good the Gods provide thee.

The Many rend the Skies, with loud Applause;
So Love was Crown'd, but Musique won the Cause.
    The Prince, unable to conceal his Pain,
        Gaz'd on the Fair
        Who caus'd his Care,
    And sigh'd and look'd, sigh'd and look'd,
    Sigh'd and look'd, and sigh'd again:
At length, with Love and Wine at once oppress'd,
The vanquish'd Victor sunk upon her Breast.

CHORUS

The Prince, unable to conceal his Pain,
    Gaz'd on the Fair,
    Who caus'd his Care,
And sigh'd and look'd, sigh'd and look'd,
Sigh'd and look'd, and sigh'd again:
At length, with Love and Wine at once oppress'd
The vanquish'd Victor sunk upon her Breast.

The Sacred Fire

Now strike the Golden Lyre again;
A lowder yet, and yet a lowder Strain.
Break his Bands of Sleep asunder,
And rouze him, like a rattling Peal of Thunder
      Hark, hark, the horrid Sound
        Has rais'd up his Head;
        As awak'd from the Dead,
      And amaz'd, he stares around.
Revenge, revenge, *Timotheus* cries,
      See the Furies arise!
      See the Snakes that they rear
      How they hiss in their Hair,
  And the Sparkles that flash from their Eyes!
      Behold a ghastly Band,
      Each a Torch in his Hand!
Those are *Grecian* Ghosts, that in Battail were slain,
        And unbury'd remain
        Inglorious on the Plain
      Give the Vengeance due
      To the Valiant Crew.
Behold how they toss their Torches on high,
      How they point to the *Persian* Abodes,
And glitt'ring Temples of their Hostile Gods.
The Princes applaud with a furious Joy;
And the King seiz'd a Flambeau with Zeal to destroy;
      Thais led the Way
      To light him to his Prey,
And, like another *Hellen,* fir'd another *Troy.*

CHORUS

And the King seiz'd a Flambeau with Zeal to destroy;
    Thais *led the Way*
    To light him to his Prey,
And, like another Hellen, *fir'd another Troy.*

VII

Thus, long ago
'Ere heaving Bellows learn'd to blow,
While Organs yet were mute,
Timotheus, to his breathing Flute
And sounding Lyre,
Cou'd swell the Soul to rage, or kindle soft Desire.
At last Divine *Cecilia* came,
Inventress of the Vocal Frame;
The sweet Enthusiast, from her Sacred Store,
Enlarg'd the former narrow Bounds,
And added length to solemn Sounds,
With Nature's Mother-Wit, and Arts unknown before.
Let old *Timotheus* yield the Prize,
Or both divide the Crown:
He rais'd a Mortal to the Skies;
She drew an Angel down.

GRAND CHORUS

At last Divine Cecilia *came,*
Inventress of the Vocal Frame;
The sweet Enthusiast, from her Sacred Store,
Enlarg'd the former narrow Bounds,
And added Length to solemn Sounds,
With Nature's Mother-Wit, and Arts unknown before.
Let old Timotheus *yield the Prize,*
Or both divide the Crown:
He rais'd a Mortal to the Skies;
She drew an Angel down.

1697   JOHN DRYDEN

XIII

Alexander Pope

Jonathan Swift

Matthew Prior

John Gay

105. Epistle to Miss Martha Blount on her leaving town after the Coronation

As some fond Virgin, whom her mother's care
Drags from the Town to wholesome Country air,
Just when she learns to roll a melting eye,
And hear a spark, yet think no danger nigh;
From the dear man unwilling she must sever,
Yet takes one kiss before she parts for ever:
Thus from the world fair Zephalinda flew,
Saw others happy, and with sighs withdrew;
Not that their Pleasures caus'd her discontent,
She sigh'd not that they stay'd but that she went.

She went to plain-work, and to purling brooks,
Old-fashion'd halls, dull aunts, and croaking rooks;
She went from Op'ra, Park, Assembly, Play,
To morning-walks, and pray'rs three hours a day;
To part her time, 'twixt reading and bohea,
To muse, and spill her solitary tea,
Or o'er cold coffee trifle with a spoon,
Count the slow clock, and dine exact at noon;
Divert her eyes with pictures in the fire,
Hum half a tune, tell stories to the squire;
Up to her godly garret after sev'n,
There starve and pray, for that's the way to heav'n.

Some Squire, perhaps, you take delight to rack,
Whose game is Whisk, whose treat a toast in sack,
Who visits with a Gun, presents you birds,
Then gives a smacking buss, and cries—"No words!"
Or with his hounds comes hallooing from the stable,
Makes love with nods and knees beneath a table;
Whose laughs are hearty, tho' his jests are coarse,
And loves you best of all things—but his horse.

In some fair ev'ning, on your elbow laid,
You dream of Triumphs in the rural shade;

I

In pensive thought recall the fancied scene,
See Coronations rise on every green;
Before you pass th' imaginary sights
Of Lords, and Earls, and Dukes, and garter'd Knights,
While the spread fan o'ershades your closing eyes;
Then give one flirt, and all the vision flies.
Thus vanish sceptres, coronets, and balls,
And leave you in lone woods or empty walls.

So when your slave, at some dear idle time,
(Not plagu'd with headachs, or the want of rhyme,)
Stands in the streets, abstracted from the crew,
And while he seems to study, thinks of you;
Just when his fancy points your sprightly eyes,
Or sees the blush of soft Parthenia rise,
Gay pats my shoulder and you vanish quite,
Streets, Chairs, and Cockscombs rush upon my sight;
Vex'd to be still in town, I knit my brow,
Look sour, and hum a Tune, as you may now.

about 1715   ALEXANDER POPE

106. *from* The Rape of the Lock

AND now, unveil'd, the *Toilet* stands display'd,
Each Silver Vase in mystic Order laid.
First, rob'd in White, the Nymph intent adores
With Head uncover'd, the *Cosmetic* Pow'rs.
A heav'nly Image in the Glass appears,
To that she bends, to that her Eyes she rears;
Th' inferior Priestess, at her Altar's side,
Trembling, begins the sacred Rites of Pride.
Unnumber'd Treasures ope at once, and here
The various Off'rings of the World appear;
From each she nicely culls with curious Toil,
And decks the Goddess with the glitt'ring Spoil.
This Casket *India's* glowing Gems unlocks,
And all *Arabia* breathes from yonder Box.

The Tortoise here and Elephant unite,
Transformed to *Combs*, the speckled and the white.
Here Files of Pins extend their shining Rows,
Puffs, Powders, Patches, Bibles, Billet-doux.
Now awful Beauty puts on all its Arms;
The Fair each moment rises in her Charms,
Repairs her Smiles, awakens ev'ry Grace,
And calls forth all the Wonders of her Face;
Sees by Degrees a purer Blush arise,
And keener Lightnings quicken in her Eyes.
The busy *Sylphs* surround their darling Care;
These set the Head, and those divide the Hair,
Some fold the Sleeve, whilst others plait the Gown;
And *Betty's* prais'd for labours not her own.

about 1711–12   ALEXANDER POPE

107. *from* The Progress of Beauty

THREE Colours, Black, and Red, and White
    So gracefull in their proper Place,
Remove them to a diff'rent Light,
    They form a frightful hideous Face:

For instance, when the Lilly slipps
    Into the Precincts of the Rose,
And takes Possession of the Lips,
    Leaving the Purple to the nose:

So Celia went entire to bed,
    All her Complexions safe and sound;
But when she rose, the black and red,
    Though still in Sight, had chang'd their Ground.

The Black, which would not be confin'd,
    A more inferior Station seeks,
Leaving the fiery red behind,
    And mingles in her muddy Cheeks.

The Sacred Fire

The Paint by Perspiration cracks
   And falls in Rivulets of Sweat,
On either Side you see the Tracks,
   While at her Chin the Confluents met.

A skilfull Houswife thus her Thumb
   With Spittle while she spins, anoints,
And thus the brown Meanders come
   In trickling Streams betwixt her Joints.

But Celia can with ease reduce,
   By help of Pencil, Paint, and Brush,
Each Colour to it's Place and Use,
   And teach her Cheeks again to blush.

She knows her Early self no more,
   But fill'd with Admiration, stands:
As Other Painters oft adore
   The Workmanship of their own Hands.

Thus after four important hours,
   Celia's the Wonder of her Sex;
Say, which among the Heav'nly Powers
   Could cause such wonderfull Effects?

Venus, indulgent to her Kind,
   Gave Women all their Hearts could wish,
When first she taught them where to find
   White Lead, and Lusitanian Dish.

Love with White lead cements his Wings;
   White lead was sent us to repair
Two brightest, brittlest, earthly Things,
   A Lady's Face, and China-ware.

She ventures now to lift the Sash;
   The Window is her proper Sphear;
Ah, Lovely Nymph! be not too rash,
   Nor let the Beaux approach too near.

Take Pattern by your Sister Star;
   Delude at once and Bless our Sight;
When you are seen, be seen from far,
   And chiefly chuse to shine by Night.

In the Pell-Mell when passing by,
   Keep up the Glasses of your Chair,
Then each transported Fop will cry,
   "G—d d—m me, Jack, she's wondrous fair!"

But, Art no longer can prevayl,
   When the materialls all are gone;
The best Mechanick Hand must fayl,
   Where Nothing's left to work upon.

Matter, as wise Logicians say,
   Cannot without a Form subsist;
And Form, say I, as well as They,
   Must fayl if Matter brings no Grist.

And this is fair Diana's case;
   For, all Astrologers maintain,
Each Night a Bit drops off her Face,
   When Mortals say she's in her Wane:

While Partridge wisely shows the Cause
   Efficient of the Moon's Decay,
That Cancer with his pois'nous Claws
   Attacks her in the milky Way:

But Gadbury in Art profound,
   From her pale Cheeks pretends to show
That Swain Endymion is not sound,
   Or else, that Mercury's her Foe.

But, let the Cause be what it will,
   In half a Month she looks so thin,
That Flamstead can, with all his Skill,
   See but her Forehead and her Chin.

Yet, as she wasts, she grows discreet,
   Till Midnight never shows her Head;
So rotting Celia strolles the Street,
   When sober Folks are all a-bed:

For sure, if this be Luna's Fate,
   Poor Celia, but of mortall Race,
In vain expects a longer Date
   To the Materialls of Her Face.

When Mercury her Tresses mows,
   To think of Oyl and Soot, is vain:
No Painting can restore a Nose,
   Nor will her Teeth return again.

Two Balls of Glass may serve for Eyes,
   White Lead may plaister up a Cleft;
But these, alas, are poor Supplyes
   If neither Cheeks, nor Lips be left.

Ye Pow'rs who over Love preside!
   Since mortal Beautys drop so soon,
If ye would have us well supplyd,
   Send us new Nymphs with each new Moon.

1719   JONATHAN SWIFT

108. A Description of a City Shower in imitation of Virgil's Georgics

CAREFUL Observers may foretel the Hour,
(By sure prognosticks) when to dread a showr.
While Rain depends, the pensive Cat gives o'er
Her Frolicks, and pursues her Tail no more.
Returning Home at Night, you'll find the Sink
Strike your offended Sense with double Stink.
If you be wise, then, go not far to dine;
You'll spend in Coach-hire more than save in Wine.

A coming Show'r your shooting Corns presage,
Old Aches throb, your hollow Tooth will rage;
Sauntering in Coffee-house is *Dulman* seen,
He damns the Climate, and complains of Spleen.

Meanwhile the South, rising with dabbled Wings,
A sable Cloud athwart the Welkin flings,
That swill'd more Liquor than it could contain,
And, like a Drunkard, gives it up again.
Brisk *Susan* whips her Linen from the Rope,
While the first drizzling Show'r is born aslope:
Such is that Sprinkling which some careless Quean
Flirts on you from her Mop, but not so clean:
You fly, invoke the Gods; then, turning, stop
To rail; she, singing, still whirls on her Mop.
Not yet, the Dust had shun'd th' unequal Strife,
But, aided by the Wind, fought still for Life,
And wafted with its Foe by violent Gust:
'Twas doubtful which was Rain, and which was Dust.
Ah! where must needy Poet seek for Aid,
When Dust and Rain at once his Coat invade?
His only coat, where dust, confus'd with Rain,
Erects the Nap, and leaves a mingled stain?

Now in contiguous Drops the Flood comes down,
Threatening with deluge this *devoted* town.
To Shops in Crowds the daggled Females fly,
Pretend to cheapen Goods, but nothing buy.
The Templer spruce, while ev'ry Spout's abroach,
Stays till 'tis fair, yet seems to call a Coach.
The tuck'd-up Sempstress walks with hasty Strides,
While Streams run down her oil'd Umbrella's sides.
Here various Kinds, by various Fortunes led,
Commence Acquaintance underneath a Shed.
Triumphant Tories and despairing Whigs,
Forget their Fewds, and join to save their Wigs.
Box'd in a Chair the Beau impatient sits,
While Spouts run clattering o'er the Roof by Fits,

And ever and anon with frightful Din
The Leather sounds; he trembles from within.
So when *Troy* Chairmen bore the Wooden Steed,
Pregnant with *Greeks* impatient to be freed,
(Those bully *Greeks*, who, as the moderns do,
Instead of paying Chairmen, ran them through)
Laocoon struck the Outside with his Spear,
And each imprison'd Hero quak'd for Fear.

Now from all Parts the swelling Kennels flow,
And bear their Trophies with them as they go:
Filths of all Hues and odours seem to tell
What Street they sail'd from, by their Sight and smell.
They, as each Torrent drives, with rapid Force,
From *Smithfield* to *St. Pulchre's* shape their Course,
And, in huge Confluent join'd at *Snowhill* Ridge,
Fall from the *Conduit* prone to *Holborn-Bridge*.
Sweepings from Butchers Stalls, Dung, Guts and Blood,
Drown'd Puppies, stinking Sprats, all drench'd in Mud,
Dead Cats, and Turnip-Tops, come tumbling down the Flood

1710   JONATHAN SWIFT

109. To a Lady: She refusing to continue a
Dispute with me, and leaving me
in the argument
An Ode

SPARE, Gen'rous Victor, spare the Slave,
    Who did unequal War pursue;
That more than Triumph he might have,
    In being overcome by You.

In the Dispute whate'er I said,
    My Heart was by my Tongue bely'd;
And in my Looks you might have read,
    How much I argu'd on your side.

You, far from Danger as from Fear,
   Might have sustain'd an open Fight:
For seldom your Opinions err:
   Your Eyes always in the right.

Why, fair One, wou'd you not rely
   On Reason's force with Beauty's join'd?
Could I their Prevalence deny,
   I must at once be Deaf and Blind.

Alas! not hoping to subdue,
   I only to the Fight aspir'd:
To keep the beauteous Foe in view
   Was all the Glory I desir'd.

But She, howe'er of Vict'ry sure,
   Contemns the Gift too long delay'd;
And, arm'd with more immediate Pow'r,
   Calls cruel Silence to her Aid.

Deeper to wound, she shuns the fight:
   She drops her Arms, to gain the Field:
Secures her Conquest by her Flight;
   And Triumphs, when she seems to yield.

So when the *Parthian* turn'd his Steed,
   And from the Hostile Camp withdrew;
With cruel Skill the backward Reed
   He sent; and as he fled, he slew.

about 1705   MATTHEW PRIOR

110. The Fable of the *Fox* at the Point of Death

A Fox, in life's extream decay,
Weak, sick, and faint, expiring lay;
All appetite had left his maw,
And age disarm'd his mumbling jaw.

His num'rous race around him stand
To learn their dying sire's command:
He rais'd his head with whining moan,
And thus was heard the feeble tone:

Ah, sons, from evil ways depart;
My crimes lye heavy on my heart.
See, see, the murder'd geese appear!
Why are those bleeding turkeys there?
Why all around this cackling train,
Who haunt my ears for chicken slain?

The hungry foxes round them star'd,
And for the promis'd feast prepar'd.

Where, Sir, is all this dainty cheer?
No turkey, goose, nor hen is here:
These are the phantoms of your brain,
And your sons lick their lips in vain.

O gluttons, says the drooping sire,
Restrain inordinate desire.
Your liqu'rish taste you shall deplore,
When peace of conscience is no more.
Does not the hound betray our pace,
And gins and guns destroy our race?
Thieves dread the searching eye of power,
And never feel the quiet hour.
Old-age (which few of us shall know)
Now puts a period to my woe.
Would you true happiness attain,
Let honesty your passions rein,
So live in credit and esteem.
And, the good name you lost, redeem.

The counsel's good, a fox replies,
Could we perform what you advise.
Think, what our ancestors have done,
A line of thieves from son to son:
To us descends the long disgrace,
And infamy hath mark'd our race.
Though we, like harmless sheep, should feed,
Honest in thought, in word, and deed,
Whatever hen-roost is decreas'd,

We shall be thought to share the feast.
The change shall never be believ'd
A lost good name is ne'er retriev'd.
　　Nay then, replies the feeble fox,
(But hark! I hear a hen that clocks)
Go, but be moderate in your food;
A chicken too might do me good.

about 1725　　　　　　　　　　　　JOHN GAY

XIV

William Collins
Thomas Gray
Christopher Smart
Oliver Goldsmith

111. Ode

written in the beginning of the Year 1746

How sleep the Brave, who sink to Rest,
By all their Country's Wishes blest!
When *Spring*, with dewy Fingers cold,
Returns to deck their hallow'd Mold,
She there shall dress a sweeter Sod,
Than *Fancy's* Feet have ever trod.

By Fairy Hands their Knell is rung,
By Forms unseen their Dirge is sung;
There *Honour* comes, a Pilgrim grey,
To bless the Turf that wraps their Clay,
And *Freedom* shall a-while repair,
To dwell a weeping Hermit there!

1746   WILLIAM COLLINS

112. Ode to Fear

THOU, to whom the world unknown
With all its shadowy Shapes, is shown;
Who see'st, appall'd, th' unreal Scene,
While Fancy lifts the Veil between:
      Ah *Fear*!   Ah frantic *Fear*!
      I see, I see Thee near.
I know thy hurried Step, thy haggard Eye!
Like Thee I start, like Thee disorder'd fly.
For lo what *Monsters* in thy *Train* appear!
Danger, whose limbs of Giant Mold
What mortal Eye can fix'd behold?
Who stalks his Round, an hideous Form,
Howling amidst the Midnight Storm,
Or throws him on the ridgy Steep
Of some loose hanging Rock to sleep:
And with him thousand Phantoms join'd,
Who prompt to deeds accurs'd the Mind:

And those, the Fiends, who near allied,
O'er Nature's Wounds, and Wrecks, preside;
Whilst *Vengeance*, in the lurid Air,
Lifts her red Arm, expos'd and bare:
On whom the rav'ning Brood of Fate,
Who lap the Blood of Sorrow, wait;
Who, *Fear*, this ghastly Train can see,
And look not madly wild, like Thee?

about 1745   WILLIAM COLLINS

113. Ode to Evening

IF aught of Oaten Stop, or Pastoral Song,
May hope, O pensive *Eve*, to soothe thine Ear,
    Like thy own brawling Springs,
    Thy Springs, and dying Gales,
O *Nymph* reserv'd, while now the bright-hair'd Sun
Sits in yon western Tent, whose cloudy Skirts,
    With Brede ethereal wove,
    O'erhang his wavy Bed:
Now Air is hush'd, save where the weak-ey'd Bat,
With short shrill Shriek flits by on leathern Wing,
    Or where the Beetle winds
    His small but sullen Horn,
As oft he rises 'midst the twilight Path,
Against the Pilgrim borne in heedless Hum:
    Now teach me, *Maid* compos'd,
    To breathe some soften'd Strain,
Whose Numbers stealing thro' thy darkning Vale,
May not unseemly with its Stillness suit,
    As musing slow, I hail
    Thy genial lov'd Return!
For when thy folding star arising shews
His paly Circlet, at his warning Lamp
    The fragrant *Hours*, and *Elves*
    Who slept in Buds the Day,

And many a *Nymph* who wreaths her Brows with Sedge,
And sheds the fresh'ning Dew, and lovelier still,
    The *Pensive Pleasures* sweet
    Prepare thy shadowy Car.
Then let me rove some wild and heathy Scene,
Or find some Ruin 'midst its dreary Dells,
    Whose Walls more awful nod
    By thy religious Gleams.
Or if chill blust'ring Winds, or driving Rain,
Prevent my willing Feet, be mine the Hut,
    That from the Mountain's side,
    Views Wilds, and swelling Floods,
And Hamlets brown, and dim-discover'd Spires,
And hears their simple Bell, and marks o'er all
    Thy Dewy Fingers draw
    The gradual dusky Veil.
While *Spring* shall pour his Show'rs, as oft he wont,
And bathe thy breathing Tresses, modest *Eve*!
    While *Summer* loves to sport,
    Beneath thy ling'ring Light:
While sallow *Autumn* fills thy Lap with Leaves,
Or *Winter* yelling thro' the troublous Air,
    Affrights thy shrinking Train,
    And rudely rends thy Robes.
So long regardful of thy quiet Rule,
Shall *Fancy*, *Friendship*, *Science*, smiling *Peace*,
    Thy gentlest Influence own,
    And love thy fav'rite Name!

about 1745   WILLIAM COLLINS

114. Dirge

    To fair Fidele's grassy tomb
      Soft maids and village hinds shall bring
    Each op'ning sweet, of earliest bloom,
      And rifle all the breathing Spring.

No wailing ghost shall dare appear
    To vex with shrieks this quiet grove:
But shepherd lads assemble here,
    And melting virgins own their love.

No wither'd witch shall here be seen,
    No goblins lead their nightly crew;
The female fays shall haunt the green,
    And dress thy grave with pearly dew!

The red-breast oft, at ev'ning hours
    Shall kindly lend his little aid:
With hoary moss, and gather'd flow'rs,
    To deck the ground where thou art laid.

When howling winds, and beating rain,
    In tempests shake the sylvan cell,
Or 'midst the chace, on ev'ry plain,
    The tender thought on thee shall dwell.

Each lonely scene shall thee restore,
    For thee the tear be duly shed:
Belov'd till life can charm no more,
    And mourn'd till Pity's self be dead.

about 1749   WILLIAM COLLINS

115. Elegy written in a Country Churchyar

THE Curfew tolls the knell of parting day,
The lowing herd wind slowly o'er the lea,
The plowman homeward plods his weary way,
And leaves the world to darkness and to me.

Now fades the glimmering landscape on the sight,
And all the air a solemn stillness holds,
Save where the beetle wheels his droning flight,
And drowsy tinklings lull the distant folds;

Save that from yonder ivy-mantled tow'r
The mopeing owl does to the moon complain
Of such, as wand'ring near her secret bow'r,
Molest her ancient solitary reign.

Beneath those rugged elms, that yew-tree's shade,
Where heaves the turf in many a mould'ring heap,
Each in his narrow cell for ever laid,
The rude Forefathers of the hamlet sleep.

The breezy call of incense-breathing Morn,
The swallow twitt'ring from the straw-built shed,
The cock's shrill clarion, or the echoing horn,
No more shall rouse them from their lowly bed.

For them no more the blazing hearth shall burn,
Or busy housewife ply her evening care:
No children run to lisp their sire's return,
Or climb his knees the envied kiss to share.

Oft did the harvest to their sickle yield,
Their furrow oft the stubborn glebe has broke;
How jocund did they drive their team afield!
How bow'd the woods beneath their sturdy stroke!

Let not ambition mock their useful toil,
Their homely joys, and destiny obscure;
Nor Grandeur hear with a disdainful smile,
The short and simple annals of the poor.

The boast of heraldry, the pomp of pow'r,
And all that beauty, all that wealth e'er gave,
Awaits alike th' inevitable hour.
The paths of glory lead but to the grave.

Nor you, ye Proud, impute to These the fault,
If Mem'ry o'er their Tomb no Trophies raise,
Where thro' the long-drawn isle and fretted vault
The pealing anthem swells the note of praise.

The Sacred Fire

Can storied urn or animated bust
Back to its mansion call the fleeting breath?
Can Honour's voice provoke the silent dust,
Or Flatt'ry sooth the dull cold ear of Death?

Perhaps in this neglected spot is laid
Some heart once pregnant with celestial fire;
Hands, that the rod of empire might have sway'd,
Or wak'd to extasy the living lyre.

But Knowledge to their eyes her ample page
Rich with the spoils of time did ne'er unroll;
Chill Penury repress'd their noble rage,
And froze the genial current of the soul.

Full many a gem of purest ray serene,
The dark unfathom'd caves of ocean bear:
Full many a flower is born to blush unseen,
And waste its sweetness on the desert air.

Some village-Hampden, that with dauntless breast
The little Tyrant of his fields withstood;
Some mute inglorious Milton here may rest,
Some Cromwell guiltless of his country's blood.

Th' applause of list'ning senates to command,
The threats of pain and ruin to despise,
To scatter plenty o'er a smiling land,
And read their hist'ry in a nation's eyes

Their lot forbad: nor circumscrib'd alone
Their growing virtues, but their crimes confin'd;
Forbad to wade through slaughter to a throne,
And shut the gates of mercy on mankind,

The struggling pangs of conscious truth to hide,
To quench the blushes of ingenuous shame,
Or heap the shrine of Luxury and Pride
With incense kindled at the Muse's flame.

Far from the madding crowd's ignoble strife,
Their sober wishes never learn'd to stray;
Along the cool sequester'd vale of life
They kept the noiseless tenor of their way.

Yet ev'n these bones from insult to protect
Some frail memorial still erected nigh,
With uncouth rhimes and shapeless sculpture deck'd,
Implores the passing tribute of a sigh.

Their name, their years, spelt by th' unlettered muse,
The place of fame and elegy supply:
And many a holy text around she strews,
That teach the rustic moralist to die.

For who to dumb Forgetfulness a prey,
This pleasing anxious being e'er resign'd,
Left the warm precincts of the chearful day,
Nor cast one longing ling'ring look behind?

On some fond breast the parting soul relies,
Some pious drops the closing eye requires;
Ev'n from the tomb the voice of Nature cries,
Ev'n in our Ashes live their wonted Fires.

For thee, who mindful of th' unhonour'd Dead
Dost in these lines their artless tale relate;
If chance, by lonely Contemplation led,
Some kindred Spirit shall inquire thy fate,

Haply some hoary-headed Swain may say,
'Oft have we seen him at the peep of dawn
'Brushing with hasty steps the dews away
'To meet the sun upon the upland lawn.

'There at the foot of yonder nodding beech
'That wreathes its old fantastic roots so high,
'His listless length at noontide would he stretch,
'And pore upon the brook that babbles by.

'Hard by yon wood, now smiling as in scorn,
'Mutt'ring his wayward fancies he would rove,
'Now drooping, woeful wan, like one forlorn,
'Or craz'd with care, or cross'd in hopeless love.

'One morn I miss'd him on the custom'd hill,
'Along the heath and near his fav'rite tree;
'Another came; nor yet beside the rill,
'Nor up the lawn, nor at the wood was he;

'The next with dirges due in sad array
'Slow thro' the church-way path we saw him born.
'Approach and read (for thou can'st read) the lay,
'Grav'd on the stone beneath yon aged thorn.'

THE EPITAPH

Here rests his head upon the lap of Earth
A youth to Fortune and to Fame unknown.
Fair Science frown'd not on his humble birth,
And Melancholy mark'd him for her own.

Large was his bounty, and his soul sincere,
Heav'n did a recompence as largely send:
He gave to Mis'ry all he had, a tear,
He gain'd from Heav'n ('twas all he wish'd) a friend.

No farther seek his merits to disclose,
Or draw his frailties from their dread abode,
(There they alike in trembling hope repose,)
The bosom of his Father and his God.

about 1748–50   THOMAS GRAY

116. Hymn to Adversity

DAUGHTER of Jove, relentless power,
   Thou tamer of the human breast,
Whose iron scourge and torturing hour
   The bad affright, afflict the best!

Bound in thy adamantine chain
The proud are taught to taste of pain,
And purple tyrants vainly groan
With pangs unfelt before, unpitied and alone.

When first thy Sire to send on earth
    Virtue, his darling child, design'd,
To thee he gave the heavenly birth
    And bade to form her infant mind.
Stern, rugged Nurse! thy rigid lore
With patience many a year she bore;
What sorrow was, thou bad'st her know,
And from her own she learn'd to melt at others' woe.

Scared at thy frown terrific, fly
    Self-pleasing Folly's idle brood,
Wild Laughter, Noise, and thoughtless Joy,
    And leave us leisure to be good.
Light they disperse, and with them go
The summer Friend, the flattering Foe;
By vain Prosperity received,
To her they vow their truth, and are again believed.

Wisdom in sable garb array'd
    Immersed in rapturous thought profound,
And Melancholy, silent maid,
    With leaden eye, that loves the ground,
Still on thy solemn steps attend:
Warm Charity, the general friend,
With Justice, to herself severe,
And Pity dropping soft the sadly pleasing tear.

O! gently on thy suppliant's head
    Dread Goddess, lay thy chastening hand!
Not in thy Gorgon terrors clad,
    Nor circled by the vengeful band
(As by the impious thou art seen)
With thundering voice, and threatening mien,
With screaming Horror's funeral cry,
Despair, and fell Disease, and ghastly Poverty;

Thy form benign, O Goddess, wear,
　　Thy milder influence impart,
Thy philosophic train be there
　　To soften, not to wound my heart.
The generous spark extinct revive,
Teach me to love and to forgive,
Exalt my own defects to scan
What others are to feel, and know myself a Man.

about 1742　　　　　　　　　　　　　THOMAS GRAY

117. Ode on the Spring

Lo! where the rosy-bosom'd Hours,
　　Fair Venus' train, appear,
Disclose the long-expecting flowers
　　And wake the purple year!
The attic warbler pours her throat
Responsive to the cuckoo's note,
The untaught harmony of Spring:
While, whispering pleasure as they fly,
Cool Zephyrs thro' the clear blue sky
　　Their gather'd fragrance fling.

Where'er the oak's thick branches stretch
　　A broader, browner shade,
Where'er the rude and moss-grown beech
　　O'er-canopies the glade,
Beside some water's rushy brink
With me the Muse shall sit, and think
(At ease reclined in rustic state)
How vain the ardour of the Crowd,
How low, how little are the Proud,
　　How indigent the Great!

Still is the toiling hand of Care;
　　The panting herds repose:
Yet hark, how thro' the peopled air
　　The busy murmur glows!

The insect youth are on the wing,
Eager to taste the honied spring
And float amid the liquid noon;
Some lightly o'er the current skim,
Some show their gaily-gilded trim
    Quick-glancing to the sun.

To Contemplation's sober eye
    Such is the race of Man:
And they that creep, and they that fly
    Shall end where they began.
Alike the busy and the gay
But flutter thro' life's little day,
In Fortune's varying colours drest:
Brush'd by the hand of rough Mischance,
Or chill'd by Age, their airy dance
    They leave, in dust to rest.

Methinks I hear in accents low
    The sportive kind reply:
Poor moralist; and what art thou?
    A solitary fly!
Thy joys no glittering female meets,
No hive hast thou of hoarded sweets,
No painted plumage to display:
On hasty wings thy youth is flown;
Thy sun is set, thy spring is gone,
    We frolic while 'tis May.

about 1742   THOMAS GRAY

118. *from* A Song to David

SWEET is the dew that falls betimes,
And drops upon the leafy limes;
    Sweet Hermon's fragrant air:
Sweet is the lily's silver bell,
And sweet the wakeful tapers smell
    That watch for early pray'r.

The Sacred Fire

Sweet the young nurse with love intense,
Which smiles o'er sleeping innocence;
    Sweet when the lost arrive:
Sweet the musician's ardour beats,
While his vague mind's in quest of sweets,
    The choicest flow'rs to hive.

Sweeter in all the strains of love,
The language of thy turtle-dove,
    Pair'd to thy swelling chord;
Sweeter with ev'ry grace endu'd,
The glory of thy gratitude,
    Respir'd unto the Lord.

Beauteous the fleet before the gale;
Beauteous the multitudes in mail,
    Rank'd arms and crested heads:
Beauteous the garden's umbrage mild,
Walk, water, meditated wild,
    And all the bloomy beds.

Beauteous the moon full on the lawn;
And beauteous, when the veil's withdrawn,
    The virgin to her spouse:
Beauteous the temple deck'd and fill'd,
When to the heav'n of heav'ns they build
    Their heart-directed vows.

Beauteous, yea beauteous more than these,
The shepherd king upon his knees,
    For his momentous trust;
With wish of infinite conceit,
For man, beast, mute, the small and great,
    And prostrate dust to dust.

Glorious the sun in mid career;
Glorious th' assembled fires appear;
    Glorious the comet's train:
Glorious the trumpet and alarm:
Glorious th' almighty stretch'd-out arm:
    Glorious th' enraptur'd main:

Glorious—more glorious is the crown
Of Him, that brought salvation down
    By meekness, called thy Son;
Thou at stupendous truth believ'd,
And now the matchless deed's achieved,
    DETERMIN'D, DAR'D, and DONE.

about 1763   CHRISTOPHER SMART

119. *from* The Deserted Village

SWEET was the sound when oft at evening's close,
Up yonder hill the village murmur rose;
There as I pass'd with careless steps and slow,
The mingling notes came softened from below;
The swain responsive as the milk-maid sung,
The sober herd that lowed to meet their young;
The noisy geese that gabbled o'er the pool,
The playful children just let loose from school;
The watch-dog's voice that bay'd the whisp'ring wind,
And the loud laugh that spoke the vacant mind;
These all in soft confusion sought the shade,
And filled each pause the nightingale had made.
But now the sounds of population fail,
No chearful murmurs fluctuate in the gale,
No busy steps the grass-grown footway tread,
For all the bloomy flush of life is fled.
All but yon widowed, solitary thing,
That feebly bends beside the plashy spring;
She, wretched matron, forced, in age, for bread,
To strip the brook with mantling cresses spread,
To pick her wintry faggot from the thorn,
To seek her nightly shed, and weep till morn;
She only left of all the harmless train,
The sad historian of the pensive plain.

Near yonder copse, where once the garden smil'd,
And still where many a garden flower grows wild;

The Sacred Fire

There, where a few torn shrubs the place disclose,
The village preacher's modest mansion rose.
A man he was to all the country dear,
And passing rich with forty pounds a year;
Remote from towns he ran his godly race,
Nor e'er had chang'd, nor wish'd to change his place;
Unskilful he to fawn, or seek for power,
By doctrines fashioned to the varying hour;
Far other aims his heart had learned to prize
More bent to raise the wretched than to rise.
His house was known to all the vagrant train,
He chid their wanderings, but reliev'd their pain;
The long remembered beggar was his guest,
Whose beard descending swept his aged breast;
The ruined spendthrift, now no longer proud,
Claimed kindred there, and had his claims allowed;
The broken soldier, kindly bade to stay,
Sat by his fire, and talked the night away;
Wept o'er his wounds, or tales of sorrow done,
Shouldered his crutch, and show'd how fields were won;
Pleased with his guests, the good man learned to glow,
And quite forgot their vices in their woe;
Careless their merits, or their faults to scan,
His pity gave ere charity began.

Thus to relieve the wretched was his pride,
And e'en his failings leaned to Virtue's side;
But in his duty prompt at every call,
He watched and wept, he prayed and felt, for all.
And, as a bird each fond endearment tries
To tempt its new-fledg'd offspring to the skies,
He tried each art, reproved each dull delay,
Allured to brighter worlds, and led the way.

Beside the bed where parting life was layed,
And sorrow, guilt, and pain, by turns dismay'd,
The reverend champion stood.   At his control
Despair and anguish fled the struggling soul;
Comfort came down the trembling wretch to raise,
And his last faultering accents whisper'd praise.

At church, with meek and unaffected grace,
His looks adorned the venerable place;
Truth from his lips prevailed with double sway,
And fools, who came to scoff, remained to pray.
The service past, around the pious man,
With ready zeal, each honest rustic ran;
Even children followed with endearing wile,
And plucked his gown, to share the good man's smile.
His ready smile a parent's warmth exprest,
Their welfare pleased him, and their cares distrest;
To them his heart, his love, his griefs were given,
But all his serious thoughts had rest in Heaven.
As some tall cliff, that lifts its awful form,
Swells from the vale, and midway leaves the storm,
Tho' round its breast the rolling clouds are spread,
Eternal sunshine settles on its head.

about 1770   OLIVER GOLDSMITH

XV

William Cowper
William Blake

The Sacred Fire

120. *from* The Task

I was a stricken deer, that left the herd
Long since: with many an arrow deep infixt
My panting side was charg'd, when I withdrew
To seek a tranquil death in distant shades.
There was I found by one who had himself
Been hurt by th' archers. In his side he bore,
And in his hands and feet, the cruel scars.
With gentle force soliciting the darts,
He drew them forth, and heal'd, and bade me live.
Since then, with few associates, in remote
And silent woods I wander, far from those
My former partners of the peopled scene;
With few associates and not wishing more.
Here much I ruminate, as much I may,
With other views of men and manners now
Than once, and others of a life to come.
I see that all are wand'rers, gone astray
Each in his own delusions; they are lost
In chase of fancied happiness, still woo'd
And never won. Dream after dream ensues;
And still they dream that they shall still succeed.
And still are disappointed. Rings the world
With the vain stir. I sum up half mankind,
And add two-thirds of the remaining half,
And find the total of their hopes and fears
Dreams, empty dreams. The million flit as gay
As if created only like the fly,
That spreads his motley wings in th' eye of noon,
To sport their season, and be seen no more.

*   *   *   *   *

England, with all thy faults, I love thee still—
My country! and, while yet a nook is left
Where English minds and manners may be found,
Shall be constrain'd to love thee. Though thy clime
Be fickle, and thy year most part deform'd
With dripping rains, or wither'd by a frost,

The Sacred Fire

I would not yet exchange thy sullen skies,
And fields without a flow'r, for warmer France
With all her vines; nor for Ausonia's groves
Of golden fruitage, and her myrtle bow'rs.

*   *   *   *   *

   Nor rural sights alone, but rural sounds,
Exhilarate the spirit, and restore
The tone of languid Nature.   Mighty winds,
That sweep the skirt of some far-spreading wood
Of ancient growth, make music not unlike
The dash of ocean on his winding shore,
And lull the spirit while they fill the mind;
Unnumber'd branches waving in the blast,
And all their leaves fast flutt'ring, all at once.
Nor less composure waits upon the roar
Of distant floods, or on the softer voice
Of neighb'ring fountain, or of rills that slip
Through the cleft rock, and, chiming as they fall
Upon loose pebbles, lose themselves at length
In matted grass, that with a livelier green
Betrays the secret of their silent course.
Nature inanimate employs sweet sounds,
But animated nature sweeter still,
To sooth and satisfy the human ear.
Ten thousand warblers cheer the days, and one
The live-long night: nor these alone, whose notes
Nice-finger'd art must emulate in vain,
But cawing rooks, and kites that swim sublime
In still repeated circles, screaming loud,
The jay, the pie, and ev'n the boding owl
That hails the rising moon, have charms for me.
Sounds inharmonious in themselves and harsh,
Yet heard in scenes where peace for ever reigns,
And only there, please highly for their sake.

*   *   *   *   *

   There is in souls a sympathy with sounds;
And, as the mind is pitch'd, the ear is pleas'd
With melting airs, or martial, brisk or grave:

Some chord in unison with what we hear
Is touch'd within us and the heart replies.
How soft the music of those village bells,
Falling at intervals upon the ear
In cadence sweet, now dying all away,
Now pealing loud again, and louder still,
Clear and sonorous, as the gale comes on!
With easy force it opens all the cells
Where mem'ry slept.   Wherever I have heard
A kindred melody, the scene recurs,
And with it all its pleasures and its pains.

*   *   *   *   *

The night was winter in his roughest mood;
The morning sharp and clear.   But now at noon
Upon the southern side of the slant hills,
And where the woods fence off the northern blast,
The season smiles, resigning all its rage,
And has the warmth of May.   The vault is blue
Without a cloud, and white without a speck
The dazzling splendour of the scene below.
Again the harmony comes o'er the vale;
And through the trees I view th' embattled tow'r
Whence all the music.   I again perceive
The soothing influence of the wafted strains,
And settle in soft musings as I tread
The walk, still verdant, under oaks and elms,
Whose outspread branches overarch the glade.
The roof, though moveable throughout its length
As the wind sways it, has yet well suffic'd,
And, intercepting in their silent fall
The frequent flakes, has kept a path for me.
No noise is here, or none that hinders thought.
The red breast warbles still, but is content
With slender notes, and more than half suppress'd:
Pleas'd with his solitude, and flitting light
From spray to spray, where'er he rests he shakes
From many a twig the pendent drops of ice,
That tinkle in the wither'd leaves below.

The Sacred Fire

Stillness, accompanied with sounds so soft,
Charms more than silence. Meditation here
May think down hours to moments. Here the heart
May give an useful lesson to the head,
And learning wiser grow without his books.

*   *   *   *   *

    He is the happy man, whose life ev'n now
Shows somewhat of that happier life to come;
Who, doom'd to an obscure but tranquil state,
Is pleas'd with it, and, were he free to choose,
Would make his fate his choice; whom peace, the fruit
Of virtue, and whom virtue, fruit of faith,
Prepare for happiness; bespeak him one
Content indeed to sojourn while he must
Below the skies, but having there his home.
The world o'erlooks him in her busy search
Of objects, more illustrious in her view;
And, occupied as earnestly as she,
Though more sublimely, he o'erlooks the world.
She scorns his pleasures, for she knows them not;
He seeks not her's, for he has prov'd them vain.
He cannot skim the ground like summer birds
Pursuing gilded flies; and such he deems
Her honours, her emoluments, her joys.
Therefore in contemplation is his bliss,
Whose pow'r is such, that whom she lifts from earth
She makes familiar with a heav'n unseen,
And shows him glories yet to be reveal'd.
Not slothful he, though seeming unemploy'd,
And censur'd oft as useless. Stillest streams
Oft water fairest meadows, and the bird
That flutters least is longest on the wing.
Ask him, indeed, what trophies he has rais'd,
Or what achievements of immortal fame
He purposes, and he shall answer—None.
His warfare is within. There unfatigu'd
His fervent spirit labours. There he fights,
And there obtains fresh triumphs o'er himself,
And never with'ring wreaths, compar'd with which

The laurels that a Caesar reaps are weeds.
Perhaps the self-approving haughty world,
That as she sweeps him with her whistling silk,
Scarce deigns to notice him, or, if she see,
Deems him a cypher in the works of God,
Receives advantage from his noiseless hours,
Of which she little dreams.   Perhaps she owes
Her sunshine and her rain, her blooming spring
And plenteous harvest, to the pray'r he makes,
When, Isaac-like, the solitary saint
Walks forth to meditate at even tide,
And think on her, who thinks not for herself.
Forgive him, then, thou bustler in concerns
Of little worth, an idler in the best,
If author of no mischief and some good,
He seeks his proper happiness by means
That may advance, but cannot hinder, thine.
Nor, though he tread the secret path of life,
Engage no notice, and enjoy much ease,
Account him an incumbrance on the state,
Receiving benefits, and rend'ring none.
His sphere though humble, if that humble sphere
Shine with his fair example, and though small
His influence, if that influence all be spent
In soothing sorrow and in quenching strife,
In aiding helpless indigence, in works
From which at least a grateful few derive
Some taste of comfort in a world of woe,
Then let the supercilious great confess
He serves his country, recompenses well
The state, beneath the shadow of whose vine
He sits secure, and in the scale of life
Holds no ignoble, though a slighted place.
The man, whose virtues are more felt than seen,
Must drop indeed the hope of public praise;
But he may boast what few that win it can—
That if his country stands not by his skill,
At least his follies have not wrought her fall.

about 1783–84   WILLIAM COWPER

121. Hymn: On opening a place for Social Prayer

Jesus, where'er Thy people meet,
There they behold Thy mercy-seat;
Where'er they seek Thee Thou art found,
And every place is hallow'd ground.

For Thou, within no walls confin'd,
Inhabitest the humble mind;
Such ever bring Thee, where they come,
And going, take Thee to their home.

Dear Shepherd of Thy chosen few!
Thy former mercies here renew;
Here to our waiting hearts, proclaim
The sweetness of Thy saving name.

Here may we prove the power of prayer,
To strengthen faith, and sweeten care;
To teach our faint desires to rise,
And bring all Heaven before our eyes.

Behold! at Thy commanding word,
We stretch the curtain and the cord;
Come Thou, and fill this wider space,
And help us with a large increase.

Lord, we are few, but Thou art near;
Nor short Thine arm, nor deaf Thine ear;
Oh rend the heavens, come quickly down,
And make a thousand hearts Thine own.

about 1771–72   WILLIAM COWPER

122. Song

How sweet I roam'd from field to field
And tasted all the summer's pride,
Till I the prince of love beheld
Who in the sunny beams did glide!

He shew'd me lilies for my hair,
And blushing roses for my brow;
He led me through his gardens fair
Where all his golden pleasures grow.

With sweet May dews my wings were wet,
And Phoebus fir'd my vocal rage;
He caught me in his silken net,
And shut me in his golden cage.

He loves to sit and hear me sing,
Then, laughing, sports and plays with me;
Then stretches out my golden wing,
And mocks my loss of liberty.

about 1775–80   WILLIAM BLAKE

123. Songs of Innocence: Introduction

PIPING down the valleys wild,
Piping songs of pleasant glee,
On a cloud I saw a child,
And he laughing said to me:
'Pipe a song about a Lamb!'
So I piped with merry chear.
'Piper pipe that song again;'
So I piped: he wept to hear.
'Drop thy pipe, thy happy pipe;
Sing thy songs of happy chear:'
So I sang the same again,
While he wept with joy to hear.

'Piper, sit thee down and write
In a book that all may read'
So he vanished from my sight,
And I pluck'd a hollow reed,
And I made a rural pen,
And I stain'd the water clear,
And I wrote my happy songs
Every child may joy to hear.

about 1785   WILLIAM BLAKE

124. Night

THE sun descending in the west,
The evening star does shine;
The birds are silent in their nest,
And I must seek for mine.
The moon, like a flower,
In heaven's high bower,
With silent delight
Sits and smiles on the night.

Farewell, green fields and happy groves,
Where flocks have took delight.
Where lambs have nibbled, silent moves
The feet of angels bright;
Unseen they pour blessing,
And joy without ceasing,
On each bud and blossom,
And each sleeping bosom.

They look in every thoughtless nest,
Where birds are cover'd warm;
They visit caves of every beast,
To keep them all from harm.
If they see any weeping
That should have been sleeping,
They pour sleep on their head,
And sit down by their bed.

When wolves and tygers howl for prey,
They pitying stand and weep;
Seeking to drive their thirst away,
And keep them from the sheep.
But if they rush dreadful,
The angels most heedful,
Receive each mild spirit,
New worlds to inherit.

And there the lion's ruddy eyes
Shall flow with tears of gold,
And pitying the tender cries,
And walking round the fold,
Saying "Wrath, by his meekness,
And by his health, sickness
Is driven away
From our immortal day.

"And now beside thee, bleating lamb,
I can lie down and sleep;
Or think on him who bore thy name,
Graze after thee and weep.
For, wash'd in life's river,
My bright mane for ever
Shall shine like the gold
As I guard o'er the fold."

about 1785   WILLIAM BLAKE

125. The Shepherd

How sweet is the Shepherd's sweet lot!
From the morn to the evening he strays;
He shall follow his sheep all the day,
And his tongue shall be filled with praise.

For he hears the lamb's innocent call,
And he hears the ewe's tender reply;
He is watchful while they are in peace,
For they know that their Shepherd is nigh.

about 1785   WILLIAM BLAKE

126. The Sick Rose

O Rose, thou art sick!
The invisible worm,
That flies in the night
In the howling storm,

Has found out thy bed
Of crimson joy;
And his dark secret love
Does thy life destroy.

about 1790 WILLIAM BLAKE

127. *from* Auguries of Innocence

To see a World in a Grain of Sand,
And a Heaven in a Wild Flower,
Hold Infinity in the palm of your hand,
And Eternity in an hour.

Joy and Woe are woven fine,
A Clothing for the soul divine.
Under every grief and pine
Runs a joy with silken twine.

Every Morn and every Night
Some are Born to Sweet Delight.
Some are Born to Sweet Delight,
Some are Born to Endless Night.
We are led to Believe a Lie
When we see not through the Eye,
Which was Born in a Night to perish in a Night,
When the Soul Slept in Beams of Light.
God appears, and God is light,
To those poor souls who dwell in Night;
But does a Human Form Display
To those who Dwell in Realms of Day.

about 1800 WILLIAM BLAKE

XVI

North-Country Ballads
S. T. Coleridge
William Wordsworth
Walter Scott
P. B. Shelley
John Keats
Elizabeth Barrett Browning
Emily Brontë

128. Fair Helen of Kirconnell

I wish I were where Helen lies!
Night and day on me she cries;
O that I were where Helen lies,
    On fair Kirconnell lea!

Curst be the heart that thought the thought,
And curst the hand that fired the shot,
When in my arms burd Helen dropt,
    And died to succour me!

O think na but my heart was sair
When my love dropt down and spake nae mair;
I laid her down with meikle care
    On fair Kirconnell lea.

As I went down the waterside,
None but my foe to be my guide,
None but my foe to be my guide,
    On fair Kirconnell lea.

I lighted down my sword to draw,
I hacked him in pieces sma',
I hacked him in pieces sma',
    For her that died for me.

O Helen fair, beyond compare!
I'll make a garland of thy hair
Shall bind my heart for evermair
    Until the day I die.

O that I were where Helen lies!
Night and day on me she cries;
Out of my bed she bids me rise
    Says, Haste and come to me!

The Sacred Fire

O Helen fair!   O Helen chaste!
If I were with thee I were blest,
Where thou li'st low and tak'st thy rest
On fair Kirconnell lea.

I wish my grave were growing green,
A winding-sheet drawn o'er my een,
And I in Helen's arms were lying
On fair Kirconnell lea.

I wish I were where Helen lies!
Night and day on me she cries.
And I am weary of the skies
Since my love died for me.

Border Ballad

129. The Wife of Usher's Well

THERE lived a wife at Usher's Well,
And a wealthy wife was she;
She had three stout and stalwart sons,
And sent them o'er the sea.

They hadna been a week from her,
A week but barely ane,
When word came to the carlin wife
That her three sons were gane.

They hadna been a week from her,
A week but barely three,
When word came to the carlin wife
That her sons she'd never see.

"I wish the wind may never cease,
Nor fashes in the flood,
Till my three sons come hame to me,
In earthly flesh and blood!"

It fell about the Martinmas
    When nights are lang and mirk,
The carlin wife's three sons came hame,
    And their hats were o' the birk.

It neither grew in syke nor ditch,
    Nor yet in any sheugh;
But at the gates o' Paradise
    That birk grew fair eneugh.

"Blow up the fire, my maidens!
    Bring water from the well,
For a' my house shall feast this night,
    Since my three sons are well."

And she has made to them a bed,
    She's made it large and wide;
And she's taen her mantle her about,
    Sat down at the bedside.

Up then crew the red, red cock,
    And up and crew the grey;
The eldest to the youngest said,
    " 'Tis time we were away."

The cock he hadna craw'd but once,
    And clapp'd his wings at a'
Whan the youngest to the eldest said
    "Brother we must awa'.

"The cock doth craw, the day doth daw,
    The channering worm doth chide;
Gin we be mist out o' our place,
    A sair pain we maun bide.

"Fare ye weel, my mother dear!
    Fareweel to barn and byre!
And fare ye weel, the bonny lass
    That kindles my mother's fire!"

Border Ballaa

130. Lord Donald

"O WHERE hae ye been a' day, Lord Donald, my son?
O where hae ye been a' day, my jollie young man?"
"I've been awa' courtin': mither, mak my bed sune,
For I'm sick at the heart, and I fain wad lie doun."

"What wad ye hae for your supper, Lord Donald, my son?
What wad ye hae for your supper, my jollie young man?"
"I've gotten my supper; mither, make my bed sune,
For I'm sick at the heart, and I fain would lie doun."

"What did ye get to your supper, Lord Donald, my son?
What did ye get to your supper, my jollie young man?"
"A dish of sma' fishes; mither, make my bed sune,
For I'm sick at the heart, and I fain wad lie doun."

"Whare gat ye the fishes, Lord Donald, my son?
Whare gat ye the fishes, my jollie young man?"
"In my father's black ditches:—mither, mak my bed sune,
For I'm sick at the heart, and I fain wad lie doun."

"What like were your fishes, Lord Donald, my son?
What like were your fishes, my jollie young man?"
"Black backs and spreckl'd bellies; mither mak my bed sune,
For I'm sick at the heart, and I fain wad lie doun."

"O I fear ye are poisoned, Lord Donald, my son!
O I fear ye are poisoned, my jollie young man!"
"O yes I am poisoned; mither mak my bed sune,
For I'm sick at the heart, and I fain would lie doun."

"What will ye leave to your father, Lord Donald, my son?
What will ye leave to your father, my jollie young man?"
"Baith my houses and land; mither mak my bed sune,
For I'm sick at the heart, and I fain wad lie doun."

"What will ye leave to your brither, Lord Donald, my son?
What will ye leave to your brither, my jollie young man?"
"My horse and the saddle; mither mak my bed sune,
For I'm sick at the heart, and I fain wad lie doun."

"What will ye leave to your sister, Lord Donald, my son?
What will ye leave to your sister, my jollie young man?"
"Baith my gold box and rings; mither mak my bed sune,
For I'm sick at the heart, and I fain wad lie doun."

"What will ye leave to your true-love, Lord Donald, my son?
What will ye leave to your true-love, my jollie young man?"
"The tow and the halter, for to hang on yon tree,
And lat her hang there for the poisoning o' me."

Scottish Ballad

131. The Rime of the Ancient Mariner

How a ship having passed the Line was driven by storms to the cold
country towards the South Pole; and how from thence she made her
course to the tropical Latitude of the Great Pacific Ocean; and of the
strange things that befell; and in what manner the Ancient Mariner
came back to his own Country.

PART I

It is an ancient Mariner,
And he stoppeth one of three.
"By thy long grey beard and glittering eye,
Now wherefore stopp'st thou me?

"The Bridegroom's doors are opened wide,
And I am next of kin;
The guests are met, the feast is set;
May'st hear the merry din."

He holds him with his skinny hand,
"There was a ship," quoth he.
"Hold off! unhand me, grey-beard loon!"
Eftsoons his hand dropt he.

An ancient
Mariner
meeteth three
Gallants
bidden to a
wedding-feast,
and detaineth
one.

The Sacred Fire

The Wedding-Guest is spell-bound by the eye of the old sea-faring man, and constrained to hear his tale.

He holds him with his glittering eye—
The Wedding-Guest stood still,
And listens like a three-years' child:
The mariner hath his will.

The Wedding-Guest sat on a stone:
He cannot choose but hear;
And thus spake on that ancient man,
The bright-eyed Mariner.

"The ship was cheered, the harbour cleared,
Merrily did we drop
Below the kirk, below the hill,
Below the lighthouse top.

The Mariner tells how the ship sailed southward with a good wind and fair weather, till it reached the Line.

"The Sun came up upon the left,
Out of the sea came he!
And he shone bright, and on the right
Went down into the sea.

"Higher and higher every day,
Till over the mast at noon"—
The Wedding-Guest here beat his breast,
For he heard the loud bassoon.

The Wedding-Guest heareth the bridal music; but the Mariner continueth his tale.

The bride hath paced into the hall,
Red as a rose is she;
Nodding their heads before her goes
The merry minstrelsy.

The Wedding-Guest he beat his breast
Yet he cannot choose but hear;
And thus spake on that ancient man,
The bright-eyed Mariner.

The ship drawn by a storm toward the South Pole.

"And now the Storm-blast came, and he
Was tyrannous and strong:
He struck with his o'ertaking wings,
And chased us south along.

"With sloping masts and dipping prow
As who pursued with yell and blow
Still treads the shadow of his foe,
And forward bends his head,
The ship drove fast, loud roared the blast,
And southward aye we fled.

"And now there came both mist and snow,
And it grew wondrous cold:
And ice, mast-high, came floating by,
As green as emerald.

"And through the drifts the snowy clifts
Did send a dismal sheen:
Nor shapes of men nor beasts we ken—
The ice was all between.

The land of ice, and of fearful sounds where no living thing was to be seen.

"The ice was here, the ice was there,
The ice was all around:
It cracked and growled, and roared and howled,
Like noises in a swound!

"At length did cross an Albatross,
Thorough the fog it came;
As it had been a Christian soul,
We hailed it in God's name.

'Till a great sea-bird called the Albatross, came through the snow-fog, and was received with great joy and hospitality.

"It ate the food it ne'er had eat,
And round and round it flew.
The ice did split with a thunder-fit:
The helmsman steered us through!

"And a good south wind sprang up behind:
The Albatross did follow,
And every day, for food or play,
Came to the mariner's hollo!

And lo! the Albatross proveth a bird of good omen, and followeth the ship as it returneth northward through fog and floating ice.

"In mist or cloud, on mast or shroud,
It perched for vespers nine;
Whiles all the night, through fog-smoke white,
Glimmered the white moon-shine."

The ancient Mariner inhospitably killeth the pious bird of good omen.

"God save thee, ancient Mariner!
From the fiends that plague thee thus!—
Why look'st thou so?"—"With my cross-bow
I shot the Albatross."

PART II

"The sun now rose upon the right:
Out of the sea came he,
Still hid in mist, and on the left
Went down into the sea.

"And the good south wind still blew behind,
But no sweet bird did follow,
Nor any day for food or play
Came to the mariner's hollo!

His shipmates cry out against the ancient Mariner, for killing the bird of good luck.

"And I had done a hellish thing,
And it would work 'em woe:
For all averred I had killed the bird
That made the breeze to blow.
Ah wretch! said they, the bird to slay,
That made the breeze to blow!

But when the fog cleared off, they justify the same, and thus make themselves accomplices in the crime.

"Nor dim, nor red, like God's own head
The glorious Sun uprist:
Then all averred I had killed the bird
That brought the fog and mist.
'Twas right, said they, such birds to slay,
That brought the fog and mist.

The fair breeze continues; the ship enters the Pacific Ocean and sails

"The fair breeze blew, the white foam flew,
The furrow followed free:
We were the first that ever burst
Into that silent sea.

An Anthology

"Down dropt the breeze, the sails dropt down
'Twas sad as sad could be;
And we did speak only to break
The silence of the sea!

"All in a hot and copper sky,
The bloody Sun, at noon,
Right up above the mast did stand,
No bigger than the Moon.

"Day after day, day after day,
We stuck, nor breath nor motion;
As idle as a painted ship
Upon a painted ocean.

"Water, water, everywhere,
And all the boards did shrink;
Water, water, everywhere,
Nor any drop to drink.

"The very deep did rot: O Christ!
That ever this should be!
Yea, slimy things did crawl with legs
Upon the slimy sea.

"About, about, in reel and rout
The death-fires danced at night;
The water, like a witch's oils,
Burnt green, and blue, and white.

"And some in dreams assured were
Of the Spirit that plagued us so,
Nine fathom deep he had followed us
From the land of mist and snow.

northward, even till it reaches the Line.
The ship hath been suddenly becalmed.

And the Albatross begins to be avenged.

A spirit had followed them; one of the invisible inhabitants of this planet,

neither departed souls nor angels; concerning whom the learned Jew, Josephus, and the Platonic Constantinopolitan, Michael Psellus, may be consulted. They are very numerous and there is no climate or element without one or more.

"And every tongue, through utter drought,
Was withered at the root;
We could not speak no more than if
We had been choked with soot.

The shipmates
in their sore
distress would
fain throw the
whole guilt on
the ancient

"Ah! well-a-day! what evil looks
Had I from old and young!
Instead of the cross, the Albatross
About my neck was hung.

Mariner; in sign whereof they hang the dead sea-bird round his neck.

PART III

The ancient
Mariner
beholdeth a
sign in the
element afar off.

"There passed a weary time. Each throat
Was parched and glazed each eye.
A weary time! a weary time!
How glazed each weary eye—
When something westward I beheld
A something in the sky.

"At first it seemed a little speck,
And then it seemed a mist;
It moved and moved, and took at last
A certain shape I wist.

"A speck, a mist, a shape, I wist!
And still it neared and neared;
As if it dodged a water-sprite,
It plunged and tacked and veered.

At its nearer
approach it
seemeth him to
be a ship; and
at a dear ran-
som he freeth
his speech from
the bonds of
thirst.

"With throats unslaked, with black lips baked,
We could nor laugh nor wail;
Through utter drought all dumb we stood!
I bit my arm, I sucked the blood,
And cried, 'A sail! a sail!'

"With throats unslaked, with black lips baked,
Agape they heard me call:
Gramercy! they for joy did grin,
And all at once their breath drew in,
As they were drinking all.

A flash of joy;

"See! see! (I cried) she tacks no more!
Hither to work us weal;
Without a breeze, without a tide,
She steadies with upright keel!

And horror follows. For can it be a ship that comes onward without wind or tide?

"The western wave was all a-flame,
The day was well-nigh done!
Almost upon the western wave
Rested the broad bright Sun;
When that strange shape drove suddenly
Betwixt us and the Sun.

"And straight the Sun was flecked with bars,
(Heaven's Mother send us grace!)
As if through a dungeon-grate he peered,
With broad and burning face.

It seemeth him but the skeleton of a ship.

"Alas! (thought I, and my heart beat loud,)
How fast she nears and nears!
Are those *her* sails that glance in the Sun,
Like restless gossameres!

"Are those *her* ribs through which the Sun
Did peer, as through a grate?
And is that Woman all her crew?
Is that a Death? and are there two?
Is Death that Woman's mate?

And its ribs are seen as bars on the face of the setting Sun. The spectre-woman and her death-mate, and no other on board the skeleton-ship. Like vessel, like crew!

"*Her* lips were red, *her* looks were free,
Her locks were yellow and gold:

The Sacred Fire

Death and
Life-in-Death
have diced for
the ship's
crew, and she
(the latter)
winneth the
ancient
Mariner.

"Her skin was white as leprosy,
The Night-Mare Life-in-Death was she,
Who thicks man's blood with cold.

"The naked hulk alongside came,
And the twain were casting dice;
'The game is done! I've won! I've won!'
Quoth she, and whistles thrice.

No twilight
within the
courts of the
sun.

"The Sun's rim dips; the stars rush out:
At one stride comes the dark;
With far-heard whisper o'er the sea,
Off shot the spectre-bark.

At the rising
of the Moon.

"We listened and looked sideways up!
Fear at my heart, as at a cup,
My life-blood seemed to sip!
The stars were dim, and thick the night,
The steersman's face by his lamp gleamed white;
From the sails the dew did drip—
Till clomb above the eastern bar
The horned Moon, with one bright star
Within the nether tip.

One after
another,

"One after one, by the star-dogged Moon,
Too quick for groan or sight
Each turned his face with a ghastly pang,
And cursed me with his eye.

His shipmates
drop down
dead.

"Four times fifty living men
(And I heard nor sigh nor groan)
With heavy thump, a lifeless lump,
They dropped down one by one.

But Life-in-
Death begins
her work on
the ancient
Mariner.

"The souls did from their bodies fly,—
They fled to bliss or woe!
And every soul it passed me by,
Like the whizz of my cross-bow."

PART IV

"I fear thee, ancient Mariner!
I fear thy skinny hand!
And thou art long, and lank, and brown,
As is the ribbed sea-sand.

The Wedding-Guest feareth that a spirit is talking to him.

"I fear thee and thy glittering eye,
And thy skinny hand so brown."—
"Fear not, fear not, thou Wedding-Guest!
This body dropped not down.

But the ancient Mariner assureth him of his bodily life, and proceedeth to relate his horrible penance.

"Alone, alone, all, all alone,
Alone on a wide wide sea!
And never a saint took pity on
My soul in agony.

"The many men, so beautiful!
And they all dead did lie;
And a thousand thousand slimy things
Lived on; and so did I.

He despiseth the creatures of the calm.

"I looked upon the rotting sea,
And drew my eyes away;
I looked upon the rotting deck,
And there the dead men lay.

And envieth that they should live and so many lie dead.

"I looked to Heaven, and tried to pray
But or ever a prayer had gusht,
A wicked whisper came and made
My heart as dry as dust.

"I closed my lids, and kept them close,
And the balls like pulses beat;
For the sky and the sea, and the sea and the sky,
Lay like a load on my weary eye,
And the dead were at my feet.

The Sacred Fire

But the curse liveth for him in the eye of the dead men.

"The cold sweat melted from their limbs,
Nor rot nor reek did they:
The look with which they looked on me
Had never passed away.

"An orphan's curse would drag to Hell
A spirit from on high;
But oh! more horrible than that
Is a curse from a dead man's eye!
Seven days, seven nights, I saw that curse,
And yet I could not die.

In his loneliness and fixedness he yearneth towards the journeying

"The moving Moon went up the sky,
And no where did abide:
Softly she was going up,
And a star or two beside—

Moon, and the stars that still sojourn, yet still move onward; and everywhere the blue sky belongs to them, and is their appointed rest, and their native country and their own natural homes, which they enter unannounced, as lords that are certainly expected and yet there is a silent joy at their arrival.

"Her beams bemocked the sultry main,
Like April hoar-frost spread;
But where the ship's huge shadow lay
The charmed water burnt alway
A still and awful red.

By the light of the Moon he beholdeth God's creatures of the great calm.

"Beyond the shadow of the ship,
I watched the water-snakes:
They moved in tracks of shining white,
And when they reared, the elfish light
Fell off in hoary flakes.

"Within the shadow of the ship
I watched their rich attire:
Blue, glossy green, and velvet black,
They coiled and swam; and every track
Was a flash of golden fire.

"O happy living things! no tongue
Their beauty might declare:
A spring of love gushed from my heart,
And I blessed them unaware:
Sure my kind saint took pity on me,
And I blessed them unaware.

*Their beauty
and their
happiness.*

*He blesseth
them in his
heart.*

"The selfsame moment I could pray:
And from my neck so free
The Albatross fell off, and sank
Like lead into the sea."

*The spell
begins to break.*

PART V

"O sleep! it is a gentle thing,
Beloved from pole to pole!
To Mary Queen the praise be given!
She sent the gentle sleep from Heaven,
That slid into my soul.

"The silly buckets on the deck,
That had so long remained,
I dreamt that they were filled with dew;
And when I woke, it rained.

*By grace of the
holy Mother,
the ancient
Mariner is
refreshed with
rain.*

"My lips were wet, my throat was cold,
My garments all were dank;
Sure I had drunken in my dreams,
And still my body drank.

"I moved, and could not feel my limbs:
I was so light—almost
I thought that I had died in sleep,
And was a blessed ghost.

"And soon I heard a roaring wind:
It did not come anear;
But with its sound it shook the sails,
That were so thin and sere.

*He heareth
sounds, and
seeth strange
sights and
commotions in
the sky and the
element.*

The Sacred Fire

"The upper air burst into life!
And a hundred fire-flags sheen,
To and fro they were hurried about!
And to and fro, and in and out,
The wan stars danced between.

"And the coming wind did roar more loud,
And the sails did sigh like sedge;
And the rain poured down from one black cloud;
The Moon was at its edge.

"The thick black cloud was cleft, and still
The Moon was at its side:
Like waters shot from some high crag,
The lightning fell with never a jag,
A river steep and wide.

The bodies of
the ship's crew
are inspired and
the ship moves
on;

"The loud wind never reached the ship,
Yet now the ship moved on!
Beneath the lightning and the Moon
The dead men gave a groan.

"They groaned, they stirred, they all uprose,
Nor spake, nor moved their eyes;
It had been strange, even in a dream,
To have seen those dead men rise.

"The helmsman steered, the ship moved on;
Yet never a breeze up blew;
The mariners all 'gan work the ropes,
Where they were wont to do:
They raised their limbs like lifeless tools—
We were a ghastly crew.

"The body of my brother's son
Stood by me, knee to knee:
The body and I pulled at one rope,
But he said nought to me."

"I fear thee, ancient Mariner!"
"Be calm, thou Wedding-Guest!
'Twas not those souls that fled in pain,
Which to their corses came again,
But a troop of spirits blest:

"For when it dawned—they dropped their arms,
And clustered round the mast;
Sweet sounds rose slowly through their mouths,
And from their bodies passed.

"Around, around, flew each sweet sound,
Then darted to the Sun;
Slowly the sounds came back again,
Now mixed, now one by one.

"Sometimes a-dropping from the sky
I heard the sky-lark sing;
Sometimes all little birds that are,
How they seemed to fill the sea and air
With their sweet jargoning!

"And now 'twas like all instruments,
Now like a lonely flute;
And now it is an angel's song,
That makes the Heavens be mute.

"It ceased; yet still the sails made on
A pleasant noise till noon
A noise like of a hidden brook
In the leafy month of June,
That to the sleeping woods all night
Singeth a quiet tune.

"Till noon we quietly sailed on,
Yet never a breeze did breathe;
Slowly and smoothly went the ship,
Moved onward from beneath.

But not by the souls of the men, nor by dæmons of earth or middle air but by a blessed troop of angelic spirits, sent down by the invocation of the guardian saint.

The Sacred Fire

The lonesome spirit from the South Pole carries on the ship as far as the Line, in obedience to the angelic troop, but still requireth vengeance.

"Under the keel nine fathom deep,
From the land of mist and snow,
The spirit slid: and it was he
That made the ship to go.
The sails at noon left off their tune,
And the ship stood still also.

"The Sun, right up above the mast,
Had fixed her to the ocean:
But in a minute she 'gan stir,
With a short uneasy motion—
Backwards and forwards half her length
With a short uneasy motion.

"Then like a pawing horse let go,
She made a sudden bound.
It flung the blood into my head,
And I fell down in a swound.

"How long in that same fit I lay,
I have not to declare;
But ere my living life returned,
I heard and in my soul discerned
Two voices in the air.

The Polar Spirit's fellow-dæmons, the invisible inhabitants of the element, take part in his wrong; and two of them relate, one to the other, that penance long and heavy for the ancient Mariner hath been accorded to the Polar Spirit, who returneth southward.

" 'Is it he?' quoth one, 'Is this the man?
By him who died on cross,
With his cruel bow he laid full low,
The harmless Albatross.

" 'The spirit who bideth by himself
In the land of mist and snow,
He loved the bird that loved the man
Who shot him with his bow.'

"The other was a softer voice,
As soft as honey-dew
Quoth he, 'The man hath penance done,
And penance more will do.' "

PART VI

First voice

" 'But tell me, tell me! speak again,
Thy soft response renewing—
What makes that ship drive on so fast?
What is the Ocean doing?'

Second voice

" 'Still as a slave before his lord,
The Ocean hath no blast;
His great bright eye most silently
Up to the Moon is cast—

" 'If he may know which way to go;
For she guides him smooth or grim.
See, brother, see! how graciously
She looketh down on him.'

First voice

" 'But why drives on that ship so fast,
Without or wave or wind?'

Second voice

" 'The air is cut away before,
And closes from behind.

" 'Fly, brother, fly! more high, more high!
Or we shall be belated:
For slow and slow that ship will go,
When the Mariner's trance is abated.'

"I woke and we were sailing on
As in a gentle weather:
'Twas night, calm night, the Moon was high;
The dead men stood together.

The Mariner hath been cast into a trance; for the angelic power causeth the vessel to drive northward faster than human life could endure.

The supernatural motion is retarded; the Mariner awakes, and his penance begins anew.

– 287 –

The Sacred Fire

"All stood together on the deck,
For a charnel-dungeon fitter:
All fixed on me their stony eyes,
That in the Moon did glitter.

"The pang, the curse, with which they died,
Had never passed away:
I could not draw my eyes from theirs,
Nor turn them up to pray.

*The curse is
finally expiated.*

"And now this spell was snapt: once more
I viewed the ocean green,
And looked far forth, yet little saw
Of what had else been seen—

"Like one, that on a lonesome road
Doth walk in fear and dread,
And having once turned round walks on
And turns no more his head;
Because he knows, a frightful fiend
Doth close behind him tread.

"But soon there breathed a wind on me,
Nor sound nor motion made:
Its path was not upon the sea,
In ripple or in shade.

"It raised my hair, it fanned my cheek
Like a meadow-gale of spring—
It mingled strangely with my fears,
Yet it felt like a welcoming.

"Swiftly, swiftly flew the ship,
Yet she sailed softly too:
Sweetly, sweetly blew the breeze—
On me alone it blew.

*And the
ancient
Mariner
beholdeth his
native country.*

"Oh! dream of joy! is this indeed
The lighthouse top I see?
Is this the hill?   Is this the kirk?
Is this my own countree?

— 288 —

"We drifted o'er the harbour-bar,
And I with sobs did pray—
'O let me be awake, my God!
Or let me sleep alway.'

"The harbour-bay was clear as glass,
So smoothly it was strewn!
And on the bay the moonlight lay,
And the shadow of the moon.

"The rock shone bright, the kirk no less,
That stands above the rock:
The moonlight steeped in silentness
The steady weathercock.

"And the bay was white with silent light,
Till rising from the same,
Full many shapes, that shadows were,
In crimson colours came.

*The angelic
spirits leave
the dead
bodies,
And appear
in their own
forms of light.*

"A little distance from the prow
Those crimson shadows were:
I turned my eyes upon the deck—
Oh, Christ! what saw I there!

"Each corse lay flat, lifeless and flat,
And, by the holy rood!
A man all light, a seraph man,
On every corse there stood.

"This seraph-band, each waved his hand:
It was a heavenly sight!
They stood as signals to the land,
Each one a lovely light:

"This seraph-band, each waved his hand,
No voice did they impart—
No voice; but oh! the silence sank
Like music on my heart.

"But soon I heard the dash of oars,
I heard the Pilot's cheer;
My head was turned perforce away,
And I saw a boat appear.

"The Pilot, and the Pilot's boy,
I heard them coming fast:
Dear Lord in Heaven! it was a joy
The dead men could not blast.

"I saw a third—I heard his voice:
It is the Hermit good!
He singeth loud his godly hymns
That he makes in the wood.
He'll shrive my soul, he'll wash away
The Albatross's blood.

PART VII

The Hermit
of the Wood,

"This Hermit good lives in that wood
Which slopes down to the sea.
How loudly his sweet voice he rears!
He loves to talk with marineres
That come from a far countree.

"He kneels at morn, and noon, and eve—
He hath a cushion plump:
It is the moss that wholly hides
The rotted old oak-stump.

"The skiff-boat neared: I heard them talk,
'Why this is strange, I trow!
Where are those lights so many and fair,
That signal made but now?'

Approacheth
the ship with
wonder.

" 'Strange, by my faith!' the Hermit said—
'And they answered not our cheer!
The planks looked warped! and see those sails
How thin they are and sere!
I never saw aught like to them,
Unless perchance it were

" 'Brown skeletons of leaves that lag
My forest-brook along;
When the ivy-tod is heavy with snow,
And the owlet whoops to the wolf below,
That eats the she-wolf's young.'

" 'Dear Lord! it hath a fiendish look—
(The Pilot made reply)
I am a-feared'—'Push on, push on!'
Said the Hermit cheerily.

"The boat came closer to the ship,
But I nor spake nor stirred;
The boat came close beneath the ship,
And straight a sound was heard.

"Under the water it rumbled on,
Still louder and more dread:
It reached the ship, it split the bay;
The ship went down like lead.

*The ship
suddenly
sinketh.*

"Stunned by that loud and dreadful sound,
Which sky and ocean smote,
Like one that hath been seven days drowned
My body lay afloat;
But swift as dreams, myself I found
Within the Pilot's boat.

*The ancient
Mariner is
saved in the
Pilot's boat.*

"Upon the whirl where sank the ship,
The boat spun round and round;
And all was still save that the hill
Was telling of the sound.

"I moved my lips—the Pilot shrieked
And fell down in a fit;
The holy Hermit raised his eyes,
And prayed where he did sit.

The Sacred Fire

"I took the oars: the Pilot's boy,
Who now doth crazy go,
Laughed loud and long, and all the while
His eyes went to and fro.
'Ha! Ha!' quoth he, 'full plain I see,
The Devil knows how to row.'

"And now, all in my own countree,
I stood on the firm land!
The Hermit stepped forth from the boat,
And scarcely he could stand.

The ancient
Mariner
earnestly
entreateth the
Hermit to
shrieve him;
and the pen-
ance of life
falls on him.

" 'O shrieve me, shrieve me, holy man!'
The Hermit crossed his brow.
'Say quick,' quoth he, 'I bid thee say—
What manner of man art thou?'

"Forthwith this frame of mine was wrenched
With a woeful agony,
Which forced me to begin my tale;
And then it left me free.

And ever and
anon through-
out his future
life an agony
constraineth
him to travel
from land to
land.

"Since then, at an uncertain hour,
That agony returns;
And till my ghastly tale is told,
This heart within me burns.

"I pass, like night, from land to land;
I have strange power of speech;
That moment that his face I see,
I know the man that must hear me;
To him my tale I teach.

"What loud uproar bursts from that door!
The wedding-guests are there:
But in the garden-bower the bride
And bridesmaids singing are;
And hark the little vesper bell,
Which biddeth me to prayer!

"O Wedding-Guest! this soul hath been
Alone on a wide, wide sea:
So lonely 'twas, that God himself
Scarce seemed there to be.

"O sweeter than the marriage-feast,
'Tis sweeter far to me,
To walk together to the kirk
With a goodly company!—

"To walk together to the kirk,
And all together pray,
While each to his great Father bends,
Old men, and babes, and loving friends,
And youths and maidens gay!

"Farewell, farewell! but this I tell
To thee, thou Wedding-Guest!
He prayeth well, who loveth well
Both man and bird and beast.

And to teach,
by his own
example, love
and reverence
to all things
that God made
and loveth.

"He prayeth best, who loveth best
All things both great and small;
For the dear God who loveth us,
He made and loveth all."

The Mariner, whose eye is bright,
Whose beard with age is hoar,
Is gone; and now the Wedding-Guest
Turned from the bridegroom's door.

He went like one that hath been stunned,
And is of sense forlorn:
A sadder and a wiser man,
He rose the morrow morn.

about 1797-98   S. T. COLERIDGE

132. Kubla Khan: or, A Vision in a Dream

In Xanadu did Kubla Khan
  A stately pleasure-dome decree:
Where Alph, the sacred river, ran
Through caverns measureless to man,
    Down to a sunless sea.

So twice five miles of fertile ground
With walls and towers were girdled round:
And there were gardens bright with sinuous rills
Where blossomed many an incense-bearing tree;
And here were forests ancient as the hills
Enfolding sunny spots of greenery.

But oh! that deep romantic chasm which slanted
Down the green hill athwart a cedarn cover!
A savage place! as holy and enchanted
As e'er beneath a waning moon was haunted
By woman wailing for her demon lover!
And from this chasm, with ceaseless turmoil seething,
As if this earth in fast thick pants were breathing,
A mighty fountain momently was forced:
Amid whose swift half-intermitted burst
Huge fragments vaulted like rebounding hail,
Or chaffy grain beneath the thresher's flail:
And mid these dancing rocks at once and ever
If flung up momently the sacred river
Five miles meandering with a mazy motion
Through wood and dale the sacred river ran,
Then reached the caverns measureless to man,
And sank in tumult to a lifeless ocean:
And mid this tumult Kubla heard from far
Ancestral voices prophecying war!

    The shadow of the dome of pleasure
    Floated midway on the waves;

Where was heard the mingled measure
From the fountain and the caves.
It was a miracle of rare device,
A sunny pleasure-dome with caves of ice!

A damsel with a dulcimer
In a vision once I saw:
It was an Abyssinian maid,
And on a dulcimer she play'd,
Singing of Mount Abora.
Could I revive within me
Her symphony and song,
To such a deep delight 'twould win me,
That with music loud and long,
I would build that dome in air,
That sunny dome! those caves of ice!
And all who heard should see them there
And all should cry, Beware! Beware!
His flashing eyes, his floating hair!
Weave a circle round him thrice,
And close your eyes with holy dread,
For he on honey-dew hath fed,
And drunk the milk of Paradise.

1797   S. T. COLERIDGE

133. *from* Christabel

PART THE FIRST

'Tis the middle of night by the castle clock,
And the owls have awaken'd the crowing cock!
Tu—whit!—Tu—whoo!
And hark, again! the crowing cock,
How drowsily it crew.

Sir Leoline, the Baron rich,
Hath a toothless mastiff, which
From her kennel beneath the rock
Maketh answer to the clock,

The Sacred Fire

Four for the quarters, and twelve for the hour;
Ever and aye, by shine and shower,
Sixteen short howls, not over loud:
Some say, she sees my lady's shroud.

Is the night chilly and dark?
The night is chilly but not dark.
The thin gray cloud is spread on high,
It covers but not hides the sky.
The moon is behind, and at the full;
And yet she looks both small and dull.
The night is chill, the cloud is gray:
'Tis a month before the month of May,
And the Spring comes slowly up this way.

The lovely lady, Christabel,
Whom her father loves so well,
What makes her in the wood so late,
A furlong from the castle gate?
She had dreams all yesternight
Of her own betrothed knight;
And she in the midnight wood will pray
For the weal of her lover that's far away.

She stole along, she nothing spoke,
The sighs she heaved were soft and low,
And naught was green upon the oak,
But moss and rarest mistletoe:
She kneels beneath the huge oak tree,
And in silence prayeth she.

The lady sprang up suddenly,
The lovely lady, Christabel!
It moaned as near, as near can be,
But what it is, she cannot tell.—
On the other side it seems to be,
Of the huge, broad-breasted, old oak tree.

The night is chill; the forest bare;
Is it the wind that moaneth bleak?
There is not wind enough in the air
To move away the ringlet curl
From the lovely lady's cheek—
There is not wind enough to twirl
The one red leaf, the last of its clan,
That dances as often as dance it can,
Hanging so light, and hanging so high,
On the topmost twig that looks up at the sky.

Hush, beating heart of Christabel!
Jesu, Maria, shield her well!
She folded her arms beneath her cloak,
And stole to the other side of the oak.
    What sees she there?

There she sees a damsel bright,
Drest in a silken robe of white,
That shadowy in the moonlight shone:
The neck that made that white robe wan,
Her stately neck, and arms were bare:
Her blue-veined feet unsandaled were;
And wildly glittered here and there
The gems entangled in her hair.
I guess, 'twas frightful there to see
A lady so richly clad as she—
Beautiful exceedingly!

Mary mother, save me now!
(Said Christabel), And who art thou?

The lady strange made answer meet,
And her voice was faint and sweet:—
Have pity on my sore distress,
I scarce can speak for weariness.
Stretch forth thy hand, and have no fear,
Said Christabel, How camest thou here?
And the lady, whose voice was faint and sweet,
Did thus pursue her answer meet:—

The Sacred Fire

My sire is of a noble line,
And my name is Geraldine:
Five warriors seized me yestermorn,
Me, even me, a maid forlorn:
They choked my cries with force and fright,
And tied me on a palfrey white.
The palfrey was as fleet as wind,
And they rode furiously behind.
They spurred amain, their steeds were white;
And once we crossed the shade of night.
As sure as Heaven shall rescue me,
I have no thought what men they be;
Nor do I know how long it is
(For I have lain entranced I wis)
Since one, the tallest of the five,
Took me from the palfrey's back,
A weary woman, scarce alive.
Some muttered words his comrade spoke:
He placed me underneath the oak,
He swore they would return with haste;
Whither they went I cannot tell—
I thought I heard, some minutes past,
Sounds as of a castle bell.
Stretch forth thy hand (thus ended she),
And help a wretched maid to flee.

Then Christabel stretched forth her hand
And comforted fair Geraldine:
O well bright dame may you command
The service of Sir Leoline;
And gladly our stout chivalry
Will he send forth and friends withal
To guide and guard you safe and free
Home to your noble father's hall.
She rose: and forth with steps they passed
That strove to be, and were not, fast.
Her gracious STARS the lady blest,
And thus spake on sweet Christabel;
All our household are at rest,

The hall as silent as the cell,
Sir Leoline is weak in health
And may not well awakened be,
But we will move as if in stealth:
And I beseech your courtesy
This night, to share your couch with me.

They crossed the moat, and Christabel
Took the key that fitted well;
A little door she opened straight,
All in the middle of the gate;
The gate that was ironed within and without,
Where an army in battle-array had marched out.
The lady sank, belike through pain,
And Christabel with might and main
Lifted her up, a weary weight,
Over the threshold of the gate:
Then the lady rose again,
And moved, as she were not in pain.

So free from danger, free from fear,
They crossed the court: right glad they were.
And Christabel devoutly cried
To the lady by her side,
Praise we the Virgin all divine
Who hath rescued thee from thy distress!
Alas, alas! said Geraldine,
I cannot speak from weariness.
So free from danger, free from fear,
They crossed the court: right glad they were.

Outside her kennel, the mastiff old
Lay fast asleep, in moonshine cold.
The mastiff old did not awake,
Yet she an angry moan did make!
And what can ail the mastiff bitch?
Never till now she uttered yell
Beneath the eye of Christabel.
Perhaps it is the owlet's scritch:
For what can ail the mastiff bitch?

The Sacred Fire

They passed the hall, that echoes still,
Pass as lightly as you will!
The brands were flat, the brands were dying,
Amid their own white ashes lying;
But when the lady passed, there came
A tongue of light, a fit of flame;
And Christabel saw the lady's eye,
And nothing else saw she thereby,
Save the boss of the shield of Sir Leoline tall,
Which hung in a murky old niche in the wall.
O softly tread, said Christabel,
My father seldom sleepeth well.

Sweet Christabel her feet doth bare,
And jealous of the listening air
They steal their way from stair to stair,
Now in glimmer, and now in gloom,
And now they pass the Baron's room,
As still as death with stifled breath!
And now have reached the chamber door;
And now doth Geraldine press down
The rushes of the chamber floor.

The moon shines dim in the open air,
And not a moonbeam enters here.
But they without its light can see
The chamber carved so curiously,
Carved with figures strange and sweet,
All made out of a carver's brain,
For a lady's chamber meet:
The lamp with twofold silver chain
Is fastened to an angel's feet.
The silver lamp burns dead and dim;
But Christabel the lamp will trim.
She trimmed the lamp, and made it bright,
And left it swinging to and fro,
While Geraldine, in wretched plight,
Sank down upon the floor below.

O weary lady, Geraldine,
I pray you, drink this cordial wine!
It is a wine of virtuous powers;
My mother made it of wild flowers.

And will your mother pity me,
Who am a maiden most forlorn?
Christabel answered—Woe is me!
She died the hour that I was born.
I have heard the gray-haired friar tell,
How on her death-bed she did say,
That she should hear the castle bell
Strike twelve upon my wedding day.
O mother dear! that thou wert here!
I would, said Geraldine, she were!

But soon with altered voice, said she—
"Off, wandering mother! Peak and pine!
I have power to bid thee flee."
Alas! what ails poor Geraldine?
Why stares she with unsettled eye?
Can she the bodiless dead espy?
And why with hollow voice cries she,
"Off, woman, off! this hour is mine—
Though thou her guardian spirit be,
Off, woman, off! 'tis given to me."

Then Christabel knelt by the lady's side,
And raised to heaven her eyes so blue—
Alas! said she, this ghastly ride—
Dear lady! it hath wildered you!
The lady wiped her moist cold brow,
And faintly said, " 'tis over now!"

Again the wild-flower wine she drank:
Her fair large eyes 'gan glitter bright,
And from the floor whereon she sank,
The lofty lady stood upright;
She was most beautiful to see,
Like a lady of a far countree.

The Sacred Fire

And thus the lofty lady spake—
All they, who live in the upper sky,
So love you, holy Christabel!
And you love them, and for their sake
And for the good which me befell,
Even I in my degree will try,
Fair maiden, to requite you well.
But now unrobe yourself; for I
Must pray, ere yet in bed I lie.

Quoth Christabel, so let it be!
And as the lady bade, did she.
Her gentle limbs did she undress,
And lay down in her loveliness.

But through her brain of weal and woe
So many thoughts moved to and fro,
That vain it were her lids to close;
So half-way from the bed she rose,
And on her elbow did recline
To look at the lady Geraldine.

Beneath the lamp the lady bowed,
And slowly rolled her eyes around;
Then drawing in her breath aloud,
Like one that shuddered, she unbound
The cincture from beneath her breast:
Her silken robe, and inner vest,
Dropt to her feet, and full in view,
Behold! her bosom and half her side—
A sight to dream of, not to tell!
O shield her! shield sweet Christabel!

Yet Geraldine nor speaks nor stirs:
Ah! what a stricken look was hers!
Deep from within she seems half-way
To lift some weight with sick assay,
And eyes the maid and seeks delay;
Then suddenly, as one defied,
Collects herself in scorn and pride,

And lay down by the Maiden's side!—
And in her arms the maid she took,
    Ah, wel-a-day!
And with low voice and doleful look
These words did say:
In the touch of this bosom there worketh a spell,
Which is lord of thy utterance, Christabel!
Thou knowest to-night, and wilt know to-morrow
This mark of my shame, this seal of my sorrow;
    But vainly thou warrest,
      For this is alone in
    Thy power to declare,
      That in the dim forest
    Thou heard'st a low moaning,
And found'st a bright lady, surpassingly fair:
And didst bring her home with thee in love and charity,
To shield her and shelter her from the damp air.

THE CONCLUSION TO PART THE FIRST

It was a lovely sight to see
The lady Christabel when she
Was praying at the old oak tree.
    Amid the jagged shadows
    Of mossy leafless boughs,
    Kneeling in the moonlight,
    To make her gentle vows;
Her slender palms together prest,
Heaving sometimes on her breast;
Her face resigned to bliss or bale—
Her face, oh call it fair not pale,
And both blue eyes more bright than clear,
Each about to have a tear.

With open eyes (ah woe is me!)
Asleep, and dreaming fearfully,
Fearfully dreaming, yet I wis,
Dreaming that alone, which is—

The Sacred Fire

O sorrow and shame!   Can this be she,
The lady, who knelt at the old oak tree?
And lo! the worker of these harms,
That holds the maiden in her arms,
Seems to slumber still and mild,
As a mother with her child.
A star hath set, a star hath risen,
O Geraldine! since arms of thine
Have been the lovely lady's prison.
O Geraldine! one hour was thine—
Thou'st had thy will!   By tairn and rill,
The night-birds all that hour were still.
But now they are jubilant anew,
From cliff and tower, tu—whoo! tu—whoo:
Tu—whoo! tu—whoo! from wood and fell!

And see! the lady Christabel
Gathers herself from out her trance;
Her limbs relax, her countenance
Grows sad and soft; the smooth thin lids
Close o'er her eyes; and tears she sheds—
Large tears that leave the lashes bright!
And oft the while she seems to smile
As infants at a sudden light!
Yea, she doth smile, and she doth weep,
Like a youthful hermitess,
Beauteous in a wilderness,
Who, praying always, prays in sleep.
And, if she move unquietly,
Perchance 'tis but the blood so free,
Comes back and tingles in her feet.
No doubt, she hath a vision sweet.
What if her guardian spirit 'twere,
What if she knew her mother near?
But this she knows, in joys and woes,
That saints will aid if men will call:
For the blue sky bends over all!

1797   S. T. COLERIDGE

134. The Solitary Reaper

BEHOLD her, single in the field,
Yon solitary Highland Lass!
Reaping and singing by herself;
Stop here or gently pass!
Alone she cuts, and binds the grain,
And sings a melancholy strain;
Oh listen! for the Vale profound
Is overflowing with the sound.

No Nightingale did ever chant
More welcome notes to weary bands
Of travellers in some shady haunt,
Among Arabian sands;
Such thrilling voice was never heard
In spring-time from the Cuckoo-bird,
Breaking the silence of the seas
Among the farthest Hebrides.

Will no one tell me what she sings?
Perhaps the plaintive numbers flow
For old, unhappy, far-off things,
And battles long ago:
Or is it some more humble lay,
Familiar matter of to-day?
Some natural sorrow, loss or pain,
That has been, and may be again!

Whate'er the theme, the Maiden sang
As if her song could have no ending;
I saw her singing at her work,
And o'er the sickle bending:—
I listened, motionless and still;
And as I mounted up the hill,
The music in my heart I bore,
Long after it was heard no more.

about 1803–05   WILLIAM WORDSWORTH

135. Ode: Intimations of immortality from recollections of early childhood

THERE was a time when meadow, grove and stream,
The earth, and every common sight,
        To me did seem
    Apparelled in celestial light,
The glory and the freshness of a dream.
It is not now as it hath been of yore;—
        Turn wheresoe'er I may,
            By night or day,
The things which I have seen I now can see no more.

    The rainbow comes and goes,
    And lovely is the rose;
    The moon doth with delight
Look round her when the heavens are bare;
    Waters on a starry night
    Are beautiful and fair;
    The sunshine is a glorious birth;
    But yet I know, where'er I go,
That there hath past away a glory from the earth.

Now, while the birds thus sing a joyous song,
    And while the young lambs bound
        As to the tabor's sound,
To me alone there came a thought of grief;
A timely utterance gave that thought relief,
        And I again am strong.
The cataracts blow their trumpets from the steep;
No more shall grief of mine the season wrong:
I hear the echoes through the mountains throng,
The winds come to me from the fields of sleep,
        And all the earth is gay;
            Land and sea
        Give themselves up to jollity,

And with the heart of May
Doth every beast keep holiday;—
Thou child of joy
Shout round me, let me hear thy shouts, thou happy
Shepherd-boy!

Ye blessed Creatures, I have heard the call
Ye to each other make; I see
The heavens laugh with you in your jubilee;
My heart is at your festival,
My head hath its coronal,
The fulness of your bliss, I feel—I feel it all.
O evil day! if I were sullen
While Earth herself is adorning
This sweet May-morning;
And the children are culling
On every side,
In a thousand valleys far and wide
Fresh flowers; while the sun shines warm
And the babe leaps up on his mother's arm;—
I hear, I hear, with joy I hear!
—But there's a tree, of many, one,
A single field which I have looked upon,
Both of them speak of something that is gone;
The pansy at my feet
Doth the same tale repeat:
Whither is fled the visionary gleam?
Where is it now, the glory and the dream?

Our birth is but a sleep and a forgetting;
The Soul that rises with us, our life's Star,
Hath had elsewhere its setting
And cometh from afar.
Not in entire forgetfulness,
And not in utter nakedness,
But trailing clouds of glory do we come
From God, who is our home:
Heaven lies about us in our infancy!

The Sacred Fire

Shades of the prison-house begin to close
     Upon the growing Boy,
But he beholds the light, and whence it flows,
     He sees it in his joy;
The Youth, who daily farther from the east
     Must travel, still is Nature's priest,
       And by the vision splendid
       Is on his way attended;
At length the Man perceives it die away
And fade into the light of common day.

Earth fills her lap with pleasures of her own;
Yearnings she hath in her own natural kind,
And, even with something of a mother's mind
       And no unworthy aim,
       The homely Nurse doth all she can
To make her foster-child, her inmate, Man,
       Forget the glories he hath known,
And that imperial palace whence he came.

Behold the Child among his new-born blisses,
A six-years' darling of a pigmy size!
See, where 'mid work of his own hand he lies,
Fretted by sallies of his mother's kisses,
With light upon him from his father's eyes!
See, at his feet, some little plan or chart,
Some fragment from his dream of human life
Shaped by himself with newly learned art;
       A wedding or a festival,
       A mourning or a funeral;
       And this hath now his heart,
       And unto this he frames his song:
       Then will he fit his tongue
To dialogues of business, love, or strife;
       But it will not be long
       Ere this be thrown aside,
       And with new joy and pride
The little actor cons another part;

Filling from time to time his 'humorous stage'
With all the Persons, down to palsied Age,
That life brings with her in her equipage;
  As if his whole vocation
  Were endless imitation.

Thou, whose exterior semblance doth belie
  Thy soul's immensity;
Thou best philosopher, who yet dost keep
Thy heritage, thou eye amongst the blind
That, deaf and silent, read'st the eternal deep,
Haunted for ever by the eternal Mind,—
  Mighty Prophet!   Seer blest!
  On whom those truths do rest
Which we are toiling all our lives to find,
In darkness lost, the darkness of the grave;
Thou, over whom thy Immortality
Broods like the day, a master o'er a slave,
A Presence which is not to be put by;
Thou little child, yet glorious in the might
Of heaven-born freedom on thy being's height,
Why with such earnest pains dost thou provoke
The years to bring the inevitable yoke,
Thus blindly with thy blessedness at strife?
Full soon thy soul shall have her earthy freight,
And custom lie upon thee with a weight
Heavy as frost, and deep almost as life!

  O joy! that in our embers
  Is something that doth live,
  That Nature yet remembers
  What was so fugitive!
The thought of our past years in me doth breed
Perpetual benediction: not, indeed,
For that which is most worthy to be blest,
Delight and liberty, the simple creed
Of Childhood, whether busy or at rest,
With new-fledged hope still fluttering in his breast:

The Sacred Fire

—Not for these I raise
    The song of thanks and praise;
But for those obstinate questionings
Of sense and outward things,
Fallings from us, vanishings;
    Blank misgivings of a creature
Moving about in worlds not realised,
High instincts, before which our mortal nature
Did tremble like a guilty thing surprised:
    But for those first affections,
    Those shadowy recollections,
        Which, be they what they may,
Are yet the fountain light of all our day,
Are yet a master-light of all our seeing;
    Uphold us, cherish, and have power to make
Our noisy years seem moments in the being
Of the eternal Silence: truths that wake,
        To perish never;
Which neither listlessness, nor mad endeavour,
        Nor man nor boy,
Nor all that is at enmity with joy,
Can utterly abolish or destroy!
    Hence, in a season of calm weather,
        Though inland far we be,
Our souls have sight of that immortal sea
        Which brought us hither;
        Can in a moment travel thither—
And see the children sport upon the shore,
And hear the mighty waters rolling evermore.

Then sing, ye birds, sing, sing a joyous song!
        And let the young lambs bound
        As to the tabor's sound!
    We, in thought, will join your throng,
        Ye that pipe and ye that play,
        Ye that through your hearts to-day
        Feel the gladness of the May!
What though the radiance which was once so bright
Be now for ever taken from my sight,

Though nothing can bring back the hour
Of splendour in the grass, of glory in the flower;
    We will grieve not, rather find
    Strength in what remains behind;
    In the primal sympathy
    Which, having been, must ever be;
    In the soothing thoughts that spring
    Out of human suffering;
    In the faith that looks through death,
In years that bring the philosophic mind.

And O, ye Fountains, Meadows, Hills and Groves,
Forbode not any severing of our Loves!
Yet in my heart of hearts I feel your might;
I only have relinquished one delight
To live beneath your more habitual sway:
I love the brooks which down their channels fret
Even more than when I tripped lightly as they;
The innocent brightness of a new-born day
      Is lovely yet;
The clouds that gather round the setting sun
Do take a sober colouring from an eye
That hath kept watch o'er man's mortality;
Another race hath been, and other palms are won.
Thanks to the human heart by which we live,
Thanks to its tenderness, its joys, and fears,
To me the meanest flower that blows can give
Thoughts that do often lie too deep for tears.

about 1803–06   WILLIAM WORDSWORTH

136. Lines composed a few miles above Tintern Abbey

FIVE years have past; five summers, with the length
Of five long winters! and again I hear
These waters, rolling from their mountain-springs
With a soft inland murmur.—Once again

The Sacred Fire

Do I behold these steep and lofty cliffs,
That on a wild secluded scene impress
Thoughts of more deep seclusion; and connect
The landscape with the quiet of the sky.
The day is come when I again repose
Here, under this dark sycamore, and view
These plots of cottage-ground, these orchard-tufts,
Which at this season, with their unripe fruits
Are clad in one green hue, and lose themselves
'Mid groves and copses.   Once again I see
These hedge-rows, hardly hedge-rows, little lines
Of sportive wood run wild: these pastoral farms,
Green to the very door; and wreaths of smoke
Sent up, in silence, from among the trees!
With some uncertain notice as might seem
Of vagrant dwellers in the houseless woods,
Or of some Hermit's cave, where by his fire
The hermit sits alone.

                              These beauteous forms,
Through a long absence, have not been to me
As is a landscape to a blind man's eye:
But oft, in lonely rooms, and 'mid the din
Of towns and cities, I have owed to them
In hours of weariness, sensations sweet,
Felt in the blood, and felt along the heart;
And passing even into my purer mind,
With tranquil restoration:—feelings too
Of unremembered pleasure: such, perhaps,
As have no slight or trivial influence
On that best portion of a good man's life,
His little, nameless, unremembered, acts
Of kindness and of love.   Nor less, I trust,
To them I may have owed another gift,
Of aspect more sublime; that blessed mood,
In which the burthen of the mystery,
In which the heavy and the weary weight
Of all this unintelligible world,
Is lightened:—that serene and blessed mood,
In which the affections gently lead us on,—

Until, the breath of this corporeal frame
And even the motion of our human blood
Almost suspended, we are laid asleep
In body, and become a living soul:
While with an eye made quiet by the power
Of harmony, and the deep power of joy,
We see into the life of things.
                                    If this
Be but a vain belief, yet, oh! how oft—
In darkness and amid the many shapes
Of joyless daylight; when the fretful stir
Unprofitable, and the fever of the world,
Have hung upon the beatings of my heart—
How oft, in spirit, have I turned to thee,
O sylvan Wye! thou wanderer through the woods,
How often has my spirit turned to thee!

And now, with gleams of half-extinguished thought,
With many recollections dim and faint,
And somewhat of a sad perplexity,
The picture of the mind revives again:
While here I stand, not only with the sense
Of present pleasure, but with pleasing thoughts
That in this moment there is life and food
For future years.   And so I dare to hope,
Though changed, no doubt, from what I was when first
I came among these hills; when like a roe
I bounded o'er the mountains, by the sides
Of the deep rivers, and the lonely streams,
Wherever Nature led: more like a man
Flying from something that he dreads, than one
Who sought the thing he loved.   For Nature then
(The coarser pleasures of my boyish days,
And their glad animal movements all gone by)
To me was all in all.—I cannot paint
What then I was.   The sounding cataract
Haunted me like a passion: the tall rock,
The mountain, and the deep and gloomy wood,
The colours and their forms, were then to me

An appetite; a feeling and a love,
That had no need of a remoter charm,
By thought supplied, nor any interest
Unborrowed from the eye.—That time is past,
And all its aching joys are now no more,
And all its dizzy raptures. Not for this
Faint I, nor mourn nor murmur; other gifts
Have followed; for such loss I would believe,
Abundant recompense. For I have learned
To look on Nature, not as in the hour
Of thoughtless youth; but hearing oftentimes
The still sad music of humanity,
Not harsh nor grating, though of ample power
To chasten and subdue. And I have felt
A presence that disturbs me with the joy
Of elevated thoughts; a sense sublime
Of something far more deeply interfused,
Whose dwelling is the light of setting suns,
And the round ocean and the living air,
And the blue sky, and in the mind of man;
A motion and a spirit, that impels
All thinking things, all objects of all thought,
And rolls through all things. Therefore am I still
A lover of the meadows and the woods
And mountains; and of all that we behold
From this green earth; of all the mighty world
Of eye, and ear,—both what they half create,
And what perceive; well pleased to recognise
In Nature and the language of the sense,
The anchor of my purest thoughts, the nurse,
The guide, the guardian of my heart, and soul
Of all my moral being.

                Nor perchance,
If I were not thus taught, should I the more
Suffer my genial spirits to decay:
For thou art with me here upon the banks
Of this fair river; thou my dearest Friend,
My dear, dear Friend; and in thy voice I catch
The language of my former heart, and read

My former pleasures in the shooting lights
Of thy wild eyes.   Oh! yet a little while
May I behold in thee what I was once,
My dear, dear Sister! and this prayer I make,
Knowing that Nature never did betray
The heart that loved her; 'tis her privilege,
Through all the years of this our life, to lead
From joy to joy: for she can so inform
The mind that is within us, so impress
With quietness and beauty, and so feed
With lofty thoughts, that neither evil tongues,
Rash judgements, nor the sneers of selfish men,
Nor greetings where no kindness is, nor all
The dreary intercourse of daily life,
Shall e'er prevail against us, or disturb
Our cheerful faith, that all which we behold
Is full of blessings.   Therefore let the moon
Shine on thee in thy solitary walk;
And let the misty mountain-winds be free
To blow against thee: and, in after years,
When these wild ecstasies shall be matured
Into a sober pleasure; when thy mind
Shall be a mansion for all lovely forms,
Thy memory be as a dwelling-place
For all sweet sounds and harmonies; oh! then,
If solitude, or fear, or pain, or grief,
Should be thy portion, with what healing thoughts
Of tender joy wilt thou remember me,
And these my exhortations!   Nor, perchance—
If I should be where I no more can hear
Thy voice, nor catch from thy wild eyes these gleams
Of past existence—wilt thou then forget
That on the banks of this delightful stream
We stood together; and that I, so long
A worshipper of Nature, hither came
Unwearied in that service: rather say
With warmer love—oh! with far deeper zeal
Of holier love.   Nor wilt thou then forget,
That after many wanderings, many years

Of absence, these steep woods and lofty cliffs,
And this green pastoral landscape, were to me,
Most dear, both for themselves and for thy sake!

1798   WILLIAM WORDSWORTH

137. MacGregor's Gathering

THE moon's on the lake, and the mist's on the brae,
And the clan has a name that is nameless by day,
   Then gather, gather, gather, Grigalach!

Our signal for fight, that from monarchs we drew,
Must be heard but by night in our vengeful haloo!
   Then haloo, Grigalach, haloo, Grigalach!

Glen Orchy's proud mountains, Coalchuirn and her towers,
Glenstrae and Glenlyon no longer are ours;
   We're landless, landless, landless, Grigalach!

But doom'd and devoted by vassal and lord,
MacGregor has still both his heart and his sword!
   Then courage, courage, courage, Grigalach!

If they rob us of name, and pursue us with beagles,
Give their roofs to the flame, and their flesh to the eagles;
   Then vengeance, vengeance, vengeance, Grigalach!

While there's leaves in the forest, and foam on the river,
MacGregor, despite them, shall flourish for ever!
   Come then, Grigalach, come then, Grigalach!

Through the depths of Loch Katrine the steed shall career,
O'er the peak of Ben Lomond the galley shall steer,
And the rocks of Craig Royston like icicles melt,
Ere our wrongs be forgot, or our vengeance unfelt!
   Then gather, gather, gather, Grigalach!

about 1816   WALTER SCOTT

138. When the lamp is shattered . . .

WHEN the lamp is shattered
The light in the dust lies dead—
    When the cloud is scattered
The rainbow's glory is shed.
    When the lute is broken,
Sweet tones are remembered not;
    When the lips have spoken,
Loved accents are soon forgot.

As music and splendour
Survive not the lamp and the lute
    The heart's echoes render
No song when the spirit is mute:—
    No song but sad dirges,
Like the wind through a ruined cell,
    Or the mournful surges
That ring the dead seaman's knell.

When hearts have once mingled
Love first leaves the well-built nest
    The weak one is singled
To endure what it once possest.
    O Love! who bewailest
The frailty of all things here,
    Why choose you the frailest
For your cradle, your home, and your bier?

Its passions will rock thee
As the storms rock the ravens on high:
    Bright reason will mock thee,
Like the sun from a wintry sky.
    From thy nest every rafter
Will rot, and thine eagle home
    Leave thee naked to laughter,
When leaves fall and cold winds come.

about 1820   P. B. SHELLEY

139.

O WORLD, O life, O time!
On whose last steps I climb,
Trembling at that where I had stood before;
When will return the glory of your prime?
No more—Oh, never more!

Out of the day and night
A joy has taken flight;
Fresh spring, and summer, and winter hoar
Move my faint heart with grief, but with delight
No more—Oh, never more!

1821   P. B. SHELLEY

140. Stanzas

AWAY! the moor is dark beneath the moon,
Rapid clouds have drunk the last pale beams of even:
Away! the gathering winds will call the darkness soon,
And profoundest midnight shroud the serene lights of heaven.
Pause not! The time is past! Every voice cries, Away!
Tempt not with one last fear thy friend's ungentle mood:
Thy lover's eye, so glazed and cold, dares not entreat thy stay:
Duty and dereliction guide thee back to solitude.
Away, away! to thy sad and silent home:
Pour bitter tears on its desolated hearth:
Watch the dim shades, as like ghosts they go and come,
And complicate strange webs of melancholy mirth.

The leaves of autumn woods shall float around thine head:
The blooms of dewy spring shall gleam beneath thy feet:
But thy soul or this world must fade in the frost that binds the dead,
Ere midnight's frown or morning's smile, ere thou and peace may
    meet.

The cloud shadows of midnight possess their own repose,
For the weary winds are silent, or the moon is in the deep:
Some respite to its turbulence unresting ocean knows:
Whatever moves, or toils, or grieves, hath its appointed sleep.

Thou in the grave shall rest—yet till the phantoms flee
Which that house and heath and garden made dear to thee ere-
    while,
Thy remembrance and repentance and deep musings are not free
From the music of two voices and the light of one sweet smile.

1814   P. B. SHELLEY

141. Ode to Psyche

O GODDESS! hear these tuneless numbers, wrung
    By sweet enforcement and remembrance dear,
And pardon that my secrets should be sung
    Even into thine own soft-conched ear;
Surely I dreamt to-day, or did I see
    The winged Psyche with awaken'd eyes?
I wandered in a forest thoughtlessly,
    And on the sudden, fainting with surprise,
Saw two fair creatures couched side by side
    In deepest grass, beneath the whispering roof
    Of leaves and trembled blossoms, where there ran
        A brooklet scarce espied:
'Mid hush'd, cool-rooted flowers fragrant-eyed,
    Blue, silver-white and budded Tyrian,
They lay calm-breathing on the bedded grass,
    Their arms embraced and their pinions too:
    Their lips touched not, but had not bade adieu
As if disjoined by soft-handed slumber,
And ready still past kisses to outnumber
    At tender eye-dawn of aurorean love:
        The winged boy I knew;
    But who wast thou, O happy, happy dove?
        His Psyche true!

The Sacred Fire

O latest-born and loveliest vision far
    Of all Olympus' faded hierarchy!
Fairer than Phoebe's sapphire-region'd star,
    Or Vesper, amorous glow-worm of the sky:
Fairer than these, though temple thou hast none,
    Nor altar heap'd with flowers;
Nor virgin-choir to make delicious moan
    Upon the midnight hours;
No voice, no lute, no pipe, no incense sweet
    From chain-swung censer teeming;
No shrine, no grove, no oracle, no heat
    Of pale-mouth'd prophet dreaming.

O brightest! though too late for antique vows,
    Too, too late for the fond believing lyre,
When holy were the haunted forest boughs,
    Holy the air, the water and the fire;
Yet even in these days so far retir'd
    From happy pieties, thy lucent fans,
    Fluttering among the faint Olympians,
I see and sing, by my own eyes inspired.
    So let me be thy choir, and make a moan
        Upon the midnight hours!
Thy voice, thy lute, thy pipe, thy incense sweet
    From swinged censer teeming;
Thy shrine, thy grove, thy oracle, thy heat
    Of pale-mouth'd prophet dreaming.

Yes, I will be thy priest, and build a fane
    In some untrodden region of my mind,
Where branched thoughts, new-grown with pleasant pain,
    Instead of pines shall murmur in the wind;
Far, far around shall those dark-cluster'd trees
    Fledge the wild-ridged mountains steep by steep;
And there by zephyrs, streams, and birds, and bees,
    The moss-lain Dryads shall be lull'd to sleep;
And in the midst of this wide quietness
A rosy sanctuary will I dress
With the wreathed trellis of a working brain,
    With buds, and shells, and stars without a name:

With all the gardener Fancy e'er could feign,
  Who, breeding flowers, shall never breed the same:
And there shall be for thee all soft delight
  That shadowy thought can win,
A bright torch, and a casement ope at night,
  To let the warm Love in!

about 1820   JOHN KEATS

142. To Homer

STANDING aloof in giant ignorance,
  Of thee I hear and of the Cyclades,
As one who sits ashore and longs perchance
  To visit dolphin-coral in deep seas.
So thou wast blind!—but then the veil was rent;
  For Jove uncurtained Heaven to let thee live,
And Neptune made for thee a spermy tent,
  And Pan made sing for thee his forest hive;
Ay, on the shores of darkness there is light,
  And precipices show untrodden green;
There is a budding morrow in midnight;
  There is a triple sight in blindness keen:
Such seeing hadst thou, as it once befel,
  To Dian, Queen of Earth, and Heaven and Hell.

about 1818   JOHN KEATS

143. To Sleep

O SOFT embalmer of the still midnight
  Shutting with careful fingers and benign
Our gloom-pleased eyes, embowered from the light,
  Enshaded in forgetfulness divine;
O soothest Sleep! if so it please thee, close,
  In midst of this thine hymn, my willing eyes,
Or wait the amen, ere thy poppy throws
  Around my bed its lulling charities;

Then save me, or the passed day will shine
    Upon my pillow, breeding many woes;
Save me from curious conscience, that still lords
    Its strength, for darkness burrowing like a mole;
Turn the key deftly in the oiled wards,
    And seal the hushed casket of my soul.

about 1819   JOHN KEATS

144. *from* Hyperion

DEEP in the shady sadness of a vale
Far sunken from the healthy breath of morn,
Far from the fiery noon, and eve's one star,
Sat gray-hair'd Saturn, quiet as a stone,
Still as the silence round about his lair;
Forest on forest hung about his head
Like cloud on cloud.   No stir of air was there,
Not so much life as on a summer's day
Robs not one light seed from the feather'd grass,
But where the dead leaf fell, there did it rest.
A stream went voiceless by, still deadened more
By reason of his fallen divinity
Spreading a shade: the Naiad 'mid her reeds
Press'd her cold finger closer to her lips.

    Along the margin-sand large foot-marks went,
No further than to where his feet had stray'd,
And slept there since.   Upon the sodden ground
His old right hand lay nerveless, listless, dead,
Unsceptred; and his realmless eyes were closed;
While his bow'd head seem'd list'ning to the Earth,
His ancient mother, for some comfort yet.

    It seem'd no force could wake him from his place;
But there came one, who with a kindred hand
Touch'd his wide shoulders, after bending low
With reverence, though to one who knew it not.

She was a Goddess of the infant world;
By her in stature the tall Amazon
Had stood a pigmy's height: she would have ta'en
Achilles by the hair and bent his neck;
Or with a finger stay'd Ixion's wheel.
Her face was large as that of Memphian sphinx,
Pedestal'd haply in a palace court,
When sages look'd to Egypt for their lore.
But oh! how unlike marble was that face:
How beautiful, if sorrow had not made
Sorrow more beautiful than Beauty's self.
There was a listening fear in her regard,
As if calamity had but begun;
As if the vanward clouds of evil days
Had spent their malice, and the sullen rear
Was with its stored thunder labouring up.
One hand she press'd upon that aching spot
Where beats the human heart, as if just there,
Though an immortal, she felt cruel pain:
The other upon Saturn's bended neck
She laid, and to the level of his ear
Leaning with parted lips, some words she spake
In solemn tenour and deep organ tone:
Some mourning words, which in our feeble tongue
Would come in these like accents; O how frail
To that large utterance of the early Gods!
"Saturn, look up!—though wherefore, poor old King?'
"I have no comfort for thee, no not one:
"I cannot say, 'O wherefore sleepest thou?'
"For heaven is parted from thee, and the earth
"Knows thee not, thus afflicted, for a God;
"And ocean too, with all its solemn noise,
"Has from thy sceptre pass'd; and all the air
"Is emptied of thine hoary majesty.
"Thy thunder, conscious of the new command,
"Rumbles reluctant o'er our fallen house;
"And thy sharp lightning in unpractised hands
"Scorches and burns our once serene domain.
"O aching time!   O moments big as years!

"All as ye pass swell out the monstrous truth,
"And press it so upon our weary griefs
"That unbelief has not a space to breathe.
"Saturn, sleep on:—O thoughtless, why did I
"Thus violate thy slumbrous solitude?
"Why should I ope thy melancholy eyes?
"Saturn, sleep on! while at thy feet I weep."

As when, upon a tranced summer night,
Those green-rob'd senators of mighty woods,
Tall oaks, branch-charmed by the earnest stars,
Dream, and so dream all night without a stir,
Save from one gradual solitary gust
Which comes upon the silence, and dies off,
As if the ebbing air had but one wave:
So came these words and went; the while in tears
She touch'd her fair large forehead to the ground,
Just where her falling hair might be outspread
A soft and silken mat for Saturn's feet.

* * * * *

All eyes were on Enceladus's face,
And they beheld, while still Hyperion's name
Flew from his lips up to the vaulted rocks,
A pallid gleam across his features stern:
Not savage, for he saw full many a God
Wroth as himself.   He look'd upon them all,
And in each face he saw a gleam of light,
But splendider in Saturn's, whose hoar locks
Shone like the bubbling foam about a keel
When the prow sweeps into a midnight cove.
In pale and silver silence they remain'd,
Till suddenly a splendour, like the morn,
Pervaded all the beetling gloomy steeps,
All the sad spaces of oblivion,
And every gulf, and every chasm old,
And every height, and every sullen depth,
Voiceless, or hoarse with loud tormented streams:
And all the everlasting cataracts,

And all the headlong torrents far and near,
Mantled before in darkness and huge shade,
Now saw the light and made it terrible.
It was Hyperion:—a granite peak
His bright feet touch'd, and there he stay'd to view
The misery his brilliance had betray'd
To the most hateful seeing of itself.
Golden his hair of short Numidian curl,
Regal his shape majestic, a vast shade
In midst of his own brightness, like the bulk
Of Memnon's image at the set of sun
To one who travels from the dusking East:
Sighs, too, as mournful as that Memnon's harp
He utter'd, while his hands contemplative
He press'd together, and in silence stood.
Despondence seiz'd again the fallen Gods
At sight of the dejected King of Day,
And many hid their faces from the light:
But fierce Enceladus sent forth his eyes
Among the brotherhood; and, at their glare,
Uprose Iäpetus, and Creüs too,
And Phorcus, sea-born, and together strode
To where he towered on his eminence.
There those four shouted forth old Saturn's name;
Hyperion from the peak loud answered, "Saturn"!
Saturn sat near the Mother of the Gods,
In whose face was no joy, though all the Gods,
Gave from their hollow throats the name of "Saturn".

*   *   *   *   *

Thus in alternate uproar and sad peace,
Amazed were those Titans utterly.
O leave them, Muse!   O leave them to their woes!
For thou art weak to sing such tumults dire:
A solitary sorrow best befits
Thy lips, and antheming a lonely grief.
Leave them, O Muse! for thou anon wilt find
Many a fallen old Divinity
Wandering in vain about bewildered shores.

The Sacred Fire

Meantime touch piously the Delphic harp,
And not a wind of heaven but will breathe
In aid soft warble from the Dorian flute;
For lo! 'tis for the Father of all verse.
Flush everything that hath a vermeil hue,
Let the rose glow intense and warm the air,
And let the clouds of even and of morn
Float in voluptuous fleeces o'er the hills;
Let the red wine within the goblet boil,
Cold as a bubbling well: let faint-lipp'd shells,
On sands, or in great deeps, vermilion turn
Through all their labyrinths; and let the maid
Blush keenly, as with some warm kiss surprised.
Chief isle of the embowered Cyclades,
Rejoice, O Delos, with thine olives green,
And poplars, and lawn-shading palms, and beech,
In which the Zephyr breathes the loudest song,
And hazels thick, dark-stemm'd beneath the shade:
Apollo is once more the golden theme!
Where was he, when the Giant of the Sun
Stood bright, amid the sorrow of his peers?
Together had he left his mother fair
And his twin-sister sleeping in their bower,
And in the morning twilight wandered forth
Beside the osiers of a rivulet,
Full ankle-deep in lilies of the vale.
The nightingale had ceased, and a few stars
Were lingering in the heavens, while the thrush
Began calm-throated.   Throughout all the isle
There was no covert, no retired cave
Unhaunted by the murmurous noise of waves,
Though scarcely heard in many a green recess.
He listen'd, and he wept, and his bright tears
Went trickling down the golden bow he held.
Thus with half-shut suffused eyes he stood,
While from beneath some cumbrous boughs hard by
With solemn step an awful Goddess came,
And there was purport in her looks for him,
Which he with eager guess began to read

Perplex'd, the while melodiously he said:
"How cam'st thou over the unfooted sea?
"Or hath that antique mien and robed form
"Mov'd in these vales invisible till now?
"Sure I have heard those vestments sweeping o'er
"The fallen leaves, when I have sat alone
"In cool mid-forest.   Surely I have traced
"The rustle of those ample skirts about
"These grassy solitudes, and seen the flowers
"Lift up their heads, as still the whisper pass'd.
"Goddess!   I have beheld those eyes before,
"And their eternal calm, and all that face,
"Or I have dream'd."—"Yes," said the supreme shape,
"Thou hast dream'd of me; and awaking up
"Didst find a lyre all golden by thy side,
"Whose strings touch'd by thy fingers, all the vast
"Unwearied ear of the whole universe
"Listen'd in pain and pleasure at the birth
"Of such new tuneful wonder.   Is't not strange
"That thou shouldst weep, so gifted?   Tell me, youth,
"What sorrow thou canst feel; for I am sad
"When thou dost shed a tear: explain thy griefs
"To one who in this lonely isle has been
"The watcher of thy sleep and hours of life,
"From the young day when first thy infant hand
"Pluck'd witless the weak flowers, till thine arm
"Could bend that bow heroic to all times.
"Show thy heart's secret to an ancient Power
"Who hath forsaken old and sacred thrones
"For prophecies of thee, and for the sake
"Of loveliness new born."—Apollo then,
With sudden scrutiny and gloomless eyes,
Thus answer'd, while his white melodious throat
Throbb'd with the syllables.—"Mnemosyne!
"Thy name is on my tongue, I know not how;
"Why should I tell thee what thou so well seest?
"Why should I strive to show what from thy lips
"Would come no mystery?   For me, dark, dark,
"And painful vile oblivion seals my eyes:

The Sacred Fire

"I strive to search wherefore I am so sad,
"Until a melancholy numbs my limbs;
"And then upon the grass I sit, and moan
"Like one who once had wings—O why should I
"Feel cursed and thwarted, when the liegeless air
"Yields to my step aspirant? why should I
"Spurn the green turf as hateful to my feet?
"Goddess benign, point forth some unknown thing:
"Are there not other regions than this isle?
"What are the stars?   There is the sun, the sun!
"And the most patient brilliance of the moon!
"And stars by thousands!   Point me out the way
"To any one particular beauteous star,
"And I will flit into it with my lyre,
"And make its silvery splendour pant with bliss.
"I have heard the cloudy thunder: Where is power?
"Whose hand, whose essence, what divinity
"Makes this alarum in the elements,
"While I here idle listen on the shores
"In fearless yet in aching ignorance?
"O tell me, lonely Goddess! by thy harp,
"That waileth every morn and eventide,
"Tell me why thus I rave, about these groves!
"Mute thou remainest—mute? yet I can read
"A wondrous lesson in thy silent face:
"Knowledge enormous makes a God of me.
"Names, deeds, gray legends, dire events, rebellions,
"Majesties, sovran voices, agonies,
"Creations and destroyings, all at once
"Pour into the wide hollows of my brain,
"And deify me, as if some blithe wine
"Or bright elixir peerless I had drunk,
"And so become immortal."—Thus the God,
While his enkindled eyes, with level glance
Beneath his white soft temples, steadfast kept
Trembling with light upon Mnemosyne.
Soon wild commotions shook him, and made flush
All the immortal fairness of his limbs:
Most like the struggle at the gate of death;

Or liker still to one who should take leave
Of pale immortal death, and with a pang
As hot as death's is chill, with fierce convulse
Die into life: so young Apollo anguish'd.

about 1818—20   JOHN KEATS

145. The Gift

WHAT can I give thee back, O liberal
    And princely giver, who hast brought the gold
    And purple of thine heart, unstained, untold,
And laid them on the outside of the wall!
For such as I to take or leave withal,
    In unexpected largesse? am I cold,
    Ungrateful, that for these most manifold
High gifts, I render nothing back at all?
Not so; not cold,—but very poor instead.
    Ask God who knows. For frequent tears have run
The colours from my life, and left so dead
    And pale a stuff, it were not fitly done
To give the same as pillow to thy head.
    Go farther! let it serve to trample on.

about 1850   ELIZABETH BARRETT BROWNING

146. The Prisoner

STILL let my tyrants know, I am not doom'd to wear
Year after year in gloom and desolate despair;
A messenger of Hope comes every night to me,
And offers for short life, eternal liberty.

He comes with Western winds, with evening's wandering airs,
With that clear dusk of heaven that brings the thickest stars:
Winds take a pensive tone, and stars a tender fire,
And visions rise, and change, and kill me with desire.

The Sacred Fire

Desire for nothing known in my maturer years,
When Joy grew mad with awe at counting future tears:
When, if my spirit's sky was full of flashes warm,
I knew not whence they came, from sun or thunderstorm.

But first, a hush of peace—a soundless calm descends;
The struggle of distress and fierce impatience ends.
Mute music soothes my breast—unutter'd harmony
That I could never dream, till Earth was lost to me.

Then dawns the Invisible; the Unseen its truth reveals;
My outward sense is gone, my inward essence feels;
Its wings are almost free—its home, its harbour found;
Measuring the gulf, it stoops, and dares the final bound.

O dreadful is the check—intense the agony—
When the ear begins to hear, and the eye begins to see;
When the pulse begins to throb—the brain to think again
The soul to feel the flesh, and the flesh to feel the chain.

Yet I would lose no sting, would wish no torture less;
The more that anguish racks, the earlier will it bless;
And robed in fires of hell, or bright with heavenly shine,
If it but herald Death, the vision is divine.

about 1845   EMILY BRONTË

XVII

Alfred, Lord Tennyson
Matthew Arnold
Robert Browning
Christina Rossetti
D. G. Rossetti

147. The Lotos-Eaters

"Courage!" he said, and pointed toward the land,
"This mounting wave will roll us shoreward soon."
In the afternoon they came unto a land,
In which it seemed always afternoon.
All round the coast the languid air did swoon,
Breathing like one that hath a weary dream.
Full-faced above the valley stood the moon;
And like a downward smoke, the slender stream
Along the cliff to fall and pause and fall did seem.

A land of streams! some, like a downward smoke,
Slow-dropping veils of thinnest lawn did go;
And some, thro' wavering lights and shadows broke,
Rolling a slumbrous sheet of foam below.
They saw the gleaming river seaward flow
From the inner land: far off, three mountain-tops,
Three silent pinnacles of aged snow,
Stood sunset-flush'd: and, dew'd with showery drops,
Up-clomb the shadowy pine above the woven copse.

The charmed sunset linger'd low adown
In the red West: thro' mountain clefts the dale
Was seen far inland, and the yellow down
Border'd with palm, and many a winding vale
And meadow, set with slender galingale;
A land where all things always seem'd the same!
And round about the keel with faces pale,
Dark faces pale against that rosy flame,
The mild-eyed melancholy Lotos-eaters came.

Branches they bore of that enchanted stem,
Laden with flower and fruit, whereof they gave
To each, but whoso did receive of them,
And taste, to him the gushing of the wave
Far far away did seem to mourn and rave
On alien shores; and if his fellow spake,

The Sacred Fire

His voice was thin, as voices from the grave;
And deep-asleep he seem'd, yet all awake,
And music in his ears his beating heart did make.

They sat them down upon the yellow sand,
Between the sun and moon upon the shore;
And sweet it was to dream of Fatherland,
Of child, and wife, and slave; but evermore
Most weary seem'd the sea, weary the oar,
Weary the wandering fields of barren foam.
Then someone said "We will return no more;"
And all at once they sang, "Our island home
Is far beyond the wave; we will no longer roam."

CHORIC SONG

I

There is sweet music here that softer falls
Than petals from blown roses on the grass,
Or night-dews on still waters between walls
Of shadowy granite, in a gleaming pass;
Music that gentlier on the spirit lies,
Than tir'd eyelids upon tir'd eyes;
Music that brings sweet sleep down from the blissful skies.
Here are cool mosses deep,
And thro' the moss the ivies creep,
And in the stream the long-leaved flowers weep,
And from the craggy ledge the poppy hangs in sleep.

2

Why are we weigh'd upon with heaviness,
And utterly consumed with sharp distress,
While all things else have rest from weariness?
All things have rest: why should we toil alone,
We only toil, who are the first of things,
And make perpetual moan,
Still from one sorrow to another thrown:
Nor ever fold our wings,
And cease from wanderings,

Nor steep our brows in slumber's holy balm;
Nor hearken what the inner spirit sings,
"There is no joy but calm!"
Why should we only toil, the roof and crown of things?

3

Lo! in the middle of the wood,
The folded leaf is woo'd from out the bud
With winds upon the branch, and there
Grows green and broad, and takes no care,
Sun-steep'd at noon, and in the moon
Nightly dew-fed; and turning yellow
Falls, and floats adown the air.
Lo! sweeten'd with the summer light,
The full-juiced apple, waxing over-mellow,
Drops in a silent autumn night.
All its allotted length of days,
The flower ripens in its place,
Ripens and fades, and falls, and hath no toil,
Fast-rooted in the fruitful soil.

4

Hateful is the dark-blue sky,
Vaulted o'er the dark-blue sea.
Death is the end of life; ah, why
Should life all labour be?
Let us alone.   Time driveth onward fast,
And in a little while our lips are dumb.
Let us alone.   What is it that will last?
All things are taken from us, and become
Portions and parcels of the dreadful Past.
Let us alone.   What pleasure can we have
To war with evil?   Is there any peace
In ever climbing up the climbing wave?
All things have rest, and ripen toward the grave
In silence; ripen, fall and cease:
Give us long rest or death, dark death, or dreamful ease.

5

How sweet it were, hearing the downward stream,
With half-shut eyes ever to seem
Falling asleep in a half-dream!
To dream and dream, like yonder amber light,
Which will not leave the myrrh-bush on the height;
To hear each other's whisper'd speech;
Eating the Lotos day by day,
To watch the crisping ripples on the beach,
And tender curving lines of creamy spray;
To lend our hearts and spirits wholly
To the influence of mild-minded melancholy;
To muse and brood and live again in memory,
With those old faces of our infancy
Heap'd over with a mound of grass,
Two handfuls of white dust, shut in an urn of brass!

6

Dear is the memory of our wedded lives,
And dear the last embraces of our wives
And their warm tears: but all hath suffer'd change;
For surely now our household hearths are cold:
Our sons inherit us: our looks are strange:
And we should come like ghosts to trouble joy.
Or else the island princes over-bold
Have eat our substance, and the minstrel sings
Before them of the ten-years' war in Troy,
And our great deeds, as half-forgotten things.
Is there confusion in the little isle?
Let what is broken so remain.
The Gods are hard to reconcile:
'Tis hard to settle once again.
There is confusion worse than death,
Trouble on trouble, pain on pain,
Long labour unto aged breath,
Sore task to hearts worn out with many wars
And eyes grown dim with gazing on the pilot-stars.

7

But, propt on beds of amaranth and moly
How sweet (while warm airs lull us, blowing lowly)
With half-dropt eyelids still,
Beneath a heaven dark and holy,
To watch the long bright river drawing slowly
His waters from the purple hill—
To hear the dewy echoes calling
From cave to cave thro' the thick-twined vine—
To watch the emerald-colour'd water falling
Thro' many a wov'n acanthus-wreath divine!
Only to hear and see the far-off sparkling brine,
Only to hear were sweet, stretch'd out beneath the pine.

8

The Lotos blooms below the barren peak:
The Lotos blows by every winding creek:
All day the wind breathes low with mellower tone:
Thro' every hollow cave and alley lone
Round and round the spicy downs the yellow Lotos-dust is blown.
We have had enough of action, and of motion we,
Roll'd to starboard, roll'd to larboard, when the surge was seething
free,
Where the wallowing monster spouted his foam-fountains in the
sea.
Let us swear an oath, and keep it with an equal mind,
In the hollow Lotos-land to live and lie reclined
On the hills like Gods together, careless of mankind.
For they lie beside their nectar, and the bolts are hurl'd
Far below them in the valleys, and the clouds are lightly curl'd
Round their golden houses, girdled with the gleaming world:
Where they smile in secret, looking over wasted lands,
Blight and famine, plague and earthquake, roaring deeps and fiery
sands,
Clanging fights, and flaming towns, and sinking ships, and praying
hands.
But they smile, they find a music centred in a doleful song
Steaming up, a lamentation and an ancient tale of wrong,
Like a tale of little meaning tho' the words are strong;

Chanted from an ill-used race of men that cleave the soil,
Sow the seed, and reap the harvest with enduring toil,
Storing yearly little dues of wheat, and wine and oil;
Till they perish and they suffer—some, 'tis whispered—down in
    hell
Suffer endless anguish, others in Elysian valleys dwell,
Resting weary limbs at last on beds of asphodel.
Surely, surely, slumber is more sweet than toil, the shore
Than labour in the deep mid-ocean, wind and wave and oar;
Oh rest ye, brother mariners, we will not wander more.

about 1830–53   ALFRED, LORD TENNYSON

148. Now sleeps the crimson petal . . .

Now sleeps the crimson petal, now the white;
Nor waves the cypress in the palace walk;
Nor winks the gold fin in the porphyry font:
The fire-fly wakens: waken thou with me.

Now droops the milk-white peacock like a ghost,
And like a ghost she glimmers on to me.

Now lies the Earth all Danaë to the stars,
And all thy heart lies open unto me.

Now slides the silent meteor on, and leaves
A shining furrow, as thy thoughts in me.

Now folds the lily all her sweetness up,
And slips into the bosom of the lake:
So fold thyself, my dearest, thou, and slip
Into my bosom and be lost in me.

about 1845   ALFRED, LORD TENNYSON

149. Come down, O maid . . .

COME down, O maid, from yonder mountain height:
What pleasure lives in height (the shepherd sang)
In height and cold, the splendour of the hills?
But cease to move so near the Heavens, and cease
To glide a sunbeam by the blasted Pine,
To sit a star upon the sparkling spire;
And come, for Love is of the valley, come,
For Love is of the valley, come thou down
And find him; by the happy threshold, he,
Or hand in hand with Plenty in the maize,
Or red with spirted purple of the vats
Or foxlike in the vine; nor cares to walk
With Death and Morning on the Silver Horns,
Nor wilt thou snare him in the white ravine,
Nor find him dropt upon the firths of ice,
That huddling slant in furrow-cloven falls
To roll the torrent out of dusky doors:
But follow; let the torrent dance thee down
To find him in the valley; let the wild
Lean-headed Eagles yelp alone, and leave
The monstrous ledges there to slope, and spill
Their thousand wreaths of dangling water-smoke,
That like a broken purpose waste in air:
So waste not thou; but come; for all the vales
Await thee; azure pillars of the hearth
Arise to thee; the children call, and I
Thy shepherd pipe, and sweet is every sound,
Sweeter thy voice, but every sound is sweet;
Myriads of rivulets hurrying thro' the lawn,
The moan of doves in immemorial elms,
And murmuring of innumerable bees.

about 1845   ALFRED, LORD TENNYSON

The Sacred Fire

150. Œnone

THERE lies a vale in Ida, lovelier
Than all the valleys of Ionian hills.
The swimming vapour slopes athwart the glen,
Puts forth an arm, and creeps from pine to pine,
And loiters, slowly drawn.   On either hand
The lawns and meadow-ledges midway down
Hang rich in flowers, and far below them roars
The long brook falling thro' the clov'n ravine
In cataract after cataract to the sea.
Behind the valley topmost Gargarus
Stands up and takes the morning: but in front
The gorges, opening wide apart, reveal
Troas and Ilion's column'd citadel,
The crown of Troas.

              Hither came at noon
Mournful Œnone, wandering forlorn
Of Paris, once her playmate on the hills.
Her cheek had lost the rose, and round her neck
Floated her hair or seem'd to float in rest.
She, leaning on a fragment twined with vine,
Sang to the stillness, till the mountain shade
Sloped downward to her seat from the upper cliff.

"O mother Ida, many-fountain'd Ida,
Dear mother Ida, harken ere I die.
For now the noonday quiet holds the hill:
The grasshopper is silent in the grass:
The lizard, with his shadow on the stone,
Rests like a shadow, and the cicala sleeps.
The purple flowers droop: the golden bee
Is lily-cradled: I alone awake.
My eyes are full of tears, my heart of love,
My heart is breaking, and my eyes are dim,
And I am all aweary of my life.

"O mother Ida, many-fountain'd Ida,
Dear mother Ida, hearken ere I die.

Hear me O Earth, hear me O Hills, O caves
That house the cold crown'd snake! O mountain brooks,
I am the daughter of a River-God,
Hear me, for I will speak, and build up all
My sorrow with my song, as yonder walls
Rose slowly to a music slowly breathed,
A cloud that gather'd shape: for it may be
That, while I speak of it, a little while,
My heart may wander from its deeper woe.

"O mother Ida, many-fountain'd Ida,
Dear mother Ida, harken ere I die.
I waited underneath the dawning hills,
Aloft the mountain lawn was dewy-dark,
And dewy-dark aloft the mountain pine:
Beautiful Paris, evil-hearted Paris
Leading a jet-black goat white-horn'd, white-hooved,
Came up from reedy Simois all alone.

"O mother Ida, harken ere I die.
Far-off the torrent call'd me from the cleft:
Far up the solitary morning smote
The streaks of virgin snow.   With down-dropt eyes
I sat alone: white-breasted like a star
Fronting the dawn he moved; a leopard skin
Droop'd from his shoulder, but his sunny hair
Cluster'd about his temples like a God's;
And his cheek brighten'd as the foam-bow brightens
When the wind blows the foam, and all my heart
Went forth to embrace him coming ere he came.

"Dear mother Ida, harken ere I die.
He smiled, and opening out his milk-white palm
Disclosed a fruit of pure Hesperian gold,
That smelt ambrosially, and while I look'd
And listen'd, the full-flowing river of speech
Came down upon my heart.
                              " 'My own Œnone,
Beautiful-brow'd Œnone, my own soul,

Behold this fruit, whose gleaming rind ingrav'n
"For the most fair," would seem to award it thine,
As lovelier than whatever Oread haunt
The knolls of Ida, loveliest in all grace
Of movement, and the charm of married brows.'

   "Dear mother Ida, harken ere I die.
He prest the blossom of his lips to mine,
And added 'This was cast upon the board,
When all the full-faced presence of the Gods
Ranged in the halls of Peleus; whereupon
Rose feud, with question unto whom 'twere due:
But light-foot Iris brought it yester-eve,
Delivering, that to me, by common voice
Elected umpire, Herè comes to-day,
Pallas and Aphrodite, claiming each
This meed of fairest.   Thou, within the cave
Behind yon whispering tuft of oldest pine,
Mayst well behold them unbeheld, unheard
Hear all, and see thy Paris judge of Gods.'

   "Dear mother Ida, harken ere I die.
It was the deep midnoon: one silvery cloud
Had lost his way between the piney sides
Of this long glen.   Then to the bower they came,
Naked they came to that smooth-swarded bower,
And at their feet the crocus brake like fire,
Violet, amaracus, and asphodel,
Lotos and lilies: and a wind arose,
And overhead the wandering ivy and vine,
This way and that, in many a wild festoon
Ran riot, garlanding the gnarled boughs
With bunch and berry and flower thro' and thro'.

   "O mother Ida, harken ere I die.
On the tree-tops a crested peacock lit,
And o'er him flow'd a golden cloud, and lean'd
Upon him, slowly dropping fragrant dew.
Then first I heard the voice of her, to whom

Coming thro' Heaven, like a light that grows
Larger and clearer, with one mind the Gods
Rise up for reverence.   She to Paris made
Proffer of royal power, ample rule
Unquestion'd, overflowing revenue
Wherewith to embellish state, 'from many a vale
And river-sunder'd champaign clothed with corn,
Or labour'd mines undrainable of ore.
Honour,' she said, 'and homage, tax and toll,
From many an inland town and haven large,
Mast-throng'd beneath her shadowing citadel
In glassy bays among her tallest towers.'

"O mother Ida, harken ere I die.
Still she spake on and still she spake of power,
'Which in all action is the end of all;
Power fitted to the season; wisdom-bred
And throned of wisdom—from all neighbour crowns
Alliance and allegiance, till thy hand
Fail from the sceptre-staff.   Such boon from me,
From me, Heaven's Queen, Paris, to thee king-born,
A shepherd all thy life but yet king-born,
Should come most welcome, seeing men, in power
Only, are likest gods, who have attain'd
Rest in a happy place and quiet seats
Above the thunder, with undying bliss
In knowledge of their own supremacy.'

"Dear mother Ida, harken ere I die.
She ceased, and Paris held the costly fruit
Out at arm's-length, so much the thought of power
Flatter'd his spirit; but Pallas where she stood
Somewhat apart, her clear and bared limbs
O'erthwarted with the brazen-headed spear
Upon her pearly shoulder leaning cold,
The while, above, her full and earnest eye
Over her snow-cold breast and angry cheek
Kept watch, waiting decision, made reply.

The Sacred Fire

" 'Self-reverence, self-knowledge, self-control,
These three alone lead life to sovereign power.
Yet not for power, (power of herself
Would come uncall'd for) but to live by law,
Acting the law we live by without fear;
And, because right is right, to follow right
Were wisdom in the scorn of consequence.

"Dear mother Ida, harken ere I die.
Again she said: 'I woo thee not with gifts.
Sequel of guerdon could not alter me
To fairer.   Judge thou me by what I am,
So shalt thou find me fairest.
                Yet, indeed,
If gazing on divinity disrobed
Thy mortal eyes are frail to judge of fair,
Unbiass'd by self-profit, oh! rest thee sure
That I shall love thee well and cleave to thee,
So that my vigour, wedded to thy blood,
Shall strike within thy pulses, like a God's,
To push thee forward thro' a life of shocks,
Dangers, and deeds, until endurance grow
Sinew'd with action, and the full-grown will,
Circled thro' all experiences, pure law,
Commeasure perfect freedom.'
                "Here she ceased,
And Paris ponder'd, and I cried, 'O Paris,
Give it to Pallas!' but he heard me not,
Or hearing would not hear me, woe is me!

"O mother Ida, many-fountain'd Ida,
Dear mother Ida, harken ere I die.
Idalian Aphrodite beautiful,
Fresh as the foam, new-bathed in Paphian wells,
With rosy slender fingers backward drew
From her warm brows and bosom her deep hair
Ambrosial, golden round her lucid throat
And shoulder: from the violets her light foot

Shone rosy-white, and o'er her rounded form
Between the shadows of the vine-bunches
Floated the glowing sunlights, as she moved.

"Dear mother Ida, harken ere I die.
She with a subtle smile in her mild eyes,
The herald of her triumph, drawing nigh
Half-whisper'd in his ear, 'I promise thee
The fairest and most loving wife in Greece.'
She spoke and laugh'd: I shut my sight for fear:
But when I look'd, Paris had raised his arm,
And I beheld great Heré's angry eyes,
As she withdrew into the golden cloud,
And I was left alone within the bower;
And from that time to this I am alone,
And I shall be alone until I die.

"Yet, mother Ida, harken ere I die.
Fairest—why fairest wife? am I not fair?
My love has told me so a thousand times.
Methinks I must be fair, for yesterday,
When I past by, a wild and wanton pard,
Eyed like the evening star, with playful tail
Crouch'd fawning in the weed.   Most loving is she?
Ah me, my mountain shepherd, that my arms
Were wound about thee, and my hot lips prest
Close, close to thine in that quick-falling dew
Of fruitful kisses, thick as Autumn rains
Flash in the pools of whirling Simois.

"O mother, hear me yet before I die.
They came, they cut away my tallest pines,
My dark tall pines, that plumed the craggy ledge
High over the blue gorge, and all between
The snowy peak and snow-white cataract
Foster'd the callow eaglet—from beneath
Whose thick mysterious boughs in the dark morn
The panther's roar came muffled, while I sat
Low in the valley.   Never, never more

The Sacred Fire

Shall lone Œnone see the morning mist
Sweep thro' them; never see them overlaid
With narrow moon-lit slips of silver cloud,
Between the loud stream and the trembling stars.

"O mother, hear me yet before I die.
I wish that somewhere in the ruin'd folds,
Among the fragments tumbled from the glens,
Or the dry thickets, I could meet with her,
The abominable, that uninvited came
Into the fair Peleïan banquet-hall,
And cast the golden fruit upon the board,
And bred this change; that I might speak my mind,
And tell her to her face how much I hate
Her presence, hated both of Gods and men.

"O mother, hear me yet before I die.
Hath he not sworn his love a thousand times,
In this green valley, under this green hill,
Ev'n on this hand, and sitting on this stone?
Seal'd it with kisses? water'd it with tears?
O happy tears, and how unlike to these!
O happy Heaven, how canst thou see my face?
O happy earth, how canst thou bear my weight?
O death, death, death, thou ever-floating cloud,
There are enough unhappy on this earth,
Pass by the happy souls, that love to live:
I pray thee, pass before my light of life,
And shadow all my soul, that I may die.
Thou weighest heavy on the heart within,
Weigh heavy on my eyelids: let me die.

"O mother, hear me yet before I die.
I will not die alone, for fiery thoughts
Do shape themselves within me, more and more,
Whereof I catch the issue, as I hear
Dead sounds at night come from the inmost hills,
Like footsteps upon wool.   I dimly see
My far-off doubtful purpose, as a mother

- 346 -

Conjectures of the features of her child
Ere it is born: her child!—a shudder comes
Across me: never child be born of me,
Unblest, to vex me with his father's eyes!

    "O mother, hear me yet before I die.
Hear me, O earth.   I will not die alone,
Lest their shrill happy laughter come to me
Walking the cold and starless road of Death
Uncomforted, leaving my ancient love
With the Greek woman.   I will rise and go
Down into Troy, and ere the stars come forth
Talk with the wild Cassandra, for she says
A fire dances before her, and a sound
Rings ever in her ears of armed men.
What this may be I know not, but I know
That, whereso'er I am by night and day,
All earth and air seem only burning fire."

about 1850   ALFRED, LORD TENNYSON

151. *from* In Memoriam (A. H. H.)

RISEST thou thus, dim dawn, again,
    So loud with voices of the birds,
    So thick with lowings of the herds,
Day, when I lost the flower of men;

Who tremblest thro' thy darkling red
    On yon swoll'n brook that bubbles fast
    By meadows breathing of the past,
And woodlands holy to the dead;

Who murmurest in the foliaged eaves
    A song that slights the coming care,
    And Autumn laying here and there
A fiery finger on the leaves;

The Sacred Fire

Who wakenest with thy balmy breath
   To myriads on the genial earth,
   Memories of bridal, or of birth,
And unto myriads more of death.

O, wheresoever those may be,
   Betwixt the slumber of the poles,
   To-day they count as kindred souls;
They know me not, but mourn with me

       *   *   *

I wake, I rise: from end to end
   Of all the landscape underneath,
   I find no place that does not breathe
Some gracious memory of my friend;

No gray old grange, or lonely fold,
   Or low morass and whispering reed,
   Or simple stile from mead to mead,
Or sheepwalk up the windy wold;

Nor hoary knoll of ash and haw
   That hears the latest linnet trill,
   Nor quarry trench'd along the hill,
And haunted by the wrangling daw;

Nor runlet tinkling from the rock;
   Nor pastoral rivulet that swerves
   To left and right thro' meadowy curves,
That feed the mothers of the flock;

But each has pleased a kindred eye,
   And each reflects a kindlier day;
   And, leaving these, to pass away,
I think once more he seems to die.

       *   *   *

Unwatch'd the garden bough shall sway,
   The tender blossom flutter down,
   Unloved that beech will gather brown,
This maple burn itself away;

Unloved, the sunflower, shining fair,
   Ray round with flames her disk of seed,
   And many a rose-carnation feed
With summer spice the humming air;

Unloved, by many a sandy bar,
   The brook shall babble down the plain,
   At noon or when the lesser wain
Is twisting round the polar star;

Uncared for, gird the windy grove,
   And flood the haunts of hern and crake;
   Or into silver arrows break
The sailing moon in creek and cove;

Till from the garden and the wild
   A fresh association blow,
   And year by year the landscape grow
Familiar to the stranger's child;

As year by year the labourer tills
   His wonted glebe, or lops the glades;
   And year by year our memory fades
From all the circle of the hills.

*   *   *

Now fades the last long streak of snow,
   Now burgeons every maze of quick
   About the flowering squares and thick
By ashen roots the violets blow.

Now rings the woodland loud and long,
   The distance takes a lovelier hue,
   And drown'd in yonder living blue
The lark becomes a sightless song.

Now dance the lights on lawn and lea,
   The flocks are whiter down the vale,
   And milkier every milky sail
On winding stream or distant sea;

The Sacred Fire

Where now the seamew pipes, or dives
   In yonder greening gleam, and fly
   The happy birds, that change their sky
To build and brood; that live their lives

From land to land; and in my breast
   Spring wakens too; and my regret
   Becomes an April violet,
And buds and blossoms like the rest.

     *   *   *

And rise, O moon, from yonder down,
   Till over down and over dale
   All night the shining vapour sail
And pass the silent-lighted town,

The white-faced halls, the glancing rills,
   And catch at every mountain head,
   And o'er the friths that branch and spread
Their sleeping silver thro' the hills;

And touch with shade the bridal doors
   With tender gloom the roof, the wall;
   And breaking let the splendour fall
To spangle all the happy shores

By which they rest, and ocean sounds,
   And, star and system rolling past,
   A soul shall draw from out the vast
And strike his being into bounds,

And, moved thro' life of lower phase,
   Result in man, be born and think
   And act and love, a closer link
Betwixt us and the crowning race

Of those that, eye to eye, shall look
   On knowledge; under whose command
   Is Earth and Earth's, and in their hand
Is Nature like an open book;

No longer half akin to brute,
    For all we thought and loved and did,
    And hoped, and suffer'd, is but seed
Of what in them is flower and fruit;

Whereof the man, that with me trod
    This planet, was a noble type
    Appearing ere the times were ripe,
That friend of mine who lives in God,

That God, which ever lives and loves,
    One God, one law, one element,
    And one far-off divine event,
To which the whole creation moves.

about 1835 to 1850   ALFRED, LORD TENNYSON

152. *from* The Strayed Reveller

THE Gods are happy.
They turn on all sides
Their shining eyes:
And see, below them,
The Earth, and men.

They see Tiresias
Sitting, staff in hand,
    On the warm, grassy
    Asopus' bank:
His robe drawn over
His old, sightless head:
    Revolving inly
    The doom of Thebes.

They see the Centaurs
In the upper glens
Of Pelion, in the streams,
Where red-berried ashes fringe
The clear-brown shallow pools;

With streaming flanks, and heads
Rear'd proudly, snuffing
The mountain wind.

They see the Indian
Drifting, knife in hand,
His frail boat moor'd to
A floating isle thick matted
With large-leav'd, low-creeping melon-plants,
And the dark cucumber.
    He reaps and stows them,
Drifting—drifting:—round him,
Round his green harvest-plot,
Flow the cool lake-waves:
The mountains ring them.

They see the Scythian
On the wide Stepp, unharnessing
His wheel'd house at noon.
He tethers his beast down, and makes his meal,
Mare's milk, and bread
Baked on the embers:—all around
The boundless waving grass-plains stretch, thick-starr'd
With saffron and the yellow hollyhock
And flag-leav'd iris-flowers.
    Sitting in his cart
He makes his meal: before him, for long miles,
Alive with bright green lizards,
And the springing bustard fowl,
The track, a straight black line,
Furrows the rich soil: here and there
Clusters of lonely mounds
Topp'd with rough-hewn,
Gray, rain-blear'd statues, overpeer
The sunny Waste.

They see the Ferry
On the broad, clay-laden
Lone Chorasmian stream: thereon
With snort and strain,

Two horses, strongly swimming, tow
The ferry-boat, with woven ropes
    To either bow
Firm-harness'd by the mane:—a Chief,
    With shout and shaken spear
Stands at the prow, and guides them: but astern,
    The cowering Merchants, in long robes,
      Sit pale beside their wealth
Of silk-bales and of balsam-drops,
      Of gold and ivory,
Of torquoise earth and amethyst,
    Jasper and chalcedony,
And milk-barr'd onyx stones.
The loaded boat swings groaning
    In the yellow eddies.
      The Gods behold them.

They see the Heroes
Sitting in the dark ship
On the foamless, long-heaving,
    Violet sea:
At sunset nearing
The Happy Islands.

These things, Ulysses,
The wise Bards also
Behold and sing.
But oh, what labour!
  O Prince, what pain!
  They too can see
Tiresias:—but the Gods,
Who gave them vision,
Added this law:
That they should bear too
    His groping blindness,
    His dark foreboding,
    His scorn'd white hairs.
    Bear Hera's anger
    Through a life lengthen'd
    To seven ages.

The Sacred Fire

They see the Centaurs
  On Pelion:—then they feel,
 They too, the maddening wine
Swell their large veins to bursting: in wild pain
  They feel the biting spears
Of the grim Lapithæ, and Theseus, drive,
Drive crashing through their bones: they feel
High on a jutting rock in the red stream
  Alcmena's dreadful son
  Ply his bow:—such a price
    The Gods exact for song;
  To become what we sing.

They see the Indian
  On his mountain lake:—but squalls
 Make their skiff reel, and worms
In the unkind spring have gnaw'd
Their melon-harvest to the heart: They see
  The Scythian:—but long frosts
Parch them in winter-time on the bare Stepp,
Till they too fade like grass: they crawl
  Like shadows forth in spring.

They see the Merchants
  On the Oxus' stream:—but care
Must visit first them too, and make them pale.
  Whether, through whirling sand,
A cloud of desert robber-horse has burst
Upon their caravan: or greedy kings,
In the wall'd cities the way passes through,
  Crush'd them with tolls: or fever-airs,
    On some great river's marge,
    Mown them down, far from home.

They see the Heroes
  Near harbour:—but they share
Their lives, and former violent toil, in Thebes,

Seven-gated Thebes, or Troy
Or where the echoing oars
Of Argo, first
Startled the unknown Sea.

The old Silenus
Came, lolling in the sunshine,
From the dewy forest coverts,
This way, at noon.
Sitting by me, while his Fauns
Down at the water side
Sprinkled and smooth'd
His drooping garland,
He told me these things.

But I, Ulysses
Sitting on the warm steps,
Looking over the valley,
All day long, have seen,
Without pain, without labour,
Sometimes a wild-hair'd Mænad;
Sometimes a Faun with torches;
And sometimes, for a moment,
Passing through the dark stems
Flowing-rob'd—the belov'd,
The desir'd, the divine,
Belov'd Iacchus.

Ah cool night-wind, tremulous stars!
Ah glimmering water—
Fitful earth-murmur—
Dreaming woods!
Ah golden-hair'd, strangely smiling Goddess,
And thou, prov'd, much enduring,
Wave-toss'd Wanderer!
Who can stand still?
Ye fade, ye swim, ye waver before me.
The cup again!

Faster, faster,
O Circe, Goddess,
Let the wild thronging train,
The bright procession
Of eddying forms,
Sweep through my soul!

about 1845–50   MATTHEW ARNOLD

153. *from* Empedocles on Etna

FULNESS of life and power of feeling, ye
Are for the happy, for the souls at ease,
Who dwell on a firm basis of content!—
But he, who has outliv'd his prosperous days,
But he, whose youth fell on a different world
From that on which his exil'd age is thrown,
Whose mind was fed on other food, was train'd
By other rules than are in vogue to-day;
Whose habit of thought is fix'd, who will not change,
But in a world he loves not must subsist
In ceaseless opposition, be the guard
Of his own breast, fetter'd to what he guards,
That the world win no mastery over him;
Who has no friend, no fellow left, not one;
Who has no minute's breathing space allow'd
To nurse his dwindling faculty of joy—
Joy and the outward world must die to him,
As they are dead to me!

And you, ye stars!
Who slowly begin to marshal,
As of old, in the fields of heaven,
Your distant melancholy lines!
Have you, too, survived yourselves?
Are you, too, what I fear to become?
You too once lived—
You too moved joyfully
Among august companions

In an older world, peopled by Gods,
In a mightier order,
The radiant, rejoicing, intelligent Sons of Heaven!
But now, you kindle
Your lonely, cold-shining lights,
Unwilling lingerers
In the heavenly wilderness,
For a younger, ignoble world;
And renew, by necessity,
Night after night your courses,
In echoing unnear'd silence,
Above a race you know not.
Uncaring and undelighted,
Without friend and without home;
Weary like us, though not
Weary with our weariness.

No, no, ye stars! there is no death with you,
No languor, no decay!   Languor and death,
They are with me, not you!   Ye are alive!
Ye and the pure dark ether where ye ride
Brilliant above me!   And thou, fiery world,
That sapp'st the vitals of this terrible mount
Upon whose charr'd and quaking crust I stand,
Thou, too, brimmest with life;—the sea of cloud
That heaves its white and billowy vapours up
To moat this isle of ashes from the world,
Lives!—and that other fainter sea, far down,
O'er whose lit floor a road of moonbeams leads
To Etna's Liparëan sister fires
And the long dusky line of Italy—
That mild and luminous floor of waters lives,
With held-in joy swelling its heart!—I only,
Whose spring of hope is dried, whose spirit has fail'd—
I, who have not, like these, in solitude
Maintain'd courage and force, and in myself,
Nurs'd an immortal vigour—I alone
Am dead to life and joy; therefore I read
In all things my own deadness.

Oh, that I could glow like this mountain!
Oh, that my heart bounded with the swell of the sea!
Oh, that my soul were full of light as the stars!
Oh, that it brooded over the world like the air!

But no, this heart will glow no more: thou art
A living man no more, Empedocles!
Nothing but a devouring flame of thought—
But a naked, eternally restless mind.

about 1850   MATTHEW ARNOLD

154. *from* Bishop Blougram's Apology

No more wine? then we'll push back chairs and talk.
A final glass for me, tho': cool, i' faith!
We ought to have our Abbey back, you see.
It's different, preaching in basilicas,
And doing duty in some masterpiece
Like this of brother Pugin's, bless his heart!
I doubt if they're half baked, those chalk rosettes,
Ciphers and stucco-twiddlings everywhere;
It's just like breathing in a lime-kiln: eh?
Those hot long ceremonies of our church
Cost us a little—oh, they pay the price,
You take me—amply pay it!   Now we'll talk.

So you despise me, Mr. Gigadibs.
No deprecation,—nay, I beg you, sir!
Besides, 'tis our engagement: don't you know,
I promised, if you'd watch a dinner out,
We'd see truth dawn together? truth that peeps
Over the glass's edge when dinner's done,
The body gets its sop and holds its noise
And leaves the soul free a little.   Now's the time—
'Tis break of day!   You do despise me then.
If I say, "despise me",—never fear—
I know you do not in a certain sense—
Not in my arm-chair, for example: here,
I well imagine you respect my place

(*Status, entourage*, worldly circumstance)
Quite to its value—very much indeed
—Are up to the protesting eyes of you
In pride at being seated here for once—
You'll turn it to such capital account!
When somebody, through years and years to come,
Hints of the bishop,—names me—that's enough—
"Blougram?—I knew him"—(into it you slide)
"Dined with him once, a Corpus Christi Day,
All alone, we two—he's a clever man—
And after dinner,—why, the wine you know,—
Oh, there was wine, and good!—What with the wine . . .
'Faith, we began upon all sorts of talk!
He's no bad fellow, Blougram—he had seen
Something of mine he relished—some review—
He's quite above their humbug in his heart,
Half-said as much, indeed—the thing's his trade—
I warrant, Blougram's sceptical at times—
How otherwise?   I liked him, I confess!"
Che che, my dear sir, as we say at Rome,
Don't you protest now!   It's fair give and take;
You have had your turn and spoken your home-truths—
The hand's mine now, and here you follow suit.

Thus much conceded, still the first fact stays—
You do despise me; your ideal of life
Is not the bishop's—you would not be I—
You would like better to be Goethe, now,
Or Buonaparte—or, bless me, lower still,
Count D'Orsay,—so you did what you preferred,
Spoke as you thought, and, as you cannot help,
Believed or disbelieved, no matter what,
So long as on that point, whate'er it was,
You loosed your mind, were whole and sole yourself.
—That, my ideal never can include,
Upon that element of truth and worth
Never be based! for say they make me Pope—
(They can't—suppose it for our argument!)
Why, there I'm at my tether's end—I've reached

The Sacred Fire

My height, and not a height which pleases you.
It's like those eerie stories nurses tell,
Of how some actor played Death on a stage
With pasteboard crown, sham orb, and tinselled dart,
And called himself the monarch of the world,
Then going in the tire-room afterward
Because the play was done, to shift himself,
Got touched upon the sleeve familiarly
The moment he had shut the closet door
By Death himself.   Thus God might touch a Pope
At unawares, ask what his baubles mean,
And whose part he presumed to play just now?
Best be yourself, imperial, plain and true!

So, drawing comfortable breath again,
You weigh and find whatever more or less
I boast of my ideal realised
Is nothing in the balance when opposed
To your ideal, your grand simple life,
Of which you will not realise one jot.
I am much, you are nothing; you would be all,
I would be merely much—you beat me there.

No, friend, you do not beat me,—hearken why!
The common problem, yours, mine, everyone's,
Is—not to fancy what were fair in life
Provided it could be,—but, finding first
What may be, then find how to make it fair,
Up to our means—a very different thing!
No abstract intellectual plan of life
Quite irrespective of life's plainest laws,
But one, a man, who is man and nothing more,
May lead within a world which (by your leave)
Is Rome or London—not Fool's-paradise.
Embellish Rome, idealise away.
Make paradise of London, if you can,
You're welcome, nay, you're wise.
                              A simile!
We mortals cross the ocean of this world

Each in his average cabin of a life—
The best's not big, the worst yields elbow-room.
Now for our six months' voyage—how prepare?
You come on shipboard with a landsman's list
Of things he calls convenient—so they are!
An India screen is pretty furniture,
A pianoforte is a fine resource,
All Balzac's novels occupy one shelf,
The new edition fifty volumes long;
And little Greek books with the funny type
They get up well at Leipsic, fill the next:
Go on! slabbed marble, what a bath it makes!
And Parma's pride, the Jerome, let us add!
'Twere pleasant could Correggio's fleeting glow
Hang full in face of one where'er one roams,
Since he more than the others brings with him
Italy's self,—the marvellous Modenese!
Yet 'twas not on your list before, perhaps.
Alas! friend, here's the agent . . . is't the name?
The captain, or whoever's master here—
You see him screw his face up; what's his cry
Ere you set foot on shipboard? "Six feet square!"
If you won't understand what six feet mean,
And if in pique because he overhauls
Your Jerome, piano and bath, you come on board
Bare—why you cut a figure at the first
While sympathetic landsmen see you off;
Not afterwards, when, long ere half seas o'er,
You peep up from your utterly naked boards
Into some snug and well-appointed berth
Like mine, for instance (try the cooler jug—
Put back the other, but don't jog the ice),
And mortified you mutter "Well and good—
He sits enjoying his sea-furniture—
'Tis stout and proper, and there's store of it,
Though I've the better notion, all agree,
Of fitting rooms up! Hang the carpenter,
Neat ship-shape fixings and contrivances—
I would have brought my Jerome, frame and all!"

The Sacred Fire

And meantime you bring nothing: never mind:
You've proved your artist-nature: what you don't,
You might bring, so despise me, as I say.

Now come, let's backward to the starting-place,
See my way: we're two college friends, suppose—
Prepare together for our voyage, then,
Each note and check the other in his work,—
Here's mine, a bishop's outfit; criticise!
What's wrong? why won't you be a bishop too?
Why first, you don't believe, you don't and can't
(Not statedly, that is, and fixedly
And absolutely and exclusively)
In any revelation called divine.
No dogmas nail your faith—and what remains
But say so, like the honest man you are?
First, therefore, overhaul theology!
Nay, I too, not a fool, you please to think,
Must find believing every whit as hard,
And if I do not frankly say as much,
The ugly consequence is clear enough.

Now, wait, my friend: well, I do not believe—
If you'll accept no faith that is not fixed,
Absolute and exclusive, as you say.
(You're wrong—I mean to prove it in due time)
Meanwhile, I know where difficulties lie
I could not, cannot solve, nor ever shall,
So give up hope accordingly to solve—
(To you, and over the wine). Our dogmas then
With both of us, tho' in unlike degree,
Missing full credence—overboard with them!
I mean to meet you on your own premise—
Good, there go mine in company with yours!

And now what are we? unbelievers both,
Calm and complete, determinately fixed
To-day, to-morrow and for ever, pray?

You'll guarantee me that? Not so, I think.
In no-wise! all we've gained is, that belief,
As unbelief before, shakes us by fits,
Confounds us like its predecessor. Where's
The gain? how can we guard our unbelief,
Make it bear fruit to us?—the problem here.
Just when we are safest, there's a sunset-touch,
A fancy from a flower-bell, some-one's death,
A chorus-ending from Euripides,—
And that's enough for fifty hopes and fears
As old and new at once as Nature's self,
To rap and knock and enter in our soul,
Take hands and dance there, a fantastic ring,
Round the ancient idol, on his base again,—
The grand Perhaps! We look on helplessly, —
There the old misgivings, crooked questions are—
This good God,—what he could do, if he would,
Would, if he could—then must have done long since:
If so, when, where, and how? Some way must be,—
Once feel about, and soon or late you hit
Some sense, in which it might be, after all.
Why not, "The Way, the Truth, the Life?"

                             —That way
Over the mountain, which who stands upon
Is apt to doubt if it's indeed a road;
While if he views it from the waste itself,
Up goes the line there, plain from base to brow,
Not vague, mistakable! what's a break or two
Seen from the unbroken desert either side?
And then (to bring in fresh philosophy)
What if the breaks themselves should prove at last
The most consummate contrivances
To train a man's eye, teach him what is faith?
And so we stumble at truth's very test!
All we have gained then by our unbelief
Is a life of doubt diversified by faith,
For one of faith diversified by doubt.
We called the chess-board white,—we call it black.

The Sacred Fire

Believe—and our whole argument breaks up.
Enthusiasm's the best thing, I repeat;
Only, we can't command it; fire and life
Are all, dead matter's nothing, we agree:
And be it a mad dream, or God's very breath,
The fact's the same,—belief's fire once in us,
Makes of all else mere stuff to show itself.
We penetrate our life with such a glow
As fire lends wood and iron—this turns steel,
That burns to ash—all's one, fire proves its power
For good or ill, since men call flare success.
But paint a fire, it will not therefore burn.
Light one in me, I'll find it food enough!
Why, to be Luther—that's a life to lead,
Incomparably better than my own.
He comes, reclaims God's earth for God, he says,
Sets up God's rule again by simple means,
Re-opens a shut book, and all is done.
He flared out in the flaring of mankind;
Such Luther's luck was—how shall such be mine?
If he succeeded nothing's left to do:
And if he did not altogether—well,
Strauss is the next advance.   All Strauss should be
I might be also.   But to what result?
He looks upon no future: Luther did.
What can I gain on the denying side?
Ice makes no conflagration.   State the facts,
Read the right text, emancipate the world—
The emancipated world enjoys itself
With scarce a thank-you—Blougram told it first
It could not owe a farthing,—not to him
More than St. Paul! 'twould press its pay, you think?
Then add there's still that plaguey hundredth chance—
Strauss may be wrong.   And so a risk is run—
For what gain? not for Luther's, who secured
A real heaven in his heart throughout his life,
Supposing death a little altered things!

"Ay, but since you really lack faith," you cry,

"You run the same risk really on all sides,
In cool indifference as bold unbelief.
As well be Strauss as swing 'twixt Paul and him.
It's not worth having, such imperfect faith,
Nor more available to do faith's work
Than unbelief like yours.   Whole faith or none!"

    Softly, my friend!   I must dispute that point.
Once own the use of faith, I'll find you faith.
We're back on Christian ground.   You call for faith:
I show you doubt, to prove that faith exists.
The more of doubt, the stronger faith I say,
If faith o'ercomes doubt.   How I know it does?
By life and man's free will, God gave for that!
To mould life as we choose it, shows our choice:
That's our one act, the previous work's His own.
You criticise the soil? it reared this tree—
This broad life and whatever fruit it bears!
What matter though I doubt at every pore,
Head-doubts, heart-doubts, doubts at my fingers' ends,
Doubts in the trivial work of every day,
Doubts at the very bases of my soul
In the grand moments when she probes herself—
If finally I have a life to show,
The thing I did, brought out in evidence
Against the thing done to me underground
By Hell and all its brood, for aught I know?
I say, whence sprang this? shows it faith or doubt?
All's doubt in me; where's break of faith in this?
It is the idea, the feeling and the love
God means mankind should strive for and show forth,
Whatever be the process to that end—
And not historic knowledge, logic sound,
And metaphysical acumen, sure!
"What think ye of Christ," friend? when all's done and said,
Like you this Christianity or not?
It may be false, but will you wish it true?
Has it your vote to be so if it can?
Trust you an instinct silenced long ago

The Sacred Fire

That will break silence and enjoin you love
What mortified philosophy is hoarse
And all in vain, with bidding you despise?
If you desire faith—then you've faith enough.
What else seeks God—nay, what else seek ourselves?
You form a notion of me, we'll suppose,
On hearsay; it's a favourable one:
"But still" (you add), "there was no such good man,
Because of the contradictions in the facts.
One proves, for instance, he was born in Rome,
This Blougram—yet throughout the tales of him
I see he figures as an Englishman."
Well, the two things are reconcileable.
But would I rather you discovered that,
Subjoining—"Still, what matter though they be?
Blougram concerns me nought, born here or there."

Pure faith indeed—you know not what you ask!
Naked belief in God the Omnipotent,
Omniscient, Omnipresent, sears too much
The sense of conscious creatures to be borne.
It were the seeing him, no flesh shall dare.
Some think, Creation's meant to show him forth:
I say, it's meant to hide him all it can,
And that's what all the blessed evil's for.
It's use in Time is to environ us,
Our breath, our drop of dew, with shield enough
Against that sight till we can bear its stress.
Under a vertical sun, the exposed brain
And lidless eye and disemprisoned heart
Less certainly would wither up at once
Than mind, confronted with the truth of Him.
But time and earth case-harden us to live;
The feeblest sense is trusted most; the child
Feels God a moment, ichors o'er the place,
Plays on and grows to be a man like us.
With me, faith means perpetual unbelief
Kept quiet like the snake 'neath Michael's foot
Who stands calm just because he feels it writhe.

Or, if that's too ambitious,—here's my box—
I need the excitation of a pinch
Threatening the torpor of the inside nose
Nigh on the imminent sneeze that never comes.
"Leave it in peace," advise the simple folk—
Make it aware of peace by itching fits,
Say I—let doubt occasion still more faith!

about 1850–55   ROBERT BROWNING

155. Mirage

THE hope I dreamed of was a dream,
    Was but a dream; and now I wake,
Exceeding comfortless, and worn, and old,
    For a dream's sake.

I hang my harp upon a tree,
    A weeping willow in a lake;
I hang my silent harp there, wrung and snapt
    For a dream's sake.

Lie still, lie still, my breaking heart;
    My silent heart, lie still and break:
Life, and the world, and mine own self, are changed
    For a dream's sake.

about 1860   CHRISTINA ROSSETTI

156. Up-hill

DOES the road wind up-hill all the way?
    Yes, to the very end.
Will the day's journey take the whole long day?
    From morn to night, my friend.

But is there for the night a resting-place?
    A roof for when the slow dark hours begin.
May not the darkness hide it from my face?
    You cannot miss that inn.

Shall I meet other wayfarers at night?
    Those who have gone before.
Then must I knock, or call when just in sight?
    They will not keep you standing at that door.

Shall I find comfort, travel-sore and weak?
    Of labour you shall find the sum.
Will there be beds for me and all who seek?
    Yea, beds for all who come.

about 1858   CHRISTINA ROSSETTI

157. The Wood-spurge

THE wind flapped loose, the wind was still,
Shaken out dead from tree and hill:
I had walked on at the wind's will,—
I sat now, for the wind was still.

Between my knees my forehead was,—
My lips drawn in, said not Alas!
My hair was over in the grass,
My naked ears heard the day pass.

My eyes, wide open, had the run
Of some ten weeds to fix upon;
Among those few, out of the sun,
The wood-spurge flowered, three cups in one

From perfect grief there need not be
Wisdom or even memory:
One thing then learnt remains to me,—
The wood-spurge has a cup of three.

about 1860–70   D. G. ROSSETTI

An Anthology

158. Sudden Light

I HAVE been here before,
   But when or how I cannot tell:
I know the grass beyond the door,
   The sweet keen smell,
The sighing sound, the lights around the shore.

You have been mine before,—
   How long ago I may not know:
But just when at that swallow's soar
   Your neck turned so,
Some veil did fall,—I knew it all of yore.

Then, now,—perchance again! . . .
   O round mine eyes your tresses shake!
Shall we not lie as we have lain
   Thus for Love's sake,
And sleep, and wake, yet never break the chain?

about 1860–70   D. G. ROSSETTI

159. Nuptial Sleep

AT length their long kiss severed with sweet smart:
   And as the last slow sudden drops are shed
   From sparkling eaves when all the storm has fled,
So singly flagged the pulses of each heart.
Their bosoms sundered, with the opening start
   Of married flowers to either side outspread
   From the knit stem; yet still their mouths, burnt red,
Fawned on each other where they lay apart.

Sleep sank them lower than the tide of dreams,
   And their dreams watched them sink, and slid away.
Slowly their souls swam up again, through gleams
   Of watered light and dull drowned waifs of day;
Till from some wonder of new woods and streams
   He woke, and wondered more. For there she lay.

about 1860–70   D. G. ROSSETTI

The Sacred Fire

160. Willowwood

O YE, all ye that walk in Willowwood,
    That walk with hollow faces burning white;
What fathom-depth of soul-struck widowhood,
    What long, what longer hours, one lifelong night,
Ere ye again, who so in vain have wooed
    Your last hope lost, who so in vain invite
Your lips to that their unforgotten food,
    Ere ye, ere ye again shall see the light!

Alas! the bitter banks in Willowwood,
    With tear-spurge wan, with blood-wort burning red:
Alas! if ever such a pillow could
    Steep deep the soul in sleep till she were dead.—
Better all life forget her than this thing,
That Willowwood should hold her wandering . . .!

about 1860–70   D. G. ROSSETTI

XVIII

William Morris

Robert Bridges

Gerard Manley Hopkins

George Meredith

161. Prologue to
The Earthly Paradise

Of Heaven or Hell I have no power to sing,
I cannot ease the burden of your fears,
Or make quick-coming death a little thing,
Or bring again the pleasure of past years.
Nor for my words shall ye forget your tears,
Or hope again for aught that I can say,
The idle singer of an empty day.

But rather, when aweary of your mirth,
From full hearts still unsatisfied ye sigh,
And, feeling kindly unto all the earth,
Grudge every minute as it passes by,
Made the more mindful that the sweet days die—
—Remember me a little then I pray,
The idle singer of an empty day.

The heavy trouble, the bewildering care
That weighs us down who live and earn our bread,
These idle verses have no power to bear;
So let me sing of names rememberèd,
Because they, living not, can ne'er be dead,
Or long time take their memory quite away
From us poor singers of an empty day.

Dreamer of dreams, born out of my due time,
Why should I strive to set the crooked straight?
Let it suffice me that my murmuring rhyme
Beats with light wing against the ivory gate,
Telling a tale not too importunate
To those who in the sleepy region stay,
Lulled by the singer of an empty day.

Folk say, a wizard to a northern king
At Christmas-tide such wondrous things did show,
That through one window men beheld the spring,

And through another saw the summer glow,
And through a third the fruited vines a-row,
While still, unheard, but in its wonted way,
Piped the drear wind of that December day.

    So with this Earthly Paradise it is,
If ye will read aright and pardon me,
Who strive to build a shadowy isle of bliss
Midmost the beating of the steely sea,
Where tossed about all hearts of men must be;
Whose ravening monsters mighty men shall slay,
Not the poor singer of an empty day.

about 1868–70   WILLIAM MORRIS

162. *from* Eros and Psyche

SHE took her then aside, and bade her heed
A heap of grains piled high upon the floor,
Millet and mustard, hemp and poppy seed,
And fern-bloom's undistinguishable spore,
All kinds of pulse, of grasses, and of spice,
Clover and linseed, rape, and corn, and rice,
Dodder, and sesame, and many more.

'Sort me these seeds' she said; 'it now is night,
I will return at morning; if I find
That thou hast separated all aright,
Each grain from other grain after its kind,
And set them in unmingl'd heaps apart,
Then shall thy wish be granted to thine heart.'
Whereat she turn'd, and closed the door behind.

A single lamp there stood beside the heap,
And shed thereon its mocking golden light;
Such as might tempt the weary eye to sleep
Rather than prick the nerve of taskèd sight.

Yet Psyche, not to fail for lack of zeal,
With good will sat her down to her ordeal,
Sorting the larger seeds as best she might.

When lo! upon the wall, a shadow past
Of doubtful shape, across the chamber dim
Moving with speed: and seeing nought that cast
The shade, she bent her down the flame to trim;
And there the beast itself, a little ant,
Climb'd up in compass of the lustre scant,
Upon the bowl of oil ran round the rim.

Smiling to see the creature of her fear
So dwarf'd by truth, she watcht him where he crept,
For mere distraction telling in his ear
What straits she then was in, and telling wept.
Whereat he stood and trim'd his horns; but ere
Her tale was done resumed his manner scare,
Ran down, and on his way in darkness kept.

But she intent drew forth with dextrous hand
The larger seeds, or push'd the smaller back,
Or light from heavy with her breathing fan'd.
When suddenly she saw the floor grow black,
And troops of ants, flowing in noiseless train,
Moved to the hill of seeds, as o'er a plain
Armies approach a city for attack;

And gathering on the grain, began to strive
With grappling horns; and each from out the heap
His burden drew, and all their motion live
Struggled and slid upon the surface steep.
And Psyche wonder'd, watching them, to find
The creatures separated kind from kind:
Till dizzied with the sight she fell asleep.

And when she woke 'twas with the morning sound
Of Aphrodite's anger at the door,
Whom high amaze stay'd backward, as she found
Her foe asleep with all her trouble o'er:

And round the room beheld, in order due,
The piles arranged distinct and sorted true,
Grain with grain, seed with seed, and spore with spore.

about 1885   ROBERT BRIDGES

163. North Wind in October

IN the golden glade the chestnuts are fallen all;
From the sered boughs of the oak the acorns fall:
The beech scatters her ruddy fire;
The lime hath stripped to the cold,
And standeth naked above her yellow attire:
The larch thinneth her spire
To lay the ways of the wood with cloth of gold.

Out of the golden-green and white
Of the brake the fir-trees stand upright
In the forest of flame, and wave aloft
To the blue of heaven their blue-green tuftings soft.

But swiftly in shuddering gloom the splendours fail,
As the harrying North-wind beareth
A cloud of skirmishing hail
The grievèd woodland to smite:
In a hurricane through the trees he teareth,
Raking the boughs and the leaves rending,
And whistleth to the descending
Blows of his icy flail.
Gold and snow he mixeth in spite,
And whirleth afar; as away on his winnowing flight
He passeth, and all again for awhile is bright.

about 1885–90   ROBERT BRIDGES

164. April, 1885

WANTON with long delay the gay spring leaping cometh;
The blackthorn starreth now his bough on the eve of May:
All day in the sweet box-tree the bee for pleasure hummeth:
The cuckoo sends afloat his note on the air all day.

Now dewy nights again and rain in gentle shower
At root of tree and flower have quenched the winter's drouth:
On high the hot sun smiles, and banks of cloud uptower
In bulging heads that crowd for miles the dazzling South.

about 1885   ROBERT BRIDGES

165. Pied Beauty

GLORY be to God for dappled things—
    For skies of couple-colour as a brinded cow;
        For rose-moles all in stipple upon trout that swim;
Fresh-firecoal chestnut-falls; finches' wings;
    Landscape plotted and pieced—fold, fallow, and plough;
        And all trades, their gear and tackle and trim.

All things counter, original, spare, strange;
    Whatever is fickle, freckled (who knows how?)
        With swift, slow; sweet, sour; adazzle, dim;
He fathers-forth whose beauty is past change:
                        Praise him.

about 1877   GERARD MANLEY HOPKINS

166. The Windhover:
To Christ our Lord

I CAUGHT this morning morning's minion, king-
    dom of daylight's dauphin, dapple-dawn-drawn Falcon, in his
        riding
Of the rolling level underneath him steady air, and striding
High there, how he rung upon the rein of a wimpling wing
In his ecstasy! then off, off forth on a swing,
    As a skate's heel sweeps smooth on a bow-bend: the hurl and
        gliding
Rebuffed the big wind.   My heart in hiding
Stirred for a bird,—the achieve of, the mastery of the thing!

Brute beauty and valour and act, oh, air, pride plume here
  Buckle! AND the fire that breaks from thee then, a billion
Times told lovelier, more dangerous, O my chevalier!

No wonder of it: shéer plód makes plough down sillion
Shine, and blue-bleak embers, ah my dear,
  Fall, gall themselves, and gash gold-vermilion.

about 1877–79   GERARD MANLEY HOPKINS

167. Harry Ploughman

HARD as hurdle arms, with a broth of goldish flue
Breathed round; the rack of ribs; the scooped flank; lank
Rope-over thigh; knee-nave; and barrelled shank—
    Head and foot, shoulder and shank—
By a grey eye's heed steered well, one crew, fall to;
Stand at stress. Each limb's barrowy brawn, his thew
That onewhere curded, onewhere sucked or sank—soared or
    sank—
Though as a beechbole firm, finds his, as at a roll-call, rank
And features, in flesh, what deed he each must do—
    His sinew-service where do.

He leans to it, Harry bends, look. Back, elbow and liquid waist
In him, all quail to the wallowing o' the plough: 's cheek crimsons;
    curls
Wag or crossbridle, in a wind lifted, windlaced—
  See his wind-lilylocks-laced;
Churlsgrace, too, child of Amansstrength, how it hangs or hurls
Them—broad in bluff hide his frowning feet lashed! raced
With, along them, cragiron under and cold furls—
    With-a-fountain's shining-shot furls.

about 1887   GERARD MANLEY HOPKINS

168. Seed-Time

FLOWERS of the willow-herb are wool;
Flowers of the briar berries red;
Speeding their seed as the breeze may rule
Flowers of the thistle loosen the thread.
Flowers of the clematis drip in beard,
Slack from the fir-tree youngly climbed;
Chaplets in air flies foliage seared;
Heeled upon earth lie clusters rimed.

Where were skies of the mantle stained
Orange and scarlet, a coat of frieze
Travels from North till day has waned,
Tattered, soaked in the ditch's dyes.
Tumbles the rook under grey or slate;
Else enfolding us damps to the bone;
Narrows the world to my neighbour's gate;
Paints me Life as a wheezy crone.

Now seems none but the spider lord;
Star in circle his web waits prey,
Silvering bush-mounds, blue brushing sward;
Slow runs the hour, swift flits the ray.
Now to his thread-shroud is he nigh,
Nigh to the tangle where wings are sealed,
He who frolicked the jewelled fly;
All is adroop on the down and the weald.

Mists more lone for the sheep-bell enwrap
Nights that tardily let slip a morn
Paler than moons, and on noontide's lap
Flame dies cold, like the rose late born.
Rose born late, born withered in bud!—
I, even I, for a zenith of sun
Cry, to fulfil me, nourish my blood:
O for a day of the long light, one!

The Sacred Fire

Master the blood, nor read by chills,
Earth admonishes: Hast thou ploughed,
Sown, reaped, harvested grain for the mills,
Thou hast the light over shadow of cloud.
Steadily eyeing, before that wail
Animal-infant, thy mind began,
Momently nearer me: should sight fail,
Plod in the track of the husbandman.

Verily now is our season of seed,
Now in our Autumn; and Earth discerns
Them that have served her in them that can read,
Glassing, where under the surface she burns,
Quick at her wheel, while the fuel, decay,
Brightens the fire of renewal; and we?
Death is the word of a bovine day,
Know you the breast of the springing To-be.

about 1888   GEORGE MEREDITH

XIX

Thomas Hardy

The Sacred Fire

169. I said to Love . . .

I SAID to Love,
"It is not now as in old days
When men adored thee and thy ways
        All else above;
Named thee the Boy, the Bright, the One
Who spread a heaven beneath the sun,"
        I said to Love.

I said to him,
"We now know more of thee than then:
We were but weak in judgement when,
        With hearts abrim,
We clamoured thee that thou would'st please
Inflict on us thine agonies,"
        I said to him.

I said to Love,
"Thou art not young, thou art not fair,
No elfin darts, no cherub air,
        Nor swan, nor dove
Are thine; but features pitiless,
And iron daggers of distress,"
        I said to Love.

"Depart then, Love! . . .
—Man's race shall perish, threatenest thou,
Without thy kindling coupling-vow?
The age to come the man of now
        Know nothing of?—
We fear not such a threat from thee;
We are too old in apathy!
Mankind shall cease.—So let it be,"
        I said to Love.

THOMAS HARDY

about 1900 or earlier

- 383 -

170. The Ghost of the Past

W<small>E</small> two kept house, the Past and I,
    The Past and I;
Through all my tasks it hovered nigh,
    Leaving me never alone.
It was a spectral housekeeping
    Where fell no jarring tone,
As strange, as still a housekeeping
    As ever has been known.

As daily I went up the stair
    And down the stair,
I did not mind the Bygone there—
    The Present once to me;
Its moving meek companionship
    I wished might ever be,
There was in that companionship
    Something of ecstasy.

It dwelt with me just as it was
    Just as it was
When first its prospects gave me pause
    In wayward wanderings,
Before the years had torn old troths
    As they tear all sweet things,
Before gaunt griefs had wrecked old troths
    And dulled old rapturings.

And then its form began to fade,
    Began to fade,
Its gentle echoes faintlier played
    At eves upon my ear
Than when the autumn's look embrowned
    The lonely chambers here,
The autumn's settling shades embrowned
    Nooks that it haunted near.

And so with time my vision less,
    Yea, less and less
Makes of that Past my housemistress,
    It dwindles in my eye;
It looms a far-off skeleton
    And not a comrade nigh,
A flitting fitful skeleton
    Dimming as days draw by.

THOMAS HARDY

about 1905 or earlier

171. I have lived with Shades . . .

I

I HAVE lived with Shades so long,
So long have talked to them,
Since from the forest's hem
I sped to street and throng,
    That sometimes they
    In their dim style
    Will pause awhile
    To hear my say;

II

And take me by the hand,
And lead me through their rooms
In the To-Be, where Dooms
Half-wove and shapeless stand:
    And show from there
    The dwindled dust
    And rot and rust
    Of things that were.

III

"Now turn," they said to me
One day: "Look whence we came,
And signify his name
Who gazes thence at thee"—

- 385 -

—"Nor name nor race
Know I, or can,"
I said, "Of man
So commonplace."

IV

"He moves me not at all:
I note no ray or jot
Of rareness in his lot,
Or star exceptional.
      Into the dim
      Dead throngs around
      He'll sink, nor sound
      Be left of him."

V

"Yet," said they, "his frail speech,
Hath accents pitched like thine—
Thy mould and his define
A likeness each to each—
      But go!   Deep pain
      Alas, would be
      His name to thee,
      And told in vain!"

1899   THOMAS HARDY

172. Thoughts of Phena
at news of her death

NOT a line of her writing have I,
      Not a thread of her hair,
No mark of her late time as dame in her dwelling, whereby
      I may picture her there;
      And in vain do I urge my unsight
      To conceive my lost prize
At her close, whom I knew when her dreams were upbrimming
            with light,
      And with laughter her eyes.

What scenes spread around her last days
    Sad, shining, or dim?
Did her gifts and compassions enray or enarch her sweet ways
    With an aureate nimb?
  Or did life-light decline from her years,
    And mischances control
Her full day-star; unease, or regret, or forebodings or fears
    Disennoble her soul?

  Thus do I but the phantom retain
    Of the maiden of yore
As my relic; yet haply the best of her—fined in my brain
    It may be the more
  That no line of her writing have I,
    Nor a thread of her hair,
No mark of her late time as dame in her dwelling, whereby
    I may picture her there.

1890
                    THOMAS HARDY

173. My spirit will not haunt the mound . . .

My spirit will not haunt the mound
    Above my breast,
But travel, memory-possessed,
To where my tremulous being found
    Life largest, best.

My phantom-footed shape will go
    When nightfall grays
Hither and thither along the ways
I and another used to know
    In backward days.

And there you'll find me, if a jot
    You still should care
For me, and for my curious air;
If otherwise, then I shall not,
    For you, be there.

                    THOMAS HARDY
    about 1910 or earlier

The Sacred Fire

174. In Tenebris

"Considerabam ad dexteram, et videbam; et non erat qui cognosceret me . . . Non est qui requirat animam meam." *Ps.* cxli.

WHEN the clouds' swoln bosoms echo back the shouts of the many and strong
That things are all as they best may be, save a few to be right ere long,
And my eyes have not the vision in them to discern what to these is so clear,
The blot seems straightway in me alone; one better he were not here.

The stout upstanders chime, All's well with us: ruers have nought to rue!
And what the potent so often say, can it fail to be somewhat true?
Breezily go they, breezily come; their dust smokes around their career,
Till I think I am one born out of due time, who has no calling here.

Their dawns bring lusty joys, it seems: their evenings all that is sweet;
Our times are blessed times, they cry: Life shapes it as is most meet,
And nothing is much the matter; there are many smiles to a tear;
Then what is the matter is I, I say. Why should such an one be here? . . .

Let him in whose ears the low-voiced Best is killed by the clash of the First,
Who holds that if way to the Better there be, it exacts a full look at the Worst,
Who feels that delight is a delicate growth cramped by crookedness, custom and fear,
Get him up and be gone as one shaped awry; he disturbs the order here.

1895–96   THOMAS HARDY

XX

The Sacred Fire

175. *from* An Anthem of Earth

WHAT is this Man, thy darling kissed and cuffed,
Thou lustingly engender'st,
To sweat, and make his brag, and rot,
Crowned with all honour and all shamefulness?
From nightly towers
He dogs the secret footsteps of the heavens,
Sifts in his hands the stars, weighs them as gold-dust,
And yet is he successive unto nothing
But patrimony of a little mould,
And entail of four planks.   Thou has made his mouth
Avid of all dominion and all mightiness,
All sorrow, all delight, all topless grandeurs,
All beauty, and all starry majesties,
And dim transtellar things;—even that it may,
Filled in the ending with a puff of dust,
Confess—"It is enough."   The world left empty
What that poor mouthful crams.   His heart is builded
For pride, for potency, infinity,
All heights, all deeps, and all immensities,
Arrased with purple like the house of kings,
To stall the grey-rat, and the carrion-worm
Statelily lodge.   Mother of mysteries!
Sayer of dark sayings in a thousand tongues,
Who bringest forth no saying yet so dark
As we ourselves, thy darkest! We the young,
In a little thought, in a little thought,
At last confront thee, and ourselves in thee,
And wake disgarmented of glory: as one
On a mount standing, and against him stands,
On the mount adverse, crowned with westering rays,
The golden sun, and they two brotherly
Gaze each on each;
He faring down
To the dull vale, his Godhead peels from him
Till he can scarcely spurn the pebble—
For nothingness of new-found mortality—
That mutinies against his gallèd foot.

The Sacred Fire

Littly he sets him to the daily way,
With all around the valleys growing grave,
And known things changed and strange; but he holds on,
Though all the land of light be widowèd,
In a little thought.

In a little dust, in a little dust,
Earth, thou reclaim'st us, who do all our lives
Find of thee but Egyptian villeinage.
Thou dost this body, this enhavocked realm,
Subject to ancient and ancestral shadows;
Descended passions sway it; it is distraught
With ghostly usurpation, dinned and fretted
With the still-tyrannous dead; a haunted tenement,
Peopled from barrows and outworn ossuaries.
Thou giv'st us life not half so willingly
As thou undost thy giving; thou that teem'st
The stealthy terror of the sinuous pard,
The lion maned with curlèd puissance,
The serpent, and all fair strong beasts of ravin,
Thyself most fair and potent beast of ravin;
And thy great eaters thou, the greatest, eat'st.
Thou hast devoured mammoth and mastodon,
And many a floating bank of fangs,
The scaly scourges of thy primal brine,
And the tower-crested plesiosaure.
Thou fill'st thy mouth with nations, gorgest slow
On purple æons of kings; man's hulking towers
Are carcase for thee, and to modern sun
Disglutt'st their splintered bones.
Rabble of Pharaohs and Arsacidæ
Keep their cold house within thee; thou has sucked down
How many Ninevehs and Hecatompyloi
And perished cities whose great phantasmata
O'erbrow the silent citizens of Dis:—
Hast not thy fill?
Tarry awhile, lean Earth, for thou shalt drink
Even till thy dull throat sicken,
The draught thou grow'st most fat on; hear'st thou not

The world's knives bickering in their sheaths?   O patience!
Much offal of a foul world comes thy way,
And man's superfluous cloud shall soon be laid
In a little blood.

In a little peace, in a little peace,
Thou dost rebate thy rigid purposes
Of imposed being, and relenting, mend'st,
Too much, with nought.   The westering Phœbus' horse
Paws i' the lucent dust as when he shocked
The East with rising; O how may I trace
In this decline that morning when we did
Sport 'twixt the claws of newly-whelped existence,
Which had not yet learned rending? we did then
Divinely stand, not knowing yet against us
Sentence had passed of life, nor commutation
Petitioning unto death.   What's he that of
The Free State argues?   Tellus! bid him stoop,
Even where the low *hic jacet* answers him;
Thus low, O Man! there's freedom's seignory,
Tellus' most reverend sole free commonweal,
And model deeply policied: there none
Stands on precedence, nor ambitiously
Woos the impartial worm, whose favours kiss
With liberal largesse all; there each is free
To be e'en what he must, which here did strive
So much to be he could not; there all do
Their uses just, with no flown questioning.
To be took by the hand of equal earth
They doff her livery, slip to the worm,
Which lacqueys them, their suits of maintenance,
And that soiled workaday apparel cast,
Put on condition: Death's ungentle buffet
Alone makes ceremonial manumission;
So are the heavenly statutes set and those
Uranian tables of the primal Law.
In a little peace, in a little peace,
Like fierce beasts that a common thirst makes brothers,
We draw together to one hid dark lake;

The Sacred Fire

In a little peace, in a little peace,
We drain with all our burdens of dishonour
Into the cleansing sands o' the thirsty grave.
The fiery pomps, brave exhalations,
And all the glistering shows o' the seeming world,
Which the sight aches at, we unwinking see
Through the smoked glass of Death; Death, wherewith's fined
The muddy wine of life; that earth doth purge
Of her plethora of man; Death, that doth flush
The cumbered gutters of humanity;
Nothing, of nothing king, with front uncrowned,
Whose hand holds crownets; playmate swart o' the strong;
Tenebrous moon that flux and refluence draws
Of the high-tided man; skull-housèd asp
That stings the heel of kings; true Fount of Youth,
Where he that dips is deathless; being's drone-pipe;
Whose nostril turns to blight the shrivelled stars,
And thicks the lusty breathing of the sun;
Pontifical Death, that doth the crevasse bridge
To the steep and frigid God; one mortal birth
That broker is of immortality.
Under this dreadful brother uterine,
This kinsman feared, Tellus, behold me come,
Thy son stern-nursed; who mortal-motherlike,
To turn thy weanlings' mouth averse, embitter'st
Thine over-childed breast.   Now mortal-sonlike
I thou hast suckled, Mother, I at last
Shall sustenant be to thee.   Here I untrammel,
Here I pluck loose the body's cerementing,
And break the tomb of life; here I shake off
The bur o' the world, man's congregation shun,
And to the antique order of the dead
I take the tongueless vows: my cell is set
Here in thy bosom; my little trouble is ended
In a little peace.

about 1894   FRANCIS THOMPSON

176. Nuns of the Perpetual Adoration

CALM, sad, secure; behind high convent walls,
  These watch the sacred lamp, these watch and pray:
And it is one with them when evening falls,
  And one with them the cold return of day.

These heed not time; their nights and days they make
  Into a long, returning rosary,
Whereon their lives are threaded for Christ's sake:
  Meekness and vigilance and chastity.

A vowed patrol, in silent companies,
  Life-long they keep before the living Christ.
In the dim church, their prayers and penances
  Are fragrant incense to the Sacrificed.

Outside, the world is wild and passionate;
  Man's weary laughter and his sick despair
Entreat at their impenetrable gate:
  They heed no voices in their dream of prayer.

They saw the glory of the world displayed:
  They saw the bitter of it and the sweet;
They knew the roses of the world should fade,
  And be trod under by the hurrying feet.

Therefore they rather put away desire,
  And crossed their hands and came to sanctuary
And veiled their heads and put on coarse attire:
  Because their comeliness was vanity.

And there they rest; they have serene insight
  Of the illuminating dawn to be;
Mary's sweet star dispels for them the night,
  The proper darkness of humanity.

Calm, sad, secure; with faces worn and mild:
　　Surely their choice of vigil is the best?
Yea! for our roses fade, the world is wild;
　　But there, beside the altar, there, is rest.

about 1895　　　　　　　　　　　　ERNEST DOWSON

177. The Garden of Shadow

LOVE heeds no more the sighing of the wind
Against the perfect flowers: thy garden's close
Is grown a wilderness, where none shall find
One strayed, last petal of one last year's rose.

O bright, bright hair!　O mouth like a ripe fruit!
Can famine be so nigh to harvesting?
Love, that was songful, with a broken lute
In grass of graveyards goeth murmuring.

Let the wind blow against the perfect flowers,
And all thy garden change and glow with spring:
Love is grown blind with no more count of hours
Nor part in seed-time nor in harvesting.

about 1895　　　　　　　　　　　　ERNEST DOWSON

178. Epigram

BECAUSE I am idolatrous and have besought,
With grievous supplication and consuming prayer,
The admirable image that my dreams have wrought
Out of her swan's neck and her dark, abundant hair:
The jealous gods, who brook no worship save their own,
Turned my live idol marble and her heart to stone.

about 1895　　　　　　　　　　　　ERNEST DOWSON

179. *from* A Shropshire Lad

WESTWARD on the high-hilled plains
    Where for me the world began,
Still, I think, in newer veins
    Frets the changeless blood of man.

Now that other lads than I
    Strip to bathe on Severn shore,
They, no help, for all they try,
    Tread the mill I trod before.

There, when hueless is the west,
    And the darkness hushes wide,
Where the lad lies down to rest
    Stands the troubled dream beside.

There, on thoughts that once were mine,
    Day looks down the eastern steep,
And the youth at morning shine
    Makes the vow he will not keep.

about 1895   A. E. HOUSMAN

180. The Immortal Part

WHEN I meet the morning beam,
Or lay me down at night to dream,
I hear my bones within me say,
"Another night, another day.

"When shall this slough of sense be cast,
This dust of thoughts be laid at last,
The man of flesh and soul be slain
And the man of bone remain?

"This tongue that talks, these lungs that shout;
These thews that hustle us about,
This brain that fills the skull with schemes,
And its humming hive of dreams,—

The Sacred Fire

"These to-day are proud in power
And lord it in their little hour:
The immortal bones obey control
Of dying flesh and dying soul.

" 'Tis long till eve and morn are gone:
Slow the endless night comes on,
And late to fulness grows the birth
That shall last as long as earth.

"Wanderers eastward, wanderers west,
Know you why you cannot rest?
'Tis that every mother's son
Travails with a skeleton.

"Lie down in the bed of dust;
Bear the fruit that bear you must;
Bring the eternal seed to light,
And morn is all the same as night.

"Rest you so from trouble sore,
Fear the heat o' the sun no more
Nor the snowing winter wild,
Now you labour not with child.

"Empty vessel, garment cast,
We that wore you long shall last.
—Another night, another day."
So my bones within me say.

Therefore they shall do my will
To-day while I am master still,
And flesh and soul, now both are strong,
Shall hale the sullen slaves along.

Before this fire of sense decay,
This smoke of thought blow clean away,
And leave with ancient night alone
The stedfast and enduring bone.

about 1895   A. E. HOUSMAN

181. *from* A Shropshire Lad

BRING, in this timeless grave to throw,
No cypress, sombre on the snow;
Snap not from the bitter yew
His leaves that live December through;
Break no rosemary, bright with rime
And sparkling to the winter clime;
Nor plod the winter land to look
For willows in the icy brook
To cast them leafless round him: bring
No spray that ever buds in spring.

But if the Christmas field has kept
Awns the last gleaner overstept,
Or shrivelled flax, whose flower is blue
A single season, never two;
Or if one haulm whose year is o'er
Shivers on the upland frore,
—Oh, bring from hill and stream and plain
Whatever will not flower again,
To give him comfort: he and those
Shall bide eternal bedfellows
Where low upon the couch he lies
Whence he never shall arise.

about 1895   A. E. HOUSMAN

182. *from* Marpessa

Marpessa, being given by Zeus her choice between the god Apollo and
Idas a mortal, chose Idas.

. . . As he was speaking, she with lips apart
Breathed, and with dimmer eyes leaned through the air
As one in dream, and now his human hand
Took in her own; and to Apollo spoke:
"O gradual rose of the dim universe!
Whose warmth steals through the grave unto the dead,

The Sacred Fire

Soul of the early sky, priest of bloom!
Who beautifully goest in the West,
Attracting as to an eternal home
The yearning soul.   Male of the female earth
O eager bridegroom springing in this world
As in thy bed prepared!   Fain would I know
Yon heavenly wafting through the heaven wide,
And the large view of the subjected seas,
And famous cities, and the various toil
Of men: all Asia at my feet spread out
In indolent magnificence of bloom!
Africa in her matted hair obscured,
And India in meditation plunged!
Then the delight of flinging the sunbeams,
Diffusing silent bliss; and yet more sweet,—
To cherish fruit on the warm wall; to raise
Out of the tomb to glory the pale wheat,
Serene ascension by the sun prepared;
To work with the benignly falling hours,
And beautiful slow Time.   But dearest, this,
To gild the face that from its dead looks up,
To shine on the rejected, and arrive
To women that remember in the night;
Or mend with sweetest surgery the mind.
And yet, forgive me if I can but speak
Most human words.   Of immortality
Thou singest: thou would'st hold me from the ground,
And this just opening beauty from the grave.
As yet I have known no sorrow; all my days
Like perfect lilies under water stir,
And God has sheltered me from his own wind;
The darling of his breezes have I been.
Yet as to one inland, that dreameth lone,
Sea-faring men with their sea-weary eyes,
Round the inn-fire tell of some foreign land;
So agèd men, much tossed about in life,
Have told me of that country, Sorrow far.
How many goodly ships at anchor lie
Within her ports; even to me indeed

Hath a sea-rumour through the night been borne.
And I myself remember, and have heard,
Of men that did believe, women that loved
That were unhappy long and now are dead,
With wounds that no eternity can close,
Life had so marked them: or of others who
Panted toward their end, and fell on death
Even as sobbing runners breast the rope.
And most I remember of all human things
My mother; often as a child I pressed
My face against her cheek, and felt her tears;
Even as she smiled on me, her eyes would fill,
Until my own grew ignorantly wet;
And I in silence wondered at sorrow.
When I remember this, how shall I know
That I myself may not, by sorrow taught,
Accept the perfect stillness of the ground?
Where, though I lie still, and stir not at all,
Yet shall I irresistibly be kind,
Helplessly sweet, a wandering garden bliss.
My ashes shall console and make for peace;
This mind that injured, be an aimless balm.
Or if there be some other world, with no
Bloom, neither rippling sound, nor early smell,
Nor leaves, nor pleasant exchange of human speech;
Only a dreadful pacing to and fro
Of spirits meditating on the sun;
A land of barèd boughs and grieving wind;
Yet would I not forego the doom, the place,
Whither my poets and my heroes went
Before me; warriors that with deeds forlorn
Saddened my youth, yet made it great to live;
Lonely antagonists of Destiny,
That went down scornful before many spears,
Who soon as we are born, are straight our friends;
And live in simple music, country songs,
And mournful ballads by the winter fire.
Since they have died, their death is ever mine;
I would not lose it.   Then, thou speak'st of joy,

Of immortality without one sigh,
Existence without tears for evermore.
Thou would'st preserve me from the anguish, lest
This holy face into the dark return.
Yet I being human, human sorrow miss.
The half of music, I have heard men say,
Is to have grieved; when comes the lonely wail
Over the mind; old men have told it me
Subdued after long life by simple sounds.
The mourner is the favourite of the moon,
And the departing sun his glory owes
To the eternal thoughts of creatures brief,
Who think the thing that they shall never see.
Since we must die, how bright the starry track!
How wonderful in a bereavèd ear
The Northern wind; how strange the summer night,
The exhaling earth to those who vainly love.
Out of our sadness have we made this world
So beautiful; the sea sighs in our brain,
And in our heart the yearning of the moon.
To all this sorrow was I born, and since
Out of a human womb I came, I am
Not eager to forego it; I would scorn
To elude the heaviness and take the joy,
For pain came with the sap, pangs with the bloom:
This is the sting, the wonder.   Yet should I
Linger beside thee in felicity,
Sliding with open eyes through liquid bliss
For ever; still I must grow old.   Ah, I
Should ail beside thee Apollo, and should note
With eyes that would not be, but yet are dim,
Ever so slight a change from day to day
In thee my husband; watch thee nudge thyself
To little offices that once were sweet:
Slow where thou once wert swift, remembering
To kiss those lips which once thou could'st not leave.
I should expect thee by the Western bay,
Faded, not sure of thee, with desperate smiles,
And pitiful devices of my dress

Or fashion of my hair: thou would'st grow kind;
Most bitter to a woman that was loved.
I must ensnare thee to my arms, and touch
Thy pity, to but hold thee to my heart.
But if I live with Idas, then we two
On the low earth shall prosper hand in hand
In odours of the open field, and live
In peaceful noises of the farm, and watch
The pastoral fields burned by the setting sun.
And he shall give me passionate children, not
Some radiant god that will despise me quite,
But clambering limbs and little hearts that err.
And I shall sleep beside him in the night,
And fearful from some dream shall touch his hand
Secure; or at some festival we two
Will wander through the lighted city streets;
And in the crowd I'll take his arm and feel
Him closer for the press.   So shall we live.
And though the first sweet sting of love be past,
The sweet that almost venom is; though youth,
With tender and extravagant delight,
The first and secret kiss by twilight hedge,
The insane farewell repeated o'er and o'er,
Pass off; there shall succeed a faithful peace;
Beautiful friendship tried by sun and wind,
Durable from the daily dust of life.
And though with sadder, still with kinder eyes,
We shall behold all frailties, we shall haste
To pardon, and with mellowing minds to bless.
Then though we must grow old, we shall grow old
Together, and he shall not greatly miss
My bloom faded, and waning light of eyes
Too deeply gazed in ever to seem dim;
Nor shall we murmur at, nor much regret
The years that gently bend us to the ground,
And gradually incline our face; that we
Leisurely stooping, and with each slow step,
May curiously inspect our lasting home.
But we shall sit with luminous holy smiles,

Endeared by many griefs, by many a jest,
And custom sweet of living side by side;
And full of memories not unkindly glance
Upon each other. Last, we shall descend
Into the natural ground—not without tears—
One must go first, ah god! one must go first;
After so long one blow for both were good;
Still like old friends, glad to have met, and leave
Behind a wholesome memory on the earth.
And thou, beautiful god, in that far time,
When in thy setting sweet thou gazest down
On this grey head, wilt thou remember then
That once I pleased thee, that I once was young?"
When she had spoken, Idas with one cry
Held her, and there was silence; while the god
In anger disappeared. Then slowly they,
He looking downward, and she gazing up,
Into the evening green wandered away.

about 1898   STEPHEN PHILLIPS

183. The Sad Shepherd

THERE was a man whom Sorrow named his friend,
    And he, of his high comrade Sorrow dreaming,
    Went walking with slow steps along the gleaming
And humming sands, where windy surges wend:
And he called loudly to the stars to bend
    From their pale thrones and comfort him, but they
    Among themselves laugh on and sing alway:
And then the man whom Sorrow named his friend
Cried out, *Dim sea, hear my most piteous cry!*
    The sea swept on and cried her old cry still,
    Rolling along in dreams from hill to hill;
He fled the persecution of her glory
And, in a far off, gentle valley stopping,
    Cried all his story to the dew-drops glistening,
    But naught they heard, for they are always listening,
The dew-drops, for the sound of their own dropping.

And then the man whom Sorrow named his friend
   Sought once again the shore, and found a shell
   And thought, *I will my heavy story tell*
Till my own words, re-echoing, shall send
Their sadness through a hollow, pearly heart;
   And my own tale again for me shall sing,
   And my own whispering words be comforting
And lo! my ancient burden may depart.
Then he sang softly nigh the pearly rim;
   But the sad dweller by the sea-ways lone
   Changed all he sang to inarticulate moan
Among her wildering whorls, forgetting him.

about 1890–95   W. B. YEATS

184. The Everlasting Voices

O SWEET everlasting Voices, be still;
Go to the guards of the heavenly fold
And bid them wander obeying your will
Flame under flame, till Time be no more;
Have you not heard that our hearts are old,
That you call in birds, in wind on the hill,
In shaken boughs, in tide on the shore?
O sweet everlasting Voices, be still.

about 1899   W. B. YEATS

185. Song

OH! Sorrow, Sorrow, scarce I knew
   Your name when, shaking down the may
In sport, a little child, I grew
   Afraid to find you at my play.
I heard it ere I looked at you;
   You sang it softly as you came
Bringing your little boughs of yew
   To fling across my gayest game.

The Sacred Fire

Oh! Sorrow, Sorrow, was I fair
    That when I decked me for a bride,
You met me stepping down the stair
    And led me from my lover's side?
Was I so dear you could not spare
    The maid to love, the child to play,
But coming always unaware,
    Must bid and beckon me away?

Oh! Sorrow, Sorrow, is my bed
    So wide and warm that you must lie
Upon it; toss your weary head
    And stir my slumber with your sigh?
I left my love at your behest,
    I waved your little boughs of yew,
But Sorrow, Sorrow, let me rest,
    For oh! I cannot sleep with you.

before 1910   CHARLOTTE MEW

186. Moorland Night

My face is against the grass—the moorland grass is wet—
    My eyes are shut against the grass, against my lips there are
      the little blades,
    Over my head the curlews call,
    And now there is the night wind in my hair;
My heart is against the grass and the sweet earth;—it has gone
      still, at last.
    It does not want to beat any more,
      And why should it beat?
    This is the end of the journey:
      The Thing is found.

    This is the end of all the roads—
  Over the grass there is the night-dew
And the wind that drives up from the sea along the moorland road;
    I hear a curlew start out from the heath

And fly off, calling through the dusk,
   The wild, long, rippling call.
The Thing is found and I am quiet with the earth.
Perhaps the earth will hold it, or the wind, or that bird's cry,
But it is not for long in any life I know. This cannot stay,
Not now, not yet, not in a dying world, with me, for very long.
   I leave it here:
   And one day the wet grass may give it back—
   One day the quiet earth may give it back—
The calling birds may give it back as they go by—
To someone walking on the moor who starves for love and will
      not know
   Who gave it to all these to give away;
   Or, if I come and ask for it again,
      Oh! then, to me.

before 1910　　　　　　　　　　　　　　CHARLOTTE MEW

187. *from* The Testament of a Man Forbid

MANKIND has cast me out. When I became
So close a comrade of the day and night,
Of earth and of the seasons of the year,
And so submissive in my love of life
And study of the world that I unknew
The past and names renowned, religion, art,
Inventions, thoughts, and deeds, as men unknow
What good and evil fate befell their souls
Before their bodies gave them residence,
(How the old letter haunts the spirit still!
As if the soul were other than the sum
The body's powers make up—a golden coin,
Amount of so much silver, so much bronze!)
I said, rejoicing, "Now I stand erect,
"And am that which I am." Compassionate
I watched a motley crowd beside me bent
Beneath unsteady burdens, toppling loads
Of volumes, news and lore antique, that showered
About their ears to be re-edified

The Sacred Fire

On aching heads and shoulders overtasked.
Yet were these hodmen cheerful, ignorant
Of woe whose character it is to seem
Predestined and an honourable care:
They read their books, re-read, and read again;
They balanced libraries upon their polls,
And tottered through the valley almost prone,
But certain they were nobler than the beasts.
I saw besides in fields and cities hordes
Of haggard people soaked in filth and slime
Wherewith they fed the jaded earth the while
Their souls of ordure stank; automata
That served machines whose tyrannous revolt
Enthralled their lords, as if the mistletoe
Displaying mournful gold and wintry pearls
On sufferance, should enchant the forest oak
To be its accident and parasite;
Wretches and monsters that were capable
Of joy and sorrow once, their bodies numbed.
Their souls deflowered, their reason disendowed
By noisome trades, or at the furnaces,
In drains and quarries and the sunless mines;
And myriads upon myriads, human still
Without redemption drudging till they died.

Aware how multitudes of those enslaved
No respite sought, but squandered leisure hours
Among the crowd whose choice or task it was
To balance libraries upon their polls,
I laughed a long low laugh with weeping strung,
A rosary of tears, to see mankind
So dauntless and so dull, and cried at last,
"Good people, honest people, cast them off
"And stand erect, for few are helped by books.
"What! will you die crushed under libraries?
"Lo! thirty centuries of literature
"Have curved your spines and overborne your brains!
"Off with it—all of it!   Stand up; behold
"The earth; life, death, and day and night!

"Think not the things that have been said of these;
"But watch them and be excellent, for men
"Are what they contemplate."

They mocked me . . .

*   *   *

. . . "we cast you out.
"Your well-earned portion of the Universe
"Is isolation and eternal death.
"Cut off, an alien, here you have no home:
"No face shall ever gladden at your step,
"No woman long to see you.   Get you hence,
"And seek the desert; or since your soul is dead,
"Return your body to the earth at once,
"And let resolved oblivion triumph now.

Gladly the World approved with hand and voice:
And one, a woman, offered me a knife:
"And let resolved oblivion triumph now,"
She echoed.   Had it been my will to die,
I should not then have made the sacrifice
At the World's bidding; but I chose to live,
For while I live the victory is mine.

So I went forth for evermore forbid
The company of men.   The Universe,
Systems and suns and all that breathes and is,
Appeared at first in that dread solitude
Only the momentary, insolent
Irruption of a glittering fantasy
Into the silent, empty Infinite.
But eyes and ears were given to me again:
With these a man may do; with these, endure.

I haunt the hills that overlook the sea.
Here in the Winter like a meshwork shroud
The sifted snow reveals the perished land,
And powders wisps of knotgrass dank and dead

The Sacred Fire

That trail like faded locks on mouldering skulls
Unearthed from shallow burial. With the Spring
The west-wind thunders through the budding hedge
That stems the furrowed steep—a sound of drums,
Of gongs and muted cymbals; yellow breasts
And brown wings whirl in gusts, fly chaffering, drop,
And surge in gusts again; in wooded coombs
The hyacinth with purple diapers
The russet beechmast, and cowslips hoard
Their virgin gold in lucent chalices;
The sombre furze, all suddenly attired
In rich brocade, the enterprise in chief
And pageant of the season, overrides
The rolling land and girds the bosomed plain
That strips her green robe to a saffron shore
And steps into the surf where threads and scales
And arabesques of blue and emerald wave
Begin to damascene the iron sea;
While faint from upland fold and covert peal
The sheep-bell and the cuckoo's mellow chime.
Then when the sovereign light from which we came,
Of earth enamoured, bends most questioning looks,
I watch the land grow beautiful, a bride
Transfigured with desire of her great lord.
Bethrothal music of the tireless larks,
Heaven-high, heaven-wide, possesses all the air,
And wreathes the shining lattice of the light
With chaplets, purple clusters, vintages
Of sound from the first fragrant breath and first
Tear-sprinkled blush of Summer to the deep
Transmuted fire, the smouldering golden moons,
The wine-stained dusk of Autumn harvest-ripe;
And I behold the period of Time,
When Memory shall devolve and Knowledge lapse
Wanting a subject, and the willing earth
Leap to the bosom of the sun to be
Pure flame once more in a new time begun:
Here as I pace the pallid doleful hills
And serpentine declivities that creep

Unhonoured to the ocean's shifting verge,
Or where with prouder curve and greener sward,
Surmounting peacefully the restless tides,
The cliffed escarpment ends in stormclad strength.

about 1900   JOHN DAVIDSON

XXI

Lascelles Abercrombie

Walter de la Mare

Rupert Brooke

Robert Frost

Edward Thomas

Wilfred Owen

D. H. Lawrence

Herbert Read

The Sacred Fire

188. Marriage Song

I

COME up, dear chosen morning, come,
Blessing the air with light,
And bid the sky repent of being dark:
Let all the spaces round the world be white,
And give the earth her green again.
Into new hours of beautiful delight,
Out of the shadow where she has lain,
Bring the earth awake for glee,
Shining with dews as fresh and clear
As my beloved's voice upon the air.
For now, O morning chosen of all days, on thee
A wondrous duty lies:
There was an evening that did loveliness foretell;
Thence upon thee, O chosen morn, it fell
To fashion into perfect destiny
The radiant prophecy.
For in an evening of young moon, that went
Filling the moist air with a rosy fire,
I and my beloved knew our love;
And knew that thou, O morning, wouldst arise
To give us knowledge of achieved desire.
For, standing stricken with astonishment,
Half terrified in the delight,
Even as the moon did into clear air move
And made a golden light,
Lo there, croucht up against it, a dark hill,
A monstrous back of earth, a spine
Of hunchèd rock, furred with great growth of pine,
Lay like a beast, snout in its paws, asleep;
Yet in its sleeping seemed it miserable,
As though strong fear must always keep
Hold of its heart, and drive its blood in dream.
Yea, for to our new love, did it not seem,
That dark and quiet length of hill,
The sleeping grief of the world?—Out of it we

Had like imaginations stept to be
Beauty and golden wonder; and for the lovely fear
Of coming perfect joy, had changed
The terror that dreamt there!
And now the golden moon had turned
To shining white, white as our souls that burned
With vision of our prophecy assured:
Suddenly white was the moon; but she
At once did on a woven modesty
Of cloud, and soon went in obscured:
And we were dark, and vanished that strange hill.
But yet it was not long before
There opened in the sky a narrow door,
Made with pearl lintel and pearl sill;
And the earth's night seem'd pressing there,—
All as a beggar on some festival would peer,—
To gaze into a room of light beyond,
The hidden silver splendour of the moon.
Yea, and we also, we
Long gazed wistfully
Towards thee, O morning, come at last,
And towards the light that thou wilt pour upon us soon!

II

O soul who still art strange to sense,
Who often against beauty wouldst complain,
Doubting between joy and pain:
If like the startling touch of something keen
Against thee, it hath been
To follow from an upland height
The swift sun hunting rain
Across the April meadows of a plain,
Until the fields would flash into the air
Their joyous green, like emeralds alight;
Or when in the blue of night's mid-noon
The burning naked moon
Draws to a brink of cloudy weather near,
A breadth of snow, firm and soft as a wing,

Stretcht out over a wind that gently goes,—
Through the white sleep of snowy cloud there grows
An azure-border'd shining ring,
The gleaming dream of the approaching joy of her;—
What now wilt thou do, Soul? What now,
If with such things as these troubled thou wert?
How wilt thou now endure, or how
Not now be strangely hurt?—
When utter beauty must come closer to thee
Than even anger or fear could be;
When thou, like metal in a kiln, must lie
Seized by beauty's mightily able flame;
Enjoyed by beauty as by the ruthless glee
Of an unescapable power;
Obeying beauty as air obeys a cry;
Yea, one thing made of beauty and thee,
As steel and a white heat are made the same!
—Ah, but I know how this infirmity
Will fail and be not, no, not memory,
When I begin the marvellous hour.
This only is my heart's strain'd eagerness,
Long waiting for its bliss.—
But from those other fears, from those
That keep to Love so close,
From fears that are the shadow of delight,
Hide me, O joys; make them unknown to-night!

III

Thou bright God that in dream camest to me last night,
Thou with the flesh made of a golden light,
Knew I not thee, thee and thy heart,
Knew I not well, God, who thou wert?
Yea, and my soul divinely understood
The light that was beneath thee a ground,
The golden light that cover'd thee round,
Turning my sleep to a fiery morn,
Was as a heavenly oath there sworn
Promising me an immortal good:

The Sacred Fire

Well I knew thee, God of marriages, thee and thy flame!
Ah, but wherefore beside thee came
That fearful sight of another mood?
Why in thy light, to thy hand chained,
Towards me its bondage terribly strained,
Why came with thee that dreadful hound,
The wild hound Fear, black, ravenous and gaunt?
Why him with thee should thy dear light surround?
Why broughtest thou that beast to haunt
The blissful footsteps of my golden dream?—
All shadowy black the body dread,
All frenzied fire the head,—
The hunger of its mouth a hollow crimson flame,
The hatred in its eyes a blaze
Fierce and green, stabbing the ruddy glaze,
And sharp white jetting fire the teeth snarl'd at me,
And white the dribbling rage of froth,—
A throat that gaped to bay and paws working violently,
Yet soundless all as a winging moth;
Tugging towards me, famishing for my heart;—
Even while thou, O golden god, wert still
Looking the beautiful kindness of thy will
Into my soul, even then must I be
With thy bright promise looking at me,
Then bitterly of that hound afraid?—
Darkness, I know, attendeth bright,
And light comes not but shadow comes:
And heart must know, if it know thy light,
Thy wild hound fear, the shadow of love's delight.
Yea, is it thus? Are we so made
Of death and darkness, that even thou,
O golden God of the joys of love,
Thy mind to us canst only prove,
The glorious devices of thy mind,
By so revealing how thy journeying here
Through this mortality, doth closely bind
Thy brightness to the shadow of dreadful Fear?
Ah no, it shall not be! Thy joyous light
Shall hide me from the hunger of fear to-night.

IV

For wonderfully to live I now begin
So that the darkness which accompanies
Our being here, is fasten'd up within
The power of light that holdeth me;
And from these shining chains, to see
My joy with bold misliking eyes,
The shrouded figure will not dare arise.
For henceforth, from to-night,
I am wholly gone into the bright
Safety of the beauty of love:
Not only all my waking vigours plied
Under the searching glory of love,
But knowing myself with love all satisfied
Even when my life is hidden in sleep;
As high clouds, to themselves that keep
The moon's white company, are all possest
Silverly with the presence of their guest;
Or as a darken'd room
That hath within it roses, whence the air
And quietness are taken everywhere
Deliciously by sweet perfume

about 1910   LASCELLES ABERCROMBIE

189. Silence

WITH changeful sound life beats upon the ear;
        Yet striving for release
    The most delighting string's
            Sweet jargonings,
        The happiest throat's
    Most easeful, lovely notes
Fall back into a veiling silentness.

Even amid the rumour of a moving host,
    Blackening the clear green earth,
        Vainly 'gainst that thin wall
            The trumpets call,

Or with loud hum
The smoke-bemuffled drum:
From that high quietness no reply comes forth.

When all at peace, two friends at ease alone
Talk out their hearts,—yet still,
Between the grace-notes of
The voice of love
From each to each
Trembles a rarer speech,
And with its presence every pause doth fill.

Unmoved it broods, this all-encompassing hush
Of one who stooping near,
No smallest stir will make
Our fear to wake;
But yet intent
Upon some mystery bent,
Hearkens the lightest word we say, or hear.

about 1912   WALTER DE LA MARE

190. All that's Past

VERY old are the woods;
And the buds that break
Out of the briar's boughs,
When March winds wake,
So old with their beauty are—
Oh, no man knows
Through what wild centuries
Roves back the rose

Very old are the brooks;
And the rills that rise
Where snow sleeps cold beneath
The azure skies

Sing such a history
     Of come and gone
Their every drop is as wise
     As Solomon.

Very old are we men;
     Our dreams are tales
Told in dim Eden
     By Eve's nightingales;
We wake and whisper awhile,
     But, the day gone by,
Silence and sleep like fields
     Of amaranth lie.

WALTER DE LA MARE

about 1912

191. The Linnet

Upon this leafy bush
     With thorns and roses in it,
Flutters a thing of light,
     A twittering linnet,
And all the throbbing world
     Of dew and sun and air
By this small parcel of life
     Is made more fair;
As if each bramble-spray
     And mounded gold-wreathed furze,
Harebell and little thyme,
     Were only hers;
As if this beauty and grace
     Did to one bird belong,
And, at a flutter of wing,
     Might vanish in song.

WALTER DE LA MARE

about 1918

The Sacred Fire

192. An Epitaph

HERE lies a most beautiful lady,
Light of step and heart was she;
I think she was the most beautiful lady
That ever was in the West Country.
But beauty vanishes; beauty passes;
However rare—rare it be;
And when I crumble, who will remember
This lady of the West Country?

about 1912   WALTER DE LA MARE

193. The Owl

WHAT if to edge of dream,
When the spirit is come,
Shriek the hunting owl,
And summon it home—
To the fear-stirred heart
And the ancient dread
Of man, when cold root or stone
Pillowed roofless head?

Clangs not at last the hour
When roof shelters not;
And ears are deaf,
And all fears forgot:
Since the spirit too far has fared
For summoning scream
Of any strange fowl on earth
To shatter its dream?

                    WALTER DE LA MARE
about 1920

194. Sonnet

Not with vain tears, when we're beyond the sun,
  We'll beat on the substantial doors, nor tread
  Those dusty high-roads of the aimless dead
Plaintive for Earth; but rather turn and run
Down some close-covered by-way of the air,
  Some low sweet alley between wind and wind,
  Stoop under faint gleams, thread the shadows, find
Some whispering ghost-forgotten nook, and there

Spend in pure converse our eternal day;
  Think each in each, immediately wise;
Learn all we lacked before; hear, know and say
  What this tumultuous body now denies;
And feel, who have laid our groping hands away;
  And see, no longer blinded by our eyes.

about 1913   RUPERT BROOKE

195. Clouds

Down the blue night the unending columns press
  In noiseless tumult, break and wave and flow,
  Now tread the far South, or lift rounds of snow
Up to the white moon's hidden loveliness.
Some pause in their grave wandering comradeless,
  And turn with profound gesture vague and slow,
  As who would pray good for the world, but know
Their benediction empty as they bless.

They say that the Dead die not, but remain
  Near to the rich heirs of their grief and mirth.
    I think they ride the calm mid-heaven, as these,
In wise majestic melancholy train,
    And watch the moon, and the still-raging seas,
And men, coming and going on the earth.

about 1913   RUPERT BROOKE

196. The Sound of the Trees

I WONDER about the trees.
Why do we wish to bear
Forever the noise of these
More than another noise
So close to our dwelling place?
We suffer them by the day
Till we lose all measure of pace,
And fixity in our joys,
And acquire a listening air.
They are that that talks of going
But never gets away;
And that talks no less for knowing,
As it grows wiser and older,
That now it means to stay.
My feet tug at the floor
And my head sways to my shoulder
Sometimes when I watch trees sway,
From the window or the door.
I shall set forth for somewhere,
I shall make the reckless choice
Some day when they are in voice
And tossing so as to scare
The white clouds over them on.
I shall have less to say,
But I shall be gone.

about 1916   ROBERT FROST

197. The Road not taken

Two roads diverged in a yellow wood,
And sorry I could not travel both
And be one traveller, long I stood
And looked down one as far as I could
To where it bent in the undergrowth;

Then took the other, as just as fair,
And having perhaps the better claim,
Because it was grassy and wanted wear;
Though as for that the passing there
Had worn them really about the same,

And both that morning equally lay
In leaves no step had trodden black.
Oh! I kept the first for another day!
Yet knowing how way leads on to way,
I doubted if I should ever come back.

And I shall be telling this with a sigh
Somewhere ages and ages hence:
Two roads diverged in a wood, and I—
I took the one less travelled by,
And that has made all the difference.

about 1916   ROBERT FROST

198. The Woodpile

Out walking in the frozen swamp one gray day
I paused and said, "I will turn back from here
No, I will go on farther—and we shall see."
The hard snow held me, save where now and then
One foot went through. The view was all in lines
Straight up and down of tall slim trees
Too much alike to mark or name a place by
So as to say for certain I was here
Or somewhere else: I was just far from home.
A small bird flew before me. He was careful
To put a tree between us when he lighted,
And say no word to tell me who he was
Who was so foolish as to think what he thought.
He thought that I was after him for a feather—
The white one in his tail; like one who takes

- 425 -

Everything said as personal to himself.
One flight out sideways would have undeceived him.
And there was a pile of wood for which
I forgot him and let his little fear
Carry him off the way I might have gone,
Without so much as wishing him good night.
He went behind it to make his last stand.
It was a cord of maple, cut and split
And piled—and measured, four by four by eight.
And not another like it could I see.
No runner tracks in this year's snow looped near it.
And it was older sure than this year's cutting,
Or even last year's or the year's before.
The wood was gray and the bark warping off it
And the pile somewhat sunken. Clematis
Had wound strings round and round it like a bundle.
What held it though on one side was a tree
Still growing, and on one a stake and prop,
These latter about to fall. I thought that only
Someone who lived in turning to fresh tasks
Could so forget his handiwork on which
He spent himself, the labour of his axe,
And leave it there far from a useful fireplace
To warm the frozen swamp as best it could
With the slow smokeless burning of decay.

about 1914   ROBERT FROST

199. After apple-picking

My long two-pointed ladder's sticking through a tree
Toward heaven still,
And there's a barrel that I didn't fill
Beside it, and there may be two or three
Apples I didn't pick upon some bough.
But I am done with apple-picking now.
Essence of winter sleep is on the night,
The scent of apples: I am drowsing off.

I cannot rub the strangeness from my sight
I got from looking through a pane of glass
I skimmed this morning from the drinking trough
And held against the world of hoary grass.
It melted, and I let it fall and break.
But I was well
Upon my way to sleep before it fell,
And I could tell
What form my dreaming was about to take.
Magnified apples appear and disappear,
Stem end and blossom end,
And every fleck of russet showing clear.
My instep arch not only keeps the ache,
It keeps the pressure of a ladder round.
I feel the ladder sway as the boughs bend.
And I keep hearing from the cellar bin
The rumbling sound
Of load on load of apples coming in.
For I have had too much
Of apple-picking: I am overtired
Of the great harvest I myself desired.
There were ten thousand thousand fruit to touch,
Cherish in hand, lift down, and not let fall.
For all
That struck the earth,
No matter if not bruised or spiked with stubble,
Went surely to the cider-apple heap
As of no worth.
One can see what will trouble
This sleep of mine, whatever sleep it is.
Were he not gone,
The woodchuck could say whether it's like his
Long sleep, as I describe its coming on,
Or just some human sleep.

about 1914   ROBERT FROST

The Sacred Fire

200. It Rains

It rains, and nothing stirs within the fence
Anywhere through the orchard's untrodden, dense
Forest of parsley.   The great diamonds
Of rain on the grass-blades there is none to break
Or the fallen petals further down to shake.

And I am as nearly happy as possible
To search the wilderness in vain though well,
To think of two walking, kissing there,
Drenched, yet forgetting the kisses of the rain:
Sad, too, to think that never, never again,

Unless alone, so happy shall I walk
In the rain.   When I turn away, on its fine stalk
Twilight has fined to naught, the parsley flower
Figures, suspended still and ghostly white,
The past hovering as it revisits the light.

about 1915   EDWARD THOMAS

201. Tall Nettles

Tall nettles cover up, as they have done
These many springs, the rusty harrow, the plough
Long worn out, and the roller made of stone:
Only the elm-butt tops the nettles now.

This corner of the farmyard I like most:
As well as any bloom upon a flower
I like the dust on the nettles, never lost
Except to prove the sweetness of a shower.

about 1915   EDWARD THOMAS

202. October

THE green elm with the one great bough of gold
Lets leaves into the grass slip, one by one—
The short hill grass, the mushrooms small milk-white,
Harebell and scabious and tormentil,
That blackberry and gorse, in dew and sun,
Bow down to; and the wind travels too light
To shake the fallen birch leaves from the fern;
The gossamers wander at their own will
At heavier steps than birds' the squirrels scold.
The late year has grown fresh again and new
As Spring and to the touch is not more cool
Than it is warm to the gaze; and now I might
As happy be as earth is beautiful,
Were I some other or with earth could turn
In alternation of violet and rose,
Harebell and snowdrop, at their season due,
And gorse that has no time not to be gay.
But if this be not happiness,—who knows?
Some day I shall think this a happy day,
And this mood by the name of melancholy
Shall no more blackened and obscured be.

about 1915   EDWARD THOMAS

203. Insensibility

I

HAPPY are men who yet before they are killed
Can let their veins run cold.
Whom no compassion fleers
Or makes their feet
Sore on the alleys cobbled with their brothers.
The front line withers,
But they are troops that fade, not flowers,

For poets' tearful fooling:
Men, gaps for filling:
Losses who might have fought
Longer; but no one bothers.

II

And some cease feeling
Even themselves or for themselves.
Dullness best solves
The tease and doubt of shelling,
And Chance's strange arithmetic
Comes simpler than the reckoning of their shilling.
They keep no check on armies' decimation.

III

Happy are these who lose imagination:
They have enough to carry with ammunition.
Their spirit drags no pack,
Their old wounds save with cold can not more ache.
Having seen all things red,
Their eyes are rid
Of the hurt of the colour of blood for ever.
And terror's first constriction over,
Their hearts remain small-drawn.
Their senses in some scorching cautery of battle
Now long since ironed,
Can laugh among the dying, unconcerned.

IV

Happy the soldier home, with not a notion
How somewhere, every dawn, some men attack,
And many sighs are drained.
Happy the lad whose mind was never trained:
His days are worth forgetting more than not.
He sings along the march
Which we march taciturn, because of dusk,
The long, forlorn, relentless tread
From larger day to huger night.

V

We wise, who with a thought besmirch
Blood over all our soul,
How should we see our task
But through his blunt and lashless eyes?
Alive, he is not vital overmuch;
Dying, not mortal overmuch;
Nor sad, nor proud,
Nor curious at all.
He cannot tell
Old men's placidity from his.

VI

But cursed are dullards whom no cannon stuns,
That they should be as stones;
Wretched are they, and mean
With paucity that never was simplicity.
By choice they made themselves immune
To pity and whatever moans in man
Before the last sea and the hapless stars;
Whatever mourns when many leave these shores;
Whatever shares
The eternal reciprocity of tears.

about 1917   WILFRED OWEN

204. "And oh!—that the man I am might cease
to be——"

No, now I wish the sunshine would stop,
and the white shining houses and the gay red flowers on the
    balconies
and the bluish mountains beyond, would be crushed out
between two valves of darkness;
the darkness falling, the darkness rising, with muffled sound
obliterating everything.
I wish that whatever props up the walls of light

would fall, and darkness come hurling heavily down,
and it would be thick black dark for ever.
Not sleep, which is grey with dreams
nor death, which quivers with birth,
but heavy sealing darkness, silence, all immovable.
What is sleep?
It goes over me, like a shadow over a hill,
but it does not alter me nor help me.
And death would ache still, I am sure;
it would be lambent, uneasy.
I wish it would be completely dark everywhere,
inside me, and out, heavily dark
utterly.

about 1917   D. H. LAWRENCE

205. Kangaroo

IN the northern hemisphere
Life seems to leap in the air, or skim under the wind
Like stags on rocky ground, or pawing horses, or springy scut-tailed
  rabbits.

Or else rush horizontal to charge at the sky's horizon,
Like bulls or bisons or wild pigs.

Or slip like water slippery towards its ends,
As foxes, stoats, and wolves, and prairie dogs.

Only mice, and moles, and rats, and badgers, and beavers, or
  perhaps bears
Seem belly-plumbed to the earth's mid-navel.
Or frogs that when they leap come flop, and flop to the centre of
  the earth.

But the yellow antipodal Kangaroo, when she sits up,
Who can unseat her, like a liquid drop that is heavy, and just
  touches earth.
The downward drip.
The down-urge.
So much denser than cold-blooded frogs.

An Anthology

Delicate mother Kangaroo
Sitting up there rabbit-wise, but huge, plumb-weighted,
And lifting her beautiful slender face, oh! so much more gently
    and finely lined than a rabbit's, or than a hare's,
Lifting her face to nibble at a round white peppermint drop, which
    she loves, sensitive mother Kangaroo.

Her sensitive, long, pure-bred face.
Her full antipodal eyes, so dark,
So big and quiet and remote, having watched so many empty dawns
    in silent Australia.

Her little loose hands, and drooping Victorian shoulders
And then her great weight below the waist, her vast pale belly
With a thin young yellow little paw hanging out, and a straggle
    of a long thin ear, like ribbon,
Like a funny trimming to the middle of her belly, thin little dangle
    of an immature paw, and one thin ear.

Her belly, her big haunches
And in addition, the great muscular python-stretch of her tail.
There, she shan't have any more peppermint drops.
So she wistfully, sensitively sniffs the air, and then turns, and goes
    off in slow sad leaps

On the long flat skis of her legs
Steered and propelled by that steel-strong snake of a tail

Stops again, half turns, inquisitive to look back.
While something stirs quickly in her belly, and a lean little face
    comes out, as from a window,
Peaked and a bit dismayed,
Only to disappear again quickly away from the sight of the world,
    to snuggle down in the warmth,
Leaving the trail of a different paw hanging out.

Still she watches with eternal, cocked wistfulness!
How full her eyes are, like the full, fathomless, shining eyes of an
    Australian black-boy
Who has been lost so many centuries on the margins of existence!

The Sacred Fire

She watches with insatiable wistfulness.
Untold centuries of watching for something to come,
For a new signal from life, in that silent lost land of the South.
Where nothing bites but insects and snakes and the sun, small life.
Where no bull roared, no cow ever lowed, no stag cried, no leopard
    screeched, no lion coughed, no dog barked,
But all was silent save for parrots occasionally, in the haunted
    blue bush.

Wistfully watching, with wonderful liquid eyes.
And all her weight, all her blood, dripping sack-wise down towards
    the earth's centre,
And the live little one taking in its paw at the door of her belly.

Leap then, and come down on the line that draws to the earth's
    deep centre.

about 1922   D. H. LAWRENCE

206. Snake

A SNAKE came to my water-trough
On a hot, hot day, and I in pyjamas for the heat,
To drink there.

In the deep, strange-scented shade of the great dark carob-tree
I came down the steps with my pitcher
And must wait, must stand and wait, for there he was at the trough
    before me.

He reached down from a fissure in the earth-wall in the gloom
And trailed his yellow-brown slackness soft-bellied down, over the
    edge of the stone trough
And rested his throat upon the stone bottom,
And where the water had dripped from the tap, in a small clearness,
He sipped with his straight mouth,
Softly drank through his straight gums, into his slack long body,
Silently.

– 434 –

Someone was before me at my water-trough,
And I, like a second comer, waiting.

He lifted his head from his drinking, as cattle do,
And looked at me vaguely, as drinking cattle do,
And flickered his two-forked tongue from his lips, and mused a
    moment,
And stooped and drank a little more,
Being earth-brown, earth-golden from the burning bowels of the
    earth
On the day of Sicilian July, with Etna smoking.

The voice of my education said to me
He must be killed,
For in Sicily the black, black snakes are innocent, the gold are
    venomous.

And voices said in me, If you were a man
You would take a stick and break him now, and finish him off.

But must I confess how I liked him,
How glad I was he had come like a guest in quiet, to drink at my
    water-trough
And depart peaceful, pacified, and thankless,
Into the burning bowels of this earth?

Was it cowardice, that I dared not kill him?
Was it perversity, that I longed to talk to him?
Was it humility, to feel so honoured?
I felt so honoured.

And yet those voices:
If you were not afraid, you would kill him!

And truly I was afraid, I was most afraid,
But even so, honoured still more
That he should seek out my hospitality
From out the dark door of the secret earth.

The Sacred Fire

He drank enough
And lifted his head, dreamily, as one who has drunken,
And flickered his tongue like a forked night on the air, so black,
And looked around like a god, unseeing, into the air,
And slowly turned his head,
And slowly, very slowly, as if thrice adream,
Proceeded to draw his slow length curving round
And climb again the broken bank of my wall-face.

And as he put his head into that dreadful hole,
And as he slowly drew up, snake-easing his shoulders, and entered
    farther,
A sort of horror, a sort of protest against his withdrawing into that
    horrid black hole,
Deliberately going into the blackness, and slowly drawing himself
    after,
Overcame me now his back was turned.

I looked round, I put down my pitcher,
I picked up a clumsy log
And threw it at the water-trough with a clatter.

I think it did not hit him,
But suddenly that part of him that was left behind convulsed in
    undignified haste,
Writhed like lightning, and was gone
Into the black hole, the earth-lipped fissure in the wall front,
At which, in the intense still noon, I stared with fascination.
And immediately I regretted it
I thought how paltry, how vulgar, what a mean act!
I despised myself and the voices of my accursed human education.

And I thought of the albatross,
And I wished he would come back, my snake.

For he seemed to me again like a king,
Like a king in exile, uncrowned in the underworld,
Now due to be crowned again.

And so, I missed my chance with one of the lords
Of life.
And I have something to expiate;
A pettiness.

about 1920   D. H. LAWRENCE

207. Men in New Mexico

MOUNTAINS blanket-wrapped
Round a white hearth of desert—

While the sun goes round
And round and round the desert,
The mountains never get up and walk about.
They can't, they can't wake.

They camped and went to sleep
In the last twilight
Of Indian gods;
And they can't wake.

Indians dance and run and stamp—
No good.
White men make gold-mines and the mountains unmake them
In their sleep.

The Indians laugh in their sleep
From fear,
Like a man when he sleeps and his sleep is over, and he can't
    wake up,
And he lies like a log and screams and his scream is silent
Because his body can't wake up;
So he laughs from fear, pure fear, in the grip of the sleep.

A dark membrane over the will, holding a man down
Even when the mind has flickered awake;
A membrane of sleep, like a black blanket.

– 437 –

The Sacred Fire

We walk in our sleep, in this land,
Somnambulist wide-eyed afraid.

We scream for someone to wake us
And our scream is soundless in the paralysis of sleep.
And we know it.

The Penitentes lash themselves till they run with blood
In their efforts to come awake for a moment;
To tear the membrane of this sleep . . .
No good.

The Indians thought the white men would awake them . . .
And instead, the white men scramble asleep in the mountains, . . .
And ride on horseback asleep forever through the desert,
And shoot one another, amazed and mad with somnambulism,
Thinking death will awaken something . . .
No good.

Born with a caul
A black membrane over the face,
And unable to tear it,
Though the mind is awake.

Mountains blanket-wrapped
Round the ash-white hearth of the desert;
And though the sun leaps like a thing unleashed in the sky
They can't get up, they are under the blanket.

about 1922   D. H. LAWRENCE

208. Autumn at Taos

OVER the rounded sides of the Rockies, the aspens of autumn,
The aspens of autumn,
Like yellow hair of a tigress brindled with pins.

Down on my hearth-rug of desert, sage of the mesa,
An ash-grey pelt
Of wolf all hairy and level, a wolf's wild pelt.

Trot-trot to the mottled foot-hills, cedar-mottled and piñon;
Did you ever see an otter?
Silvery-sided, fish-fanged, fierce-faced whiskered, mottled.

When I trot my little pony through the aspen-trees of the cañon
Behold me trotting at ease betwixt the slopes of the golden
Great and glistening-feathered legs of the hawk of Horus;
The golden hawk of Horus
Astride above me.

But under the pines
I go slowly
As under the hairy belly of a great black bear.

Glad to emerge and look back
On the yellow pointed aspen trees laid one on another like feathers,
Feather over feather on the breast of the great and golden
Hawk as I say of Horus.

Pleased to be out in the sage and the pine fish-dotted foothills
Past the otter's whiskers,
On to the fur of the wolf-pelt that strews the plain.

And then to look back to the rounded sides of the squatting Rockies,
Tigress brindled with aspen
Jaguar-splashed, puma-yellow, leopard-livid slopes of America.

Make big eyes, little pony
At all these skins of wild beasts;
They won't hurt you.

Fangs and claws and talons and beaks and hawk-eyes
Are nerveless just now.
So be easy.

about 1922   D. H. LAWRENCE

209. Shadows

AND if to-night my soul may find her peace
in sleep, and sink in good oblivion,
and in the morning wake like a new-opened flower
then I have been dipped again in God, and new created.

And if, as weeks go round, in the dark of the moon
my spirit darkens and goes out, and soft strange gloom
pervades my movements and my thoughts and words
then shall I know that I am walking still
with God, we are close together now the moon's in shadow.

And if, as autumn deepens and darkens
I feel the pain of falling leaves, and stems that break in storms
and trouble and dissolution and distress
and then the softness of deep shadows folding, folding
around my soul and spirit, around my lips
so sweet, like a swoon, or more like the drowse of a low, sad song
singing darker than the nightingale, on, on to the solstice
and the silence of short days, the silence of the year, the shadow,
then I shall know that my life is moving still
with the dark earth, and drenched
with the deep oblivion of earth's lapse and renewal.

And if, in the changing phases of man's life
I fall in sickness and in misery
my wrists seem broken and my heart seems dead
and strength is gone, and my life
is only the leavings of a life:

and still, among it all, snatches of lovely oblivion, and snatches of
     renewal
odd, wintry flowers upon the withered stem, yet new, strange
     flowers
such as my life has not brought forth before, new blossoms of me,

then I must know that still
I am in the hands of the unknown God,
he is breaking me down to his own oblivion
to send me forth on a new morning, a new man.

about 1931   D. H. LAWRENCE

210. Three Eclogues

1. *The Orchard*

GROTESQUE patterns of blue-gray mould
Cling to my barren apple-trees:
But in spring
Pale blossoms break like flames
Along black wavering twigs:
And soon
Rains wash the cold frail petals
Downfalling like tremulous flakes
Even within my heart.

2. *April*

To the fresh wet fields
and the white
froth of flowers

Came the wild errant
swallows with a scream.

3. *Curfew*

LIKE a faun my head uplifted
In delicate mists:

And breaking on my soul
Tremulous waves that beat and cling
To yellow leaves and dark green hills:

Bells in the autumn evening.

about 1914   HERBERT READ

XXII

Herbert Read
T. S. Eliot
W. B. Yeats

211. Mutations of the Phœnix

Beauty, truth and rarity,
Grace in all simplicity,
Here enclosed in cinders lie.

I

We have rested our limbs
    in some forsaken cove
where wide black horns of rock
Weigh on the subdued waters
    the waters
        menaced to quiet.

Our limbs
    settle into the crumbling sand.
There will be our impress here
    until the flowing tide
        erases
all designs the fretful day leaves here.

The blood burns in our limbs with an even flame.
The same sundering flame
    has burnt the world and left these crumbling sands.
The one flame
    burns many phenomena.

The limbs
    have their arcadian lethargy
holding the included flame
    to a temporal submission.

The flame
    burns all
    uses
the ducts and chambers of our tunnelled flesh
    to focus flame
        to its innate intensity.

The Sacred Fire

Flame
    is a whirl of atoms.
At one moment a whorl of what is seen—
    a shell

A shell
    convoluted through time—
        endless and beginningless time.

Will this sea
    throw such symbols round our limbs
        when the white surf recedes?
Does a white flame
    burn among the waves?

Will a phœnix arise
    from a womb evolved
        among the curved crests of foam?
At Aphrodite's birth
    were the waters in white flame?

2

Why should I dwell in individual ecstasy?
It is a hollow quarry of the mind
rilled with rock drippings, smoothed with silt;
And only the whorlminded Hamlet walks there
musing in the gutters.

We now leave this infinite well,
where naught is found—naught is definite,
to emerge:
to scan the round of vision,
a greedy eye wanting things finite
and enumerate to the mind.

3

Mind wins deciduously,
hibernating through many years.
Impulse alone is immutable sap
and flowing continuance

extending life to leafy men.
Effort of consciousness
    carries from origin
        the metamorphic clue.
The cap is here
in conscience humanly unique;
and conscience is control, ordaining the strain
to some perfection
    not briefly known.

4

We must not be oversubtle with these fools
else we defeat ourselves, not urging them.
They are in the filmy undergrowth
driven by frenzies whom they see
seductively mirrored in their minds.
Yet how persuade a mind that the thing seen
is habitant of the cerebral cave
and has elsewhere no materiality?
    But like a lily lust
    haunting the withered groins of crones
    is a phantom desperate to reason.
Shall the phœnix devour
    the horrid insurrection?
His flames are incinerary of much evil—
of all evil evident to the mind.
But here where naught but sick moonshine
is thrown from reflective facets
the seductive are the more lustreful phantoms.
In the clearing: in solar ruddiness
ends lunar moodiness.
There silhouettes are etched
    not phantomly
but in living areas of the mind.

5

    The sea fringe breaks
along the yellow shore
and is finite to the vision.

So time breaks in spume and fret
of intersifted worlds.
Our world is invisible
    till vision
        makes a finite reflection.
Then the world is finite—
    cast in the mould and measure
        of a finite instrument.

You can't escape: don't escape
poor easeless human mind.
Better leave things finite.
See where that curled surf clashes
in a wreath, in a running crest,
    in a fan of white flame!
All the past lives there—
    lives as time breaks
        in spume and frets of intersifted worlds.

All existence
    past, present and to be
        is in this sea fringe.
There is no other temporal scene.

6

The phœnix burns spiritually
    among the fierce stars
    and in the docile brain's recesses.
Its ultimate spark
you cannot trace.
Its spark out
and out is existence.
Time ends: time being vision—
reflected interaction of any elements.
But vision is fire.
Light burns the world in the focus of an eye.
The eye is all: is hierarch of the finite world.
Eye gone light gone, and the unknown is very near.

7

Phœnix, bird of terrible pride,
ruddy eye and iron beak!
Come, leave the incinerary nest;
spread your red wings.

And soaring in the golden light
survey the world;
hover against the highest sky;
menace men with your strange phenomena.

For a haunt seek a coign
in a rocky land;
when the night is black
settle on the bleak headlands.

Utter shrill warnings in the cold dawn sky;
let them descend
into the shuttered minds below you.
Inhabit our withered nerves.

8

This is the holy phœnix time.
The sun is sunken in a deep abyss
and her dying life transpires.

Each bar and boss
of rallied cloud the fire receives.

Till the ashen sky dissolves.

The mind seeks ease
        now that the moon has risen
                and the world itself is full of ease.

The embers of the world
        settle with a sigh, a bird's wing, a leaf.
There is a faint glow of embers
        in the ashen sky.

These stars
> are your final ecstasy,
and the moon now risen
> golden, easeful.

The hills creep in mistily—
> the tide is now a distant sigh—
like hounds outstretched
they guard the included peace—
> the tide a muted ecstasy.

The river carries in its slaty bed
> an echo from the sea.

But we leave
> even the river is lost.

No sound now.
No colour: all black: a cave.

In the cavern's mouth
the moon is hidden.

Yet still the stars—
> intense remnants of time.

O phœnix,
O merciful bird of fire,
Extinguish your white
> hungry flames.

about 1923,   HERBERT READ

212. The White Isle of Leuce

LEAVE Helen to her lover.   Draw away
before the sea is dark.   Frighten with your oars
the white sea-birds till they rise
on wings that veer
against the black sentinels
> of the silent wood.

The oars beat off; Achilles cannot see
the prows that dip against the dim shore's line.
But the rowers as they rest on the lifting waves
hear the revelry of Helen and a voice singing
of battle and love.   The rowers hear and rest
and tremble for the limbs of Helen and the secrets
     of the sacred isle.

about 1925   HERBERT READ

213. Gerontion

Thou hast nor youth nor age
But as it were an after dinner sleep
Dreaming of both.

Here I am, an old man in a dry month,
Being read to by a boy, waiting for rain.
I was neither at the hot gates
Nor fought in the warm rain
Nor knee deep in the salt marsh, heaving a cutlass,
Bitten by flies, fought.
My house is a decayed house,
And the jew squats on the window sill, the owner,
Spawned in some estaminet of Antwerp,
Blistered in Brussels, patched and peeled in London.
The goat coughs at night in the field overhead;
Rocks, moss, stonecrop, iron, merds.
The woman keeps the kitchen, makes tea,
Sneezes at evening, poking the peevish gutter.

                     I am an old man,
A dull head among windy spaces.

Signs are taken for wonders.   "We would see a sign!"
The word within a word, unable to speak a word,
Swaddled with darkness.   In the juvescence of the year
Came Christ the tiger.

– 451 –

The Sacred Fire

In depraved May, dogwood and chestnut, flowering judas,
To be eaten, to be divided, to be drunk
Among whispers; by Mr. Silvero
With caressing hands, at Limoges
Who walked all night in the next room;

By Hakagawa bowing among the Titians;
By Madame de Tornquist, in the dark room
Shifting the candles; Fräulein von Kulp
Who turned in the hall, one hand on the door.
    Vacant shuttles
Weave the wind. I have no ghosts,
An old man in a draughty house
Under a windy knob.

After such knowledge, what forgiveness? Think now
History has many cunning passages, contrived corridors
And issues, deceives with whispering ambitions,
Guides us by vanities. Think now
She gives when our attention is distracted
And what she gives, gives with such supple confusions
That the giving famishes the craving. Gives too late
What's not believed in, or if still believed,
In memory only, reconsidered passion. Gives too soon
Into weak hands, what's thought can be dispensed with
Till the refusal propagates a fear. Think
Neither fear nor courage saves us. Unnatural vices
Are fathered by our heroism. Virtues
Are forced upon us by our impudent crimes.
These tears are shaken from the wrath-bearing tree.

The tiger springs in the new year. Us he devours.
    Think at last
We have not reached conclusion, when I
Stiffen in a rented house. Think at last
I have not made this show purposely
And it is not by any concitation
Of the backward devils.
I would meet you upon this honestly.

— 452 —

I that was near your heart was removed therefrom
To lose beauty in terror, terror in inquisition.
I have lost my passion: why should I need to keep it
Since what is kept must be adulterated?
I have lost my sight, smell, hearing, taste and touch:
How should I use it for your closer contact?

These with a thousand small deliberations
Protract the profit, of their chilled delirium,
Excite the membrane, when the sense has cooled,
With pungent sauces, multiply variety
In a wilderness of mirrors.   What will the spider do,
Suspend its operations, will the weevil
Delay? De Bailhache, Fresca, Mrs. Cammel, whirled
Beyond the circuit of the shuddering Bear
In fractured atoms.   Gull against the wind, in the windy straits
Of Belle Isle, or running on the Horn,
White feathers in the snow, the Gulf claims,
And an old man driven by the Trades
To a sleepy corner.
                              Tenants of the house,
Thoughts of a dry brain in a dry season.

about 1920   T. S. ELIOT

214. *from* Ash-Wednesday

IV

Who walked between the violet and the violet
Who walked between
The various ranks of varied green
Going in white and blue, in Mary's colour,
Talking of trivial things
In ignorance and in knowledge of eternal dolour
Who moved among the others as they walked,
Who then made strong the fountains and made fresh the springs

Made cool the dry rock and made firm the sand
In blue of larkspur, blue of Mary's colour,
Sovegna vos

Here are the years that walk between, bearing
Away the fiddles and the flutes, restoring
One who moves in the time between sleep and waking, wearing

White light folded, sheathed about her, folded.
The new years walk, restoring
Through a bright cloud of tears, the years, restoring
With a new verse the ancient rhyme.   Redeem
The time.   Redeem
The unread vision in the higher dream
While jewelled unicorns draw by the gilded hearse.

The silent sister veiled in white and blue
Between the yews, behind the garden god,
Whose flute is breathless, bent her head and signed but spoke no
       word

But the fountain sprang up and the bird sang down
Redeem the time, redeem the dream
The token of the word unheard, unspoken

Till the wind shake a thousand whispers from the yew

And after this our exile

about 1930   T. S. ELIOT

215. *from* Ash-Wednesday

V

IF the lost word is lost, if the spent word is spent
If the unheard, unspoken
Word is unspoken, unheard;
Still is the unspoken word, the Word unheard,
The Word without a word, the Word within
The world and for the world;

And the light shone in darkness and
Against the Word the unstilled world still whirled
About the centre of the silent Word.

O my people, what have I done unto thee.

Where shall the word be found, where will the word
Resound?   Not here, there is not enough silence
Not on the sea or on the islands, not
On the mainland, in the desert or the rain land,
For those who walk in darkness
Both in the day time and in the night time
The right time and the right place are not here
No place of grace for those who avoid the face
No time to rejoice for those who walk among noise and deny
    the voice

Will the veiled sister pray for
Those who walk in darkness, who chose thee and oppose thee,
Those who are torn on the horn between season and season, time
    and time, between
Hour and hour, word and word, power and power, those who
    wait
In darkness?   Will the veiled sister pray
For children at the gate
Who will not go away and cannot pray:
Pray for those who chose and oppose

O my people, what have I done unto thee.

Will the veiled sister between the slender
Yew trees pray for those who offend her
And are terrified and cannot surrender
And affirm before the world and deny between the rocks
In the last desert between the last blue rocks
The desert in the garden the garden in the desert
Of drouth, spitting from the mouth the withered apple seed.

O my people.

about 1930   T. S. ELIOT

216. Marina

Quis hic locus, quae regio, quae mundi plaga?

WHAT seas what shores what grey rocks and what islands
What water lapping the bow
And scent of pine and the woodthrush singing through the fog
What images return
O my daughter.

Those who sharpen the tooth of the dog, meaning
Death
Those who glitter with the glory of the hummingbird, meaning
Death
Those who sit in the stye of contentment, meaning
Death
Those who suffer the ecstasy of the animals, meaning
Death

Are become unsubstantial, reduced by a wind,
A breath of pine, and the woodsong fog
By this grace dissolved in place

What is this face, less clear and clearer
The pulse in the arm, less strong and stronger—
Given or lent? more distant than stars and nearer than the eye
Whispers and small laughter between leaves and hurrying feet
Under sleep, where all the waters meet.

Bowsprit cracked with ice and paint cracked with heat.
I made this, I have forgotten
And remember.
The rigging weak and the canvas rotten
Between one June and another September.
Made this unknowing, half conscious, unknown, my own.
The garboard strake leaks, the seams need caulking.
This form, this face, this life
Living to live in a world of time beyond me; let me
Resign my life for this life, my speech for that unspoken,
The awakened, lips parted, the hope, the new ships.

What seas what shores what granite islands towards my timbers
And woodthrush calling through the fog
My daughter.

about 1930   T. S. ELIOT

217. Byzantium

THE unpurged images of day recede;
The Emperor's drunken soldiery are abed;
Night resonance recedes, night-walkers' song
After great cathedral gong;
A starlit or a moonlit dome disdains
All that man is,
All mere complexities,
The fury and the mire of human veins.

Before me floats an image, man or shade,
Shade more than man, more image than a shade;
For Hades' bobbin bound in mummy-cloth
May unwind the winding path;
A mouth that has no moisture and no breath
Breathless mouths may summon;
I hail the superhuman;
I call it death-in-life and life-in-death.

Miracle, bird or golden handiwork,
More miracle than bird or handiwork,
Planted on the starlit golden bough,
Can like the cocks of Hades crow,
Or, by the moon embittered, scorn aloud
In glory of changeless metal
Common bird or petal
And all complexities of mire or blood.

At midnight on the Emperor's pavement flit
Flames no faggot feeds, nor steel has lit,
Nor storm disturbs, flames begotten of flame,
Where blood-begotten spirits come

And all complexities of fury leave,
Dying into a dance,
An agony of trance,
An agony of flame that cannot singe a sleeve.

Astraddle on the dolphin's mire and blood,
Spirit after spirit!   The smithies break the flood,
The golden smithies of the Emperor!
Marbles of the dancing floor
Break bitter furies of complexity,
Those images that yet
Fresh images beget,
That dolphin-torn, that gong-tormented sea.

1930   W. B. YEATS

218. A Prayer for Old Age

GOD guard me from those thoughts men think
In the mind alone;
He that sings a lasting song
Thinks in a marrow-bone;

From all that makes a wise old man
That can be praised of all;
O what am I that I should seem
For the song's sake a fool?

I pray—for fashion's word is out
And prayer comes round again—
That I may seem, though I die old,
A foolish passionate man.

1935   W. B. YEATS

XXIII

C. Day Lewis
Louis MacNeice
Stephen Spender
W. H. Auden

The Sacred Fire

219. You that love England . . .

You that love England, who have an ear for her music,
The slow movement of clouds in benediction,
Clear arias of light thrilling over her uplands,
Over the chords of summer sustained peacefully;
Ceaseless the leaves' counterpoint in a west wind lively,
Blossom and river rippling loveliest allegro,
And the storms of wood strings brass at year's finale:
Listen. Can you not hear the entrance of a new theme?

You who go out alone, on tandem or on pillion,
Down arterial roads riding in April,
Or sad beside lakes where hill-slopes are reflected
Making fires of leaves, your high hopes fallen:
Cyclists and hikers in company, day excursionists,
Refugees from cursed towns and devastated areas;
Know you seek a new world, a saviour to establish
Long-lost kinship and restore the blood's fulfilment.

You who like peace, good sticks, happy in a small way
Watching birds or playing cricket with schoolboys,
Who pay for drinks all round, whom disaster chose not;
Yet passing derelict mills and barns roof-rent
Where despair has burnt itself out—hearts at a standstill,
Who suffer loss, aware of a lowered vitality;
We can tell you a secret, offer a tonic; only
Submit to the visiting angel, the strange new healer.

You above all who have come to the far end, victims
Of a run-down machine, who can bear it no longer;
Whether in easy chairs chafing at impotence
Or against hunger, bullies and spies preserving
The nerve for action, the spark of indignation—
Need fight in the dark no more, you know your enemies.
You shall be leaders when zero hour is signalled,
Wielders of power and welders of a new world.

about 1935   C. DAY LEWIS

The Sacred Fire

220. Wolves

I DO not want to be reflective any more
Envying and despising unreflective things
Finding pathos in dogs and undeveloped handwriting
And young girls doing their hair and all the castles of sand
Flushed, by the children's bed-time level with the shore.

The tide comes in and goes out again, I do not want
To be always stressing either its flux or its permanence,
I do not want to be a tragic or philosophic chorus
But to keep my eye only on the nearer future
And after that to let the sea flow over us.

Come then all of you, come closer, form a circle
Join hands and make believe that joined
Hands will keep away the wolves of water
Who howl along our coast.   And be it assumed
That no one hears them among the talk and laughter.

about 1935   LOUIS MACNEICE

221. After they have tired . . .

AFTER they have tired of the brilliance of cities
And of striving for office where at last they may languish
Hung round with easy chains until
Death and Jerusalem glorify also the crossing-sweeper:
Then those streets the rich built and their easy love
Fade like old cloths, and it is death stalks through life
Grinning white through all faces
Clean and equal like the shine from snow.

In this time when grief pours freezing over us,
When the hard light of pain gleams at every street corner,
When those who were pillars of that day's gold roof
Shrink in their clothes; surely from hunger
We may strike fire, like fire from flint?

And our strength is now the strength of our bones
Clean and equal like the shine from snow
And the strength of fame and our enforced idleness,
And it is the strength of our love for each other.

Readers of this strange language
We have come at last to a country
Where light equal, like the shine from snow, strikes all faces,
Here you may wonder
How it was that works, money, interest, building, could ever hide
The palpable and obvious love of man for man.

Oh comrades, let not those who follow after
—The beautiful generation that shall spring from our sides—
Let them not wonder how after the failure of banks
The failure of cathedrals and the declared insanity of our rulers,
We lacked the Spring-like resources of the tiger
Or of plants who strike out new roots to gushing waters.
But through torn-down portions of old fabric let their eyes
Watch the admiring dawn explode like a shell
Around us, dazing us with its light like the shine from snow.

about 1933   STEPHEN SPENDER

222. Journey to Iceland

AND the traveller hopes: 'Let me be far from any
Physician'; and the ports have names for the sea:
    The citiless, the corroding, the sorrow;
    And North means to all: 'Reject.'

And the great plains are for ever where the cold fish is hunted,
And everywhere; the light birds flicker and flaunt;
    Under the scolding flag the lover
    Of islands may see at last,

Faintly, his limited hope; and he nears the glitter
Of glaciers, the sterile immature mountain intense
    In the abnormal day of this world, and a river's
    Fan-like polyp of sand.

The Sacred Fire

Then let the good citizen here find natural marvels;
The horse-shoe ravine, the issue of steam from a cleft
    In the rock, and rocks, and waterfalls brushing the
    Rocks, and among the rocks birds.

And the student of prose and conduct, places to visit;
The site of a church where a bishop was put in a bag,
    The bath of a great historian, the rock where
    An outlaw dreaded the dark.

Remember the doomed man thrown by his horse and crying:
'Beautiful is the hillside, I will not go';
    The old woman confessing: 'He that I loved the
    Best, to him I was worst.'

For Europe is absent. This is an island and therefore
Unreal. And the steadfast affections of its dead may be bought
    By those whose dreams accuse them of being
    Spitefully alive, and the pale

From too much passion of kissing feel pure in its deserts.
Can they? For the world is, and the present, and the lie.
    And the narrow bridge over the torrent,
    And the small farm under the crag

Are the natural setting for the jealousies of a province;
And the weak vow of fidelity is formed by the cairn;
    And within the indigenous figure on horseback
    On the bridle path down by the lake

The blood moves also by crooked and furtive inches,
Asks all your questions: 'Where is the homage? When
    Shall justice be done? O who is against me?
    Why am I always alone?'

Present then the world to the world with its mendicant shadow;
Let the suits be flash, the Minister of Commerce insane;
    Let jazz be bestowed on the huts, and the beauty's
    Set cosmopolitan smile.

For our time has no favourite suburb; no local features
Are those of the young for whom all wish to care;
    The promise is only a promise, the fabulous
    Country impartially far.

Tears fall in all the rivers.   Again the driver
Pulls on his gloves and in a blinding snowstorm starts
    Upon his deadly journey; and again the writer
    Runs howling to his art.

1936   W. H. AUDEN

NOTES TO THE
INTRODUCTION

[1] "He has no taste whose taste is for one sort of thing only, though one-sided partisanship of this kind is common enough. True taste is all-embracing, comprehending beauty of every kind, never expecting from any a greater or different delight or satisfaction than it can by its nature give."

[2] The case may be compared with the sculpture nowadays called Romantic, which is the illustrative "expression" of human feeling and character and should be contrasted with the creative or Classical art in which the forms—whatever their origin in feeling or otherwise —have become satisfying and beautiful in themselves.

[3] Even its separation in argument suggests the linguistic fiction or nominalist fallacy most familiar in theology, whereby the name takes the place of the reality, or aspect of reality, it was used arbitrarily to define; and the mind proceeds with no sense of error to the imagined essence or abstraction.

[4] The drama is obviously in a different case; but drama is not con-terminous with poetry though their bounds overlap. Nor can narrative verse be all poetry in the sense here discussed; it may almost be regarded as a surviving primitive form.

[5] I cannot imagine a greater disservice to poetry than the current attempt made in schools to find a short cut to appreciation by formal instruction in the subject. It seems to be supposed that the long process of personal trial and testing, following some spontaneous kindling experience, by which alone a genuine taste can be formed, can be omitted and a short cut be found by presenting a child with the final results of other (adult) people's experience. The error in this attempt to mass-produce culture lies in its proposal to multiply effects instead of setting in motion causes. The actual result is either to create an odious literary snobbishness or (much more often) to impart a permanent dislike and distrust of a meaningless school "subject". It is well to teach children self-expression in prose in the best English traditions, and let them be given access to libraries, but the delicate plant of a sensibility to poetry (rare enough at all times) should be left to grow

to maturity unforced. The drama is in the same predicament. It undoubtedly appeals to children, but only in those aspects which are concerned with make-believe and external action; it is wanton and disastrous to waste Shakespeare to satisfy this need.

[6] An intellectualist (as opposed to an empiricist) criticism, depending on absolutes no matter how fictitious, will of course have none of this anarchical toleration.

[7] *Dresden China*, pp. 12–14.

[8] Indignation at the perverted efforts of those who treat poetry as no more than meaning, who write notes to "elucidate" it and research endlessly into the lives and waste-paper baskets of poets in search of "human" interest, is perhaps after all misplaced. These creatures who torment the body of poetry are perhaps least harmfully employed in thus avoiding her vital parts. For just as absolute beauty is not reached by a direct striving after it, so perhaps it is better for the reader to avoid too direct a consciousness of the purely poetical qualities. Analysis is here as always a danger; the bloom is easily lost by "handling" and over-familiarity. I remember a remark of Bacon, a warning to the effect that atheism is found less often in those who deny, than in those whose minds are cauterised and made insensitive by too much handling of holy things. That is the danger here, and there is thus cause for satisfaction that no adequate terminology for the discussion of poetry itself has yet been found. Even the mode of approach indicated in this introduction is not without its dangers; but it may be justified as needed to remove prejudice and misconception, and after that is done is better dismissed from the mind.

[9] A glossary is given on page 478. This doctrine of the inviolability of the words of a poem must carry also a conviction that their translation into another language is impossible. Translation is possible with writing that merely conveys information or argument, but even this needs qualification, since thought may be shaped by the very structure of a language. Translation begins to be impossible when the words are given by the writer a significance beyond their mere intellectual content, in fact when the writing begins to be a work of art, and reaches the extreme limit of absurdity in the attempted translation of a poem. The ideas of a poem may be rendered into another language, the poetic qualities may be given in the nearest equivalent and the translation may even be greater than the original; but it will be the translator's and not the poet's poem.

[10] It was the age of Thomas Tallis, whose sombre music expresses its spirit with overwhelming power.

[11] I have ventured to include some passages from the Authorized Version of the Bible, set out, as I have for long thought they could

be, in the form of irregular verse. I have avoided any discussion of the relation of prose to verse, but I may state here that I am of the opinion that the passages quoted belong to the latter as plainly as do the best poems of D. H. Lawrence and other recent writers of *vers libre*.

[12] I have left aside as too difficult to be argued in the brief space available here the question whether there may be degrees in the value of poetry according to the importance of its subject-matter. It may be engendered at one end of the scale by a passionate care for style and at the other by vision and prophetic insight into the deeper concerns of the human race. From the point of view of one concerned with pure poetry, importance of subject is irrelevant; but if the work is considered as a contribution to the heritage of the race, it is by no means irrelevant, and so much the worse for pure poetry it may be said. It is obvious that the latter sort of poetry stirs most of us more profoundly; its incandescence is fiercer than the none-the-less authentic flame of the other. I am in fact conscious that certain poems (such as Greville's *Chorus Sacerdotum* and others, especially in Book VIII and IX) have been included in this anthology partly because they so admirably embody the English vision and response to those concerns and experiences. But I do not think this affects the general arguments I have here put forward.

[13] His drawings, for all their wild imaginative content, belong in their formal character to the 18th Century.

[14] I distrust those re-discoveries of poets supposedly neglected by their time on account of their then unfashionable style. It would be a far better occupation to vindicate the reputation of poets blackened by the reactions of their immediate successors.

[15] A few ballads are included in my series, somewhat arbitrarily perhaps, at this point. It is arguable, however, that in the form in which we have them they were a creation of this time.

[16] The music of Beethoven, also.

[17] This was the "Revived Rococo" or "Rockingham china" period of English decorative art, the most vulgar and insensitive in its history.

[18] But these are the lyrics by which alone he is usually represented in anthologies.

[19] The experience so common among the young, of a first and exclusive devotion to the nascent "modern" art of their own day, is, I think, a natural and healthy one. No adjustment of the point of view is required and often enough the excitement of a revelation of beauty is strengthened by an enthusiasm for the poet's themes, together with (it must be granted) a satisfaction also at the bewilderment of elders and especially of the schoolmasters; these, by their boring presentation of the past only, had made into a hateful task what should have been a

spontaneous delight. In such cases a sensitive mind unprejudiced by "a training in appreciation" will normally proceed to the discovery that the poets of the past achieved a beauty no less authentic than their modern successors, though their occasions no longer have the urgency of those of the contemporary poet. A passionate liking for modern art is in fact the best possible starting point for an educational process designed to lead to an understanding of the past and a proper valuing of tradition.

[20] "Romantic" is still (as it has been for at least thirty years) the current term of strongest abuse. In 1937 a leading anti-romantic critic could accuse the poets of "twenty years ago" of "admiring their own nobility", illustrating this by a quotation from W. E. Henley. The claim often made by and for the contemporary poets, that they have abandoned "poetical" for everyday language, is a perennial one also; it is part of the English tradition to do this from time to time, and the cases of Wordsworth, Hardy and Robert Frost (to mention only a few) are enough to show that it is no novelty.

BIBLIOGRAPHY AND NOTES

The following notes refer to the source of the text used, which is in most cases an early edition. For the titles of the current editions of contemporary authors, the *Acknowledgements* on page xi should be consulted. Many of the original editions in the Dyce Collection in the Library of the Victoria and Albert Museum have been used in the revision of the texts, and my thanks are due to the staff there for facilities granted.

1. British Museum, Harleian MS. 2253. Believed to have been written at Leominster Abbey. Printed in E. K. Chambers and F. Sidgwick, *Early English Lyrics* (1907), the most attractively presented collection of poems of this period.

2. The same manuscript as the last. First three verses only. Printed in full by Chambers and Sidgwick.

3. British Museum, Harleian MS. 913. Believed to have been written at Gray Abbey, Kildare, between 1308 and 1318. Printed by Chambers and Sidgwick.

4. From the Prologue to *The Legend of Fair Women*. Text from W. W. Skeat, *Complete Works of Geoffrey Chaucer* (1894).

5. British Museum, Sloane MS. 2593. Printed by Chambers and Sidgwick, and in the original spelling by B. Fehr, in *Archiv für das Studium der neueren Sprachen und Litteraturen*, cix, p. 150.

6. Scott's *Minstrelsy of the Scottish Border*, 1802-3 and later; ed. T. F. Henderson (1902), III, p. 170. This I feel is mediæval in spirit, distinct from the narrative ballads printed on pages 269 to 273.

7. British Museum, Harleian MS. 7578. Printed by Chambers and Sidgwick. The text here follows the manuscript as published by B. Fehr, in *Archiv für das Studium der neueren Sprachen und Litteraturen*, cvii, p. 68. Part of a composite poem of which the remainder is of no merit.

8. British Museum, Royal Appendix MS. 58. Printed by Chambers and Sidgwick. The text here follows the manuscript as published by E. Flügel in *Anglia: Zeitschrift für englische Philologie*, xii, p. 260.

9, 10 and 11. Published under this title in *Tottel's Miscellany*, 1557. Texts from this and Miss A. K. Foxwell's edition of Wyat's poems (London University, 1913), based on the manuscripts.

12. Title and text from *Tottel's Miscellany*, 1557, in which Surrey's poems achieved a great popular success, largely due to the circumstances of his death. He is not to be compared with his master Wyat, whose name is usually linked with his.

13. *The Shepheardes Calendar*, 1579; reprinted in *Spenser's Minor Poems* (ed. E. de Selincourt), 1910.

14. *Tamburlaine the Great, who from a Scythian Shephearde, by his rare and wonderfull Conquests became a most puissant and mightye Monarque, and (for his tyranny, and terrour in Warre) was tearmed The Scourge of God*, 1590. Text reprinted in C. F. Tucker Brooke, *The Works of Christopher Marlowe* (Oxford University Press, 1910).

15. *Hero and Leander*, 1598. Written in or before 1593, when Marlowe was killed. Text reprinted by C. F. Tucker Brooke as above.

16. *Venus and Adonis*, 1593.

17 and 18. From *Rosalynde: Eupheues Golden Legacie*, 1590. Text from a reprint of the 1592 edition by "S. W. S.", in *Glaucus and Silla with other lyrical and pastoral poems*, Chiswick Press, 1819.

19. From *A Margarite of America*, 1596. Text as last.

20. *Amoretti and Epithalamion, written not long since by Edmund Spenser*, 1595. Reprinted by E. de Selincourt as above.

21. From *The Merchant of Venice*, 1623.

22. From *First Book of Songs or Airs by John Dowland, Bachelor of Music*, 1597. Reprinted by A. H. Bullen, *Shorter Elizabethan Poems*, 1903.

23. From *Polyhymnia*, 1590, as reprinted by A. Dyce, *Works of George Peele* (1828–39).

24. From *Observations on the Art of English Poesie*, by Thomas Campion, 1602. Reprinted by A. H. Bullen, *Thomas Campion*, 1903.

25. From *A Booke of Ayres by Philip Rosseter and Thomas Campion*, 1601. Reprinted by A. H. Bullen as above.

26. From *The Third and Fourth Booke of Ayres by Thomas Campion*, 1617. Reprinted by A. H. Bullen as above.

27. From *Measure for Measure*, 1623.

28. From *The Tempest*, 1623.

29. From Tobias Hume's *First Booke of Ayres*, 1605. Reprinted by A. H. Bullen, *Lyrics from Elizabethan Song Books*, 1897.

30. From *Valentinian*, published in *Comedies and Tragedies written by Francis Beaumont and John Fletcher, gentlemen*, 1634.

31. From *Two Noble Kinsmen*, published as last, 1634.

32. *Certaine sonets by Sir Philip Sidney never before printed*, in the 1598 folio of *Arcadia;* "ill" for "evill" in line 11 is an emendation generally accepted.

33 to 36. *Amoretti . . . written not long since by Edmund Spenser*, 1595. Reprinted as above.

37 to 40. *Shakespeares Sonnets, never before imprinted*, 1609. Written at least fifteen years earlier.

41 and 42. From *Idea: in Sixtie three sonnets*, 1619; originally published in 1594, but subsequently revised by the author.

43. From *Odes with other lyric Poesies*, 1619. This is a remarkably successful piece of patriotic writing, and no picture of the Elizabethan poetic achievement would be complete without the inclusion of at least one example of Drayton's quite admirable poetry in this manner.

44 to 47. *Poems, by J. D.*, 1633. I have omitted the second and third stanzas of *The Anniversary* to leave the opening—perhaps the finest of all the fine "onsets" in Donne's poems—to make its effect unspoilt by the slight weakening of the rest.

48. *Ovid's Banquet of Sence: A Coronet for his Mistresse Philosophie and his amorous Zodiacke*, 1595.

49. *Euthymiæ Raptus; or The Teares of Peace*, 1609.

50. From *Mustapha*, 1609.

51. *Measure for Measure*, 1623.

52. *Macbeth*, 1623.

53. From *Cymbeline*, 1623.

54. From *The White Divel . . . or Vittoria Corombona*, 1612.

55. From *The Tragedy of the Dutchesse of Malfy*, 1623.

56. From *The Devil's Law-Case*, 1623.

57. From *The Broken Heart*, 1633.

58. *Job*, Chapters iii, xxxviii and xxxix.

59. *Ecclesiastes*, Chapter xii.

60. *First Epistle of Paul the Apostle to the Corinthians*, Chapter xiii.

61 and 62. *Poems, Elegies, Paradoxes and Sonnets*, 1657. The title of No. 62 in various manuscripts is "*The Exequy to his Matchless never to be forgotten Freind.*" A few lines omitted. The reading "hallow" for "hollow" in the familiar couplet is that of the printed editions and some of the manuscripts. Reprinted by L. Mason (1914). These

An Anthology

poems by Bishop Henry King could as fittingly be included in the next section, with Godolphin's *Hymn*; they show a serenity that is typically early Caroline, rather than the shattering despair characteristic of the age of James I.

63 to 65. *The Temple*, 1633.

66. *Steps to the Temple, with other Delights of the Muses*, 1646, where it bears the title given here, and in *Carmen Deo Nostro*, Paris, 1652, where it is fantastically set out, with an elaborate title, perhaps not the poet's own (he died in 1649); it is likely, however, that the revisions embodied in the later edition were made by him. Reprinted by A. R. Waller (Cambridge University Press, 1904). I have deliberately chosen this as the most exaggerated and "excessive" poem in Crashaw's characteristic manner; its moral tone is odious, but its poetry is magnificent.

67. *Silex Scintillans . . . by Henry Vaughan, Silurist*, 1650. Reprinted by L. C. Martin (Oxford University Press, 1914).

68. Printed from the author's manuscript in *Poetical Works of Thomas Traherne*, ed. G. I. Wade (London, 1932).

69 to 71. *Poems of Mr. John Milton composed at several times*, 1645. Reprinted by H. C. Beeching (Oxford University Press, 1913).

72. From [*Comus:*] *A Mask presented at Ludlow Castle*, 1634.

73. *Poems*, 1645.

74 to 76. *Hesperides*, 1648.

77. From *Wit Restored*, 1658; also in other collections of the 17th Century.

78. *Fragmenta aurea*, 1646.

79 and 80. *The Works of Sir John Suckling*, 1696.

81 and 82. Printed from a manuscript in *Poems by Sidney Godolphin*, ed. W. Dighton (Oxford University Press, 1931).

83 and 84. *Poems*, 1642.

85 to 89. *Poems*, 1681 (the first printed edition of Marvell's poems).

90. First printed by Captain Edward Thompson in 1776. Text from A. B. Grosart's edition (1872).

91. Text from *Paradise Lost*, 1667. Reprinted by H. C. Beeching, Oxford University Press, 1913, in an arrangement into books following the edition of 1674. Book III, 1–56; II, 927–67; II, 1034–55; IV, 589–609; III, 540–71; IV, 970–1015; VIII, 1–39; V, 153–208; IV, 639–56; IX, 412–33; XII, 625–49.

92. *Samson Agonistes*, 1671. Ed. Beeching, as last. Lines 1–109; 606–51.

93. *Works of Abraham Cowley, . . . out of the author's original copies*, 1681. I find Cowley's "serious" poems laborious and uninspired; but in such works as this he delightfully anticipates one of the more attractive manners of the age of Cotton and Dryden.

94 and 95. *Poems on several occasions*, 1689.

96. Apparently in *Selected Poetical Works of the Earls of Rochester, Roscomon and Dorset*, 1757.

97 and 98. *Works of Sir George Etherege*, ed. A. W. Verity (1888).

99. From *The Lucky Chance*, 1687.

100. From *An Evening's Love*, 1671.

101. From *Miscellany Poems*, 1704.

102. Prefixed to the collected poems of Mrs. Killigrew, printed after her death (1686). Text here taken from the edition of 1693.

103. *Absalom and Achitophel*, 1681.

104. *Alexander's Feast*, 1697. This is Dryden at his most artificial. A Poussinesque stage-scene, masterly in design and richly coloured, it is far better appreciated in the baroque trappings of its original spelling and setting out (which are here reproduced) than when barbarously pruned to meet a Victorian demand for "naturalness".

105. The coronation was that of George I in 1715. Text from *Works*, 1757.

106. *The Rape of the Lock: An Heroi-Comical Poem*, 1712; revised and reissued in 1714.

107. *The Progress of Beauty*, 1719; text from the copy transcribed by Stella, reprinted in *Poems of Jonathan Swift*, ed. Harold Williams, 1937.

108. *A Description of a City Shower, in imitation of Virgil's Georgics*, written in October, 1710; first printed in *The Tatler*, No. 238 (17th October, 1710).

109. *Poems on several occasions*, 1709.

110. *Fables by Mr. Gay*, 1728.

111 to 113. *Odes on several Descriptive and Allegoric subjects*, 1747.

114. First published as *Elegiac Song* in the *Gentleman's Magazine*, October, 1749. Printed with corrections by Dodsley in his *Collection of Poems by Several Hands*, Vol. 4, 1755.

115. *An Elegy wrote in a Country Church Yard*, 1751.

116. First printed in *Designs by Mr. R. Bentley for six poems by Mr. T. Gray*, 1753. The text is here taken from *Poems*, 1768, corrected by Gray himself.

117. First printed in Dodsley's *Collection of Poems by Several Hands*, Vol. 2, 1748. The text is here taken from *Poems*, 1768, corrected by Gray himself.

118. From *A Song by David and other poems by Christopher Smart*, ed. Edmund Blunden (1924).

119. *The Deserted Village*, 1770.

120. *The Task: a Poem in Six Books by William Cowper of the Inner Temple*. 1785: II (*The Time-Piece*), 206–15; I (*The Sofa*), 181–209; III (*The Garden*), 108–36; VI (*The Winter Walk at Noon*), 1–14, 57–

87, and 906–76. It is a remarkable confirmation of the theories put forward in the introduction to this book that Cowper's poetry shows its greatest beauty of rhythm and language when he is most deeply moved by human feeling.

121. From *Olney Hymns*, 1779.

122. *Poetical Sketches by W. B.*, 1783.

123 to 125. *Songs of Innocence*, 1789.

126. *Songs of Experience*, 1794.

127. From a manuscript formerly in the possession of Basil Montague Pickering, son of the publisher. Much of the long poem from which this is taken is doggerel, but there are occasional flashes of wild beauty and significance, as in these readily separated lines.

128. Published in part by Joseph Ritson, *Scottish Songs*, 1794; text from Scott's *Minstrelsy of the Scottish Border* (1802–3 and later), ed. T. F. Henderson (1902).

129. Text from the same source as the last.

130. From G. R. Kinloch, *Ancient Scottish Ballads*, 1827.

131. First printed in *Lyrical Ballads* (by Wordsworth and Coleridge), 1798, as "The Ancyent Marinere"; reprinted in 1800, 1802, 1805, etc. The text is here taken from the author's final version of 1834. It is in such poems as this and the two next following, that Coleridge's gifts as a poet are most evident. In his more "intellectual" verses the words are hardly kindled, and the strange enchantment of the others is entirely lacking.

132 and 133. *Christabel, Kubla Khan: A Vision*, and *The Pains of Sleep*, 1816.

134 and 135. *Poems in Two Volumes by William Wordsworth, author of Lyrical Ballads*, 1807.

136. *Lyrical Ballads* (by Wordsworth and Coleridge), 1798.

137. *Albyn's Anthology*, 1816.

138 and 139. *Posthumous Poems of Percy Bysshe Shelley*, 1824.

140. *Alastor, or the Spirit of Solitude, and other poems*, 1816.

141. *Lamia, Isabella, The Eve of St. Agnes, and other poems*, 1820.

142 and 143. *Life, Letters and Literary Remains of John Keats*, ed. Richard Monckton Milnes (1848).

144. *Lamia . . . and other poems*, 1820.

145. *Sonnets from the Portuguese*, 1850.

146. *Poems by Currer, Ellis and Acton Bell*, 1846.

147. First published in *Poems*, 1833; reprinted with revised text in 1853.

148 and 149. From *The Princess: A Medley*, 1847.

150. First published in *Poems*, 1833; reprinted with revised text in 1853.

The Sacred Fire

151. From *In Memoriam* (*A. H. H.*), 1850.

152. First published in the volume entitled *The Strayed Reveller*, 1849; revised and reprinted 1853.

153. *Empedocles on Etna*, 1852; revised and reprinted 1853.

154. *Men and Women*, 1855.

155 and 156. *Goblin Market and other poems*, 1862.

157 to 160. From *The House of Life*, in *Poems*, 1870.

161. Prologue to *The Earthly Paradise*, 1870.

162. *Eros and Psyche*, 1885. Reprinted in *The Poetical Works of Robert Bridges*. 6 vols. Oxford University Press (1929).

163. *Shorter Poems*, Book V, 1894. Reprinted in *The Shorter Poems of Robert Bridges*. (Clarendon Press, 1931.) This and the next have been chosen from a very large number of shorter poems all of nearly equal merit. The case of Robert Bridges is interesting. His gift was not (as in Swinburne) merely metrical, but sprang from a nice appreciation of the value of words and a discriminating ear for subtleties of rhythm. His work in my opinion fails in being in this extended sense decorative only. It would almost seem that human passion and poetic passion must kindle each other. But within its limitations his was a consummate art.

164. *Shorter Poems*, Book IV, 1890. Reprinted in *The Shorter Poems of Robert Bridges* (Clarendon Press, 1931).

165 to 167. *Poems of Gerard Manley Hopkins*, ed. R. Bridges (1918).

168. *A Reading of Earth*, 1888.

169. *Poems of the Past and the Present*, 1901.

170. *Satires of Circumstance: Lyrics and Reveries*, 1914.

171. *Poems of the Past and the Present*, 1901.

172. *Wessex Poems*, 1898.

173. *Satires of Circumstances: Lyrics and Reveries*, 1914.

174. *Poems of the Past and the Present*, 1901.

175. *New Poems*, 1897.

176 to 178. *Verses*, 1896.

179 to 181. *A Shropshire Lad*, 1896.

182. *Marpessa*, 1897, and *Poems*, 1898.

183. *Poems*, 1895.

184. *The Wind Among the Reeds*, 1899.

185 and 186. *The Rambling Sailor*, 1929. No. 186 was certainly written before 1910, and probably before 1900.

187. *The Testament of a Man Forbid*, 1901.

188. *Emblems of Love*, 1912.

189 to 191. *The Listeners*, 1912.

192. *Motley*, 1918.

193. *The Veil*, 1921.

An Anthology

GLOSSARY OF SOME 14TH AND 15TH CENTURY WORDS

betacht	.	gave	*mandeth*	.	sends forth, yieldeth
bleo	. .	complexion	*meneth*	.	complains
briddès	.	brood or young ones	*milès*	. .	wild creatures
brol	.	child	*moder*	.	mother
breme	.	valiantly	*mody*	. .	moody, passionate
cloude	.	rock	*mund*	. .	memory
dawès	.	days	*murgeth*	.	make merry
deme	. .	judge	*nulle*	. .	will not
deorès	.	deer	*ore*	. .	favour, mercy, pity
derne	. .	secret, dark	*rayleth*	.	decks
domès	.	dooms, judgements	*rode*	. .	branch
donketh	.	moistens	*roune*	. .	rune, round
ertow	. .	art thou	*schef*	. .	creature
fele	. .	many	*sikèd*	. .	sighed
fenyl	. .	fennel	*striketh*	.	flows
ferly	. .	wondrous	*tene*	. .	vex, grieve
fille	. .	thyme	*the*	. .	prosper
fleme	. .	put to flight	*tristou*	.	trust thou
ful	. .	foul	*weole*	. .	wealth
horre	. .	mist, fog, cloud	*wille*	. .	joy
isette	. .	set, placed, appointed	*wlyteth*	.	look
iyarkid	.	prepared	*woderove*	.	woodruff
leche	. .	doctor.	*wreche*	.	poor
lemmon	.	mistress	*wunnè*	.	joy
lossom	.	lovesome	*wyht*	. .	creature, wight
make	. .	mate	*vore*	. .	past times

INDEX OF AUTHORS

The numbers refer to pages

Index of Authors

Index of Authors

INDEX OF FIRST LINES

Index of First Lines

Index of First Lines

Index of First Lines

Index of First Lines

Index of First Lines

Index of First Lines